Religion of Surrender

How to use the 5 Pillars to hear God

By

Nahida Nabulsi

To the Hand

Table of Contents

Semantics - An Opening Message: i

From the Author iv

Chapter 0: Introduction 1

Chapter 1: Intention 42

Chapter 2: Prayer 89

Chapter 3: Fasting 169

Chapter 4: Charity 221

Chapter 5: Pilgrimage 305

Semantics - An Opening Message:

This text is peppered with quotes from many ancient texts, and many times, the pronoun used was "he/him." I didn't change that to "they" or something more inclusive to keep the integrity of the exact energy used, but hopefully, if I share my perspective, it will allow people to soften their trigger to those words.

For me, within myself, I have a myriad of personalities, a true spectrum, and at each point, there is a personality that is a unique mixture of masculine and feminine energy. Masculine energy is active, it goes and gets, it reaches. Feminine energy receives, it holds, it allows. We need a balance of these energies to be complete, which is why I can easily go from throwing punches and grappling at my MMA gym to being the most elegant ballerina in my yoga class and every combination in between.

Because of this ability – that I believe all of us have – when I read things with an open heart, I am able to identify with any pronoun. I know what it feels like to be in my "him" energy, my "her" energy, and the "they" between them. I never feel excluded, even though externally I identify as a "she"; internally, I am everything.

People generally like to narrow things down and define themselves, but what I am asking for here is the opposite. Instead of defining yourself, allow yourself a moment to forget which color you are and be open to being the entire rainbow.

Another word that is very triggering is God. People have placed so many beliefs into this word, and sometimes I interchange it with Source energy, Allah, Creator, Great Spirit, etc., to show the different names we call the same unfathomable and undefinable power. But it isn't just the word; it's what the word means to us.

Shortly after my nephew died, my sister came to me and declared very confidently:

"God is evil."

I nodded, understanding where that was coming from, but internally, I know that by a stretch, it may be accurate to say 'Evil is God,' but it is not accurate to say 'God is evil.' God is everything. Undefinable. Just as much the Creator and Sustainer, as the Destroyer.

Suffering is the greatest question humanity has; it makes us question our belief in God. How could someone so loving and benevolent allow such evil things to happen?

God manifests a myriad of forms from his image, and although we love the creator aspect, we have grown to hate the destroyer.

In Islam, God has 99 names that describe his essence.

Some of these names are gentle, like: "The Most Forgiving," "The Just," "The Merciful," "The Light."

Others are more foreboding: "The Harmful, The Distressor, The Afflicter," "The Destroyer, The Slayer."

Each of our souls is made of a perfectly unique combination of those names, but we've unknowingly created many out of one, and what I am attempting to do here is collapse them all. To see the light in the dark and the shadows cast by the light.

I discovered in my life that God was not just a warm hug and a safe space. God also had an iron fist and nailed 'his own son to a cross' (See **Note 1** below). Not being able to comprehend suffering in the short term, I mistook God and suffering as my worst enemy. Not understanding that good and evil are a duality of the same essence, masculine and feminine, night and day - none can exist without the other. With time and perspective, I learned the wisdom of "Love your enemy"[1] the hard way.

All I ask is that if you've gotten this far, to open your heart and mind to things that before were triggering in the least and unforgivable at worst. Without stretching beyond our current boundaries, all the concepts and teachings in this book will be contained where they need to be unlimited. If there are words in this text that trigger you, then please be patient with me and see past the words to the essence of what I am trying to convey.

Note 1: Christian vs Islamic interpretation: This statement is from the Christian perspective of Jesus*. Muslims believe that Jesus* was a prophet who was conceived when "God cast his spirit and word"[2] into the Virgin Mary. Instead of being crucified, Muslims believe that someone took his place prior to the crucifixion, allowing him to ascend to heaven, where he awaits until God sends him back to Earth to save humanity. At which point, the Muslims have been instructed to protect Jesus* and follow the order he reestablishes on Earth.

The point of this strong statement is to illustrate that throughout time, God has allowed people He created, and many who served Him unwaveringly, to suffer and die in horrific ways and did nothing to stop it. Serving God does not save us from pain. Surrendering to God only teaches us to understand the wisdom of suffering.

The Buddha* discovered the four noble truths[3] about life and suffering long ago:

Life is suffering.
The cause of suffering is craving.
The end of suffering comes with an end to craving.
There is a path which leads one away from craving and suffering.

From the Author

Surrender - the English translation of the Arabic word - Islam.

Surrendering is a universal experience.

We must surrender to evolve into the greatest version of ourselves.

It starts with the act of letting go, willingly or unwillingly, of something so dear it is often painful. But surrendering is not just letting go, it is also then attaching - to what is real.

While going through this process, we can feel lost or alone, but that pain doesn't come from letting go; it comes from feeling disconnected from our Source.

The Religion of Surrender is elegant in its simplicity,
and is the sum of five pillars:

Intention • Prayer • Fasting • Charity • Pilgrimage

We've been prescribed these tools to strengthen our direct connection with God. So that we can access Source energy with certainty, while on our endless journey of self-discovery.

To connect it only requires willingness.

Following your will.

Following God's will within you.

This is my story about how Islam surrendered me.

I woke up suddenly. Grabbing my chest, trying to reinforce it from the outside.

Nightmares had started terrorizing me a few years after my son was born.

Awake, I could write them off as irrational fears. But while I slept, I had no control. My dreams were overwhelmed with this eerie certainty that one day, too soon, he wouldn't be here.

Once the relief set in that it was just a bad dream, I laid back down and closed my eyes, feeling high off the adrenaline that always follows the anxious fits.

Listening and feeling my heartbeat go from hard drumming to soft beating to a flow. My breath relaxed, tucked under the drowsy exhaustion. gently, slowly, I drifted There again… the scenes playing on repeat.

Too defeated to fight it, I lay there paralyzed   as my heart set on fire.

Burning a hole through me, so deep, it could be a portal to another world.

As if by premonition, a man's hand aggressively reaches through the hole and grabs me by the neck, not to hurt me but to focus my attention. Fear and familiarity flicker across my mind, but in that moment, I couldn't tell whether this was God's hand or my father's.

The thought no sooner passed before I found myself transported back to my childhood.

Not this again! I thought I had already dealt with all that. Until I felt something I hadn't felt in years. Buried under a mountain of disappointment - memories of all the hope I had as a child.

Hope for kindness and mercy.

Hope that God would save me.

But that hope was crushed by the reality that no one would ever come.

The hand tightened its grip, bringing my attention back.

Then silently, it conveyed:

'When you were young, you had so much hope, but hope is weak. I had to kill your hope, so that you could become certain'.

Religion of Surrender

"Convey from me, even if it is one verse."[4]

-Muhammad*

*This symbol represents the salutations we say every time we remember the light bringers of the past, who suffered to bring messages far ahead of their time. *'Peace be upon them all'*.

Chapter 0: Introduction

Feeling Like A Fraud

There is a verse in *the Recitations* that was passed down from the Angel Gabriel to Muhammad* describing the shallowness of prayers in the age before revelation:

"Their prayers were nothing but whistling and hand clapping"[1]. It stripped me bare.

All other parts of faith were very socially and externally driven; praying, however, was the only thing I had to do alone, internally, and I never felt like I was doing it right. I felt seen through, God knew I was an imposter, and deep inside, I knew it, too.

For so long, I was going through the motions of life like an alien on *Prozac*. Since childhood, I felt like I was living in a foreign world. My innocent mind couldn't understand how people could knowingly cause harm to others, and so it assumed that's just how this world was – harsh. When I tried to emulate that behavior in order to relate to the world by being insensitive back, I found that I was the one who was looked at as foreign. Not only did I not know how to relate to other people, but not feeling accepted felt so uncomfortable in my body, I figured the only way to survive was to completely detach from emotions to the point that even when I prayed, I felt nothing.

It's not really that I didn't feel anything at all but that the feelings didn't last because, whether good or bad, I pushed them down quickly. Achievements and distractions only tickled a moment of my life, but mainly, all I remember was keeping busy all the time, unconsciously wanting to avoid being alone with my thoughts. I didn't know that this trance was by my own design; back then, no one knew or talked about survival mode. We just thought that's how you live a normal life: work, struggle, and let loose on the weekend.

I look back now and laugh at some of survival mode's funny quirks, like how much I hated flowers. I thought they were the biggest scam and waste of money, especially when they hiked up the price on Valentine's day – which I also believed was the biggest scam of all. Also, I didn't understand fashion, only utility. Steve Jobs and his daily black shirt and jeans uniform made complete sense to me.

But there were parts that weren't funny at all, like my foregoing of all fun and my constant need to hustle and make money. It was so severe that it cut off my ability to understand art and creativity. They were the furthest thing from survival, and I remember thinking to myself, 'Wow, it must be nice to be so rich that you just have hobbies you do all day.' I believed art was a luxury reserved for the rich or eccentric, and I wasn't able to comprehend why someone would starve for their art. Stability and safety were more important to me than the 'feeling' I got when I drew a picture.

So, feeling like a fraud never bothered me, with that one exception - when I prayed. I was raised in a God-conscious household, and as Muslims, I saw my mom praying a lot. As I got older, I tried to join her as she went through the postures and words of surrender, hoping that if I did them sincerely, they would somehow count. But because I was only ever taught how to worship God and never how to connect with Him internally, it always felt like I was putting on an awkward show for the air around me.

I knew it was wrong to feel so numb all the time and that I should feel something. I saw so much happiness and love around me and wondered why I couldn't feel it, but because I didn't know how to connect with the Source of love within me, I was stuck in a vicious cycle of believing that love was something I reach for externally, and even then it only lasted a moment. As a defense mechanism, for so long, I projected out cold confidence and even tricked myself into believing that I don't need love, all while constantly betraying myself to feel something. Eventually, I had to take an inventory of how I got to this place in life, which is when I found out that I had no one to blame but myself. It was the purest form of innocent ignorance in that I just didn't know what I didn't know.

What Is The Disconnect?

With the force of an entire country, we declare that:

"We hold these truths to be self-evident,
that all men are created equal, that they are endowed by their Creator with certain unalienable Rights, that among these are Life, Liberty and the **pursuit of** Happiness."[2]

I chased - whatever happiness means – for 33 years, and what I found perplexed me. I collected all the things my world told me I needed to be happy. My husband was devour-able, half Egyptian, half British, over six feet tall, with a British accent, a master's degree from Oxford, and the build of a tight end. Our kids were equally beautiful. The mortgage on our home was paid off within five years of marriage, and I had the corner office at work, with a window and a six-figure salary. By any definition, my life looked perfect, which is why I couldn't understand - Why I felt so empty?

Worse than an illusion, it felt like a lie. Reality fell so far short of my expectations that I didn't know who to blame for the deceit: the world or myself.

My wedding day, which I thought was supposed to be the best day of my life, was more like a funeral. I was getting my hair and makeup done before the reception when he called:

"I need to see you."

"No, please. I want you to wait to see me once I'm all done up, I wanna surprise you." I mistook need for desire.

"I need to see you immediately." It was a demand.

There was an urgency in his voice that he was covering because his family was around, and although I was concerned, I was also incredibly distracted with excitement, it wasn't every day I spoiled myself. So, after relenting and agreeing to see him halfway through my transformation process, I rushed back to *bareMinerals*. They had a deal where if I bought $50 worth of makeup, I got a free makeover. It was a splurge for me. The cosmetic specialist got my foundation and bronzer on and was working on one of my eyes when my phone buzzed. I excused myself again and quickly put on sunglasses and a light veil over my hair so he wouldn't see my progress, and went out to meet him.

He made a beeline to me once he saw me, his gaze unwavering, froze me to my place. He came with such intensity that my arms were already pinned down by my side before he firmly held them in place. He towered over me. Never breaking eye contact, he looked down and tightly said:

"Take your glasses off."

I tried to protest, but he was forceful, "Take them off! I need to see your eyes."

He scared me; I could see just how serious this was, so I took them off, and we looked at each other. I silently communicated my surprised concern, but his look I couldn't decipher. His eyes and eyebrows were pinched, the way they do when he is trying to solve a problem and is on the brink of giving up. He was desperate for something, consolation? Reassurance? He looked me dead in the eyes and said:

"Today is the worst day of my life," and he meant it.

A really long time ago, when I was a kid, I learned that I should never hope too much. That I should never be too happy because, inevitably, someone would come and crush it. Between the ages of five to eight is when most people lose their innocence, but speaking only of my personal experience, that is when my disconnection happened. The physical and emotional pain I experienced between those ages was so intense that the only way to survive it was to turn my feelings off. I had prayed for help, but when it didn't come, I realized I would have to take matters into my own little hands. So, I shut down my senses to the point that I would even forget memories. I hadn't consciously used this ability to mute feelings in such a long time that, ironically, I almost forgot I had this skill. But right then, at the start of what was supposed to be the best part of forever. My husband put a metaphorical shotgun to my heart and pulled the trigger point blank.

The look in his eyes suggested that he had no clue he had just detonated a landmine buried in my chest and that he expected Me to console him. After taking a moment to steady myself and for the ringing in my ears to stop deafening me, it took everything in me just to ask:

"why?"

After getting it off his chest that he felt it was unfair to have to go through an Islamic ceremony to marry me, I reminded him that it was his idea. He insisted we do it to maintain a good relationship with my mother, but I told him before that he was marrying me, not her. I don't know if he was testing me now, but I reassured him that it didn't matter to me what religion he was. To prove it, I told him that when we got home, if he wanted to, we could tear up the marriage contract from the mosque, which was different from the marriage license we had already filed with the state. As if I had said exactly what he wanted to hear, his mood immediately lifted, and he gave me a big, grateful hug without seeming to notice how stiff my body was. He apologized for being so dramatic, and as quickly as he arrived, he left, leaving me stunned not only by his harsh words but by how cowardly he was with his own commitment. I had never asked him for an Islamic ceremony, I was happy getting married in the courthouse. He forced the issue, and when it came time to do it, he attacked me. It was so illogical I couldn't wrap my mind around what had just happened.

He may have felt reassured, but I felt exactly the opposite. I didn't know who I was marrying anymore, and it was as if, in just one conversation, the man I admired and respected so much completely fell off his pedestal. He was no longer an idol I looked up to, he was a coward and hypocrite. It was in that state of mind that I went through the motions for the rest of that day. So much family had come from overseas, and everyone was so excited. No one knew what had just happened, and not wanting to ruin it for everyone else, I held it in so that everyone around me could stay happy. I had an aversion to chaos, and in always wanting to maintain stability, I rationalized that it would hurt more to tell them. I was a master at masking pain, so I put the feeling into a box and once again hid the truth so that the image of perfection could reign. Not knowing that by burying it, I would carry this pain with me into every fight we had for the next eight years.

This ability to mask and suppress pain, which I developed as a child, was just a surface-level band-aid. I didn't know it at the time, but when I buried these experiences in the furthest depths of me, I also blocked the door to receive internal communication and guidance. Which, for the overwhelming majority of my life, left me believing that feeling lost and alone all the time was normal. I never knew there was any other way to feel.

What Happens When We Don't Reconnect?

I still get triggered every time I watch the wedding scene from the *Sex and The City* movie where Big stands Carrie up at the altar. When she discovers he isn't coming, she rushes out of the building, running away from her humiliation. Their limos cross paths as she is leaving, and he is arriving - too late. They both stop in the middle of the road, and she doesn't wait to hear what he has to say, she just explodes. Beating him over and over with her delicate flower bouquet, we see the roses smash into him or snap into the air and then fall wilted on the ground. Everyone who watches that scene immediately recognizes that universal feeling. The specific kind of rage that only pure love can evoke.

Somewhere deep inside, she knew he would betray her, but she buried and blocked that knowledge from coming to the surface. Then, in true loves fashion, on what was supposed to be the happiest day of their lives, he confirmed her darkest fear. Not that he would betray her, but that, in essence, she betrayed herself — by not listening to her internal knowing. Deep inside, she knew he was untrustworthy, but that battled with her other instinct, that love conquers all.

Our sin was the same. We didn't know what love meant, so when self-love tried to contact and warn us, we ignored all its red flags and lowered our boundaries and standards. The words of real love within were harsh truths we weren't ready to swallow. They told us that there was something wrong, that although we waited so long, this wasn't the one, that something in us hurt when he was around, but we chose to ignore it. We were learning the hard way that love isn't blind, it blinds us, and in not knowing what true love was, we mistook it for mysterious men. So life used them to teach us the first lesson it teaches us all:

Love is not outside. It's inside.
And if we ever go looking for love outside,
we will feel betrayed, because it will always go.
Everything outside is temporary, we must learn to look within.

If we had been connected with the light inside of us, it would've shown us our true worth, what behaviors to tolerate, and what true love should feel like so that we don't mistake it for lust. But we weren't connected, so through the pain of betrayal, life was teaching us in a very severe way how to relinquish external images of love so that we could find the source of it within and stop being a slave for someone else's crumbs.

But no matter where I looked, I couldn't find what I was looking for; externally, all I found was betrayal, and internally, I was cold and lonely. It would take years for me to discover that the cause of all this drama was my own simple misinterpretation of my buried feelings. For my entire life, my mind was filled with thoughts of: 'I am not whole or complete. I am an unworthy fraud. Just pretend to be perfect.,' which was compounded because I believed the world when it told me that happiness was something you acquire to fill that hole within. Until one day, I stopped to look around and realized it made no sense; how could so many other people also have the same problem? How did Carrie and I share the exact same story of betrayal? It wasn't until I looked inside and faced my black hole of loneliness that I discovered what it was actually trying to tell me.

How Do We Reconnect?

In the silence of meditation, I dived into the abyss of my emptiness and found that deep inside, loneliness was not an enemy but actually a holy messenger that we are all born with. We misinterpret it as 'I am incomplete, so I am unworthy,' but really, it is an undying impulse reminding us that 'something is missing,' which is subtly different. My impulse was coded like an alarm clock, to go off when it was time for me to start my journey to find the Source of its emanation - the 'something that was missing.' Without its self-embedded programming that ignited when divine timing dictated, I could've lived my entire life in a state of ignorance, just trying to survive and not knowing what my feelings were communicating. But one fateful day, Grace rang loud and clear within, waking every sleeping cell in my body as if I were made out of goosebumps and heralding a visceral and unexplainable truth. It felt like the first and thickest of the 70,000 veils between me and the One Truth had been lifted, revealing that everything I truly need is inside of me.

Please don't allow my romantic description of this experience to fool you into thinking it was immediately pleasant. This alarm, which I describe as Grace, was set off by the most severe pain I had yet to experience. My marriage, which I write about in more detail later, ended the same way it started, a mirror image of that same massive blow to my heart. But because I had grown and learned so much over those eight years, I reflected on the pain from a much higher vantage point and saw that the same pain that shattered me opened me, which made all the difference in shifting my perspective from being a victim to the pain, to feeling empowered by it.

Pain made me realize my limits, that even though I was strong and capable, it didn't mean I was responsible for carrying the whole world on my shoulders, and it taught me how to put down things that didn't serve me anymore. It also showed me that because I had spent my life running after happiness, I didn't have much time left and that life is too short to keep chasing something that couldn't be caught. I had spent the majority of my life a slave to feeling safe by acquiring money to afford external comfort and suppressing my feelings to gain internal peace because I thought that would make me happy. But In the end, that didn't save me from discomfort and turmoil, it just made my outside world boring, and internally, I was exhausted from always pushing the lid down over my emotions.

When the pain became too great, it forced me to let go, and years of suppressed emotions exploded up to the surface, unlocking the primal feelings within me. For the first time, I looked at my raw, untamed emotions and realized they weren't monsters to be afraid of, they were messengers with critical information. Overnight, Pandora's box became a treasure chest, and I found what I had always been searching for, the 'something' everyone is searching for whether they know it or not - I found my connection to the One Love.

Reconnecting with myself in that way was life-altering. I remembered who I AM, and I didn't just love it; I realized I AM love. It filled me with peace, knowing that everything that happened in my life was to bring me to this realization and that nothing had happened in vain. Nothing I had ever acquired or experienced came anywhere close to everything this connection gave me: It spiritually guided, inspired, educated, protected, fed, and loved me – It met every need I had and ones I didn't know I had.

Because I had rejected and suppressed my internal light for so long, and rejection breeds obsession, connecting to that light became the sole focus of my life. But the pain that blew me open only gave me a taste of it; I still didn't know how to reconnect at will, and it only seemed to happen when I experienced massive amounts of pain. Innately, I knew there had to be a less painful way to access it, and I wanted to explore it more deeply and make its effect on my life stronger, so I threw myself headfirst into a journey of self-discovery.

Intuitively, I was guided to read the words of old mystics, which stirred the knowing of truth inside of me. They described perfectly what I had experienced, confirming that they knew the way, which convinced me to follow them. In studying the greatest spiritual teachers in the world, I discovered their methods weren't just similar, they were identical.

There was a formula for finding God.

Stories Of How The Greats Did It

I heard about Jesus* and Muhammad* a lot, living in a Muslim home in Texas, but I had never really taken the time to know them. It wasn't until I embarked on my own journey to uncover my truth that their stories became relevant to me.

Muhammad*, being the most recent, has the most documented life of all the light-bringers. Virtually everything he said or did was documented, not just how he prayed and handled conflict or helped others, but even funny stories of the way his wives would collude to tell him that his breath stank. He was incredibly conscious of the way he smelled, and knowing this, three of his wives decided that after he visited a specific other wife for too long, they would tell him his breath smelled bad, hoping to dissuade him from visiting her as often. She had his favorite honey (this is not a pun or innuendo), and when she would offer it to him, he would always stay a little longer to eat it, making the other wives jealous.

I only tell this story to illustrate how in-depth the details of his life are recorded. After reading many of these accounts, I strangely felt like I really knew him, and I am very grateful for those in the past who had the foresight to record this information. Before getting to know him in this way, his polyamorous stories used to be so completely unrelatable to me (and put a bit of a wedge between us), but after experiencing enough of life, I realize now I am no longer one to judge different cultures or different times. I understand that, at his time, this was a normal practice and that he would probably find our current epidemic of divorced single parenthood unbearable. Back then, no woman was allowed to go uncared for or unsupported, and as a single mother, I can finally understand the benefits of this kind of societal system. My favorite book about him is *In the Footsteps of the Prophet* by Tariq Ramadan. It's modern storytelling, and it connected me to him the most.

One by one, I read about the lives of all these great teachers, and what struck me was how similar their practices were **before** they broke through and started communing with God. Beyond their professions, which they were all completely ordinary working-class people: shepherds, carpenters, and tradesmen. They were all doing the exact same thing the moment the spark was lit within them, and they went from being blessed to blessings to the world. Their formula included a combination of intentional silence, meditation, and fasting.

Muhammad* would sit alone in the caves of Mount Hira for weeks at a time, with only a small rationing of food. The practices of silence, meditation, and fasting were well known by the Hanifs, who were the spiritual Gnostics of the region, and although Muhammad* didn't identify as a Hanif, after establishing Islam, he instructed his people never to disturb them.

After years of this consistent practice, he finally made his first connection at 40 years old, and it scared him half to death. The Angel Gabriel appeared to him, who he did not know, and said:

"Read!"

Muhammad* responded: "I am not of those who read."

Three times, they went back and forth, the intensity of command getting stronger. Muhammad* felt like he was being squeezed when, finally, Gabriel said:

"Read in the name of your lord (Educator), who created humankind out of a clinging clot. Read, and your Lord is most bountiful, he who taught by means of the pen, taught humankind that which they did not know."
- Quran 96:1-5

Muhammad* was terrified. Thinking he had been possessed, he immediately went straight home to seek the comfort of his wife, Khadija*. He put his head in her lap and said:

"Cover me. Cover me!"

He was cold and shaking as he relayed what he had just experienced to her:

"I was afraid for myself."

She firmly reassured him: "You have nothing to fear. Have a rest and calm down. God will not let you suffer any humiliation because you are kind to your kinsfolk, you speak the truth, you help those in need, you are generous to your guests, and you support every just cause."[3]

She was the first to believe in him, even before he believed in himself. He was experiencing doubt and needed the same validation and reassurance all humans need in those moments of feeling overwhelmed. Nonetheless, it was alone that he received his first message in silence.

Jesus* was about 30 years old when he went alone into the desert and fasted for 40 days and nights. He was tempted with hunger and power when he proved that:

"Man does not live on bread alone, but on every word that proceeds from the mouth of God"[4]. After surrendering his desires, he went on to start his ministry.

Moses* was 80 years old when he went up Mount Sinai alone and received the 10 commandments. He fasted for 40 days and nights – three consecutive times, totaling 120 days of fasting. When he came down after the third time, his face shined so bright people were afraid to look at him.

Abraham* was 14 years old and alone while meditating on the rising and setting of the sun, moon, and stars when he made the natural realization that there must be an intelligent architect and that there must only be one. Otherwise, they would be at war with each other, and the world would only be chaos.

The Buddha* having spent years in states of extreme fasting, eating as little as a grain of wheat and a sesame seed a day, finally discovered the middle way after hearing the song of the lute and realizing:

"When the strings of the lute are loose, its sound won't carry. When the strings are too tight, they break. When the strings are neither too loose nor too tight, the music is beautiful. I'm pulling my strings too tightly. I cannot find the Way to Truth, living a life of luxury, or with my body so weak."[5]

Afterwards, he sat alone under the bodhi tree, silently meditating without moving from his seat for 49 days until he reached enlightenment.

Getting Past Limits

I know what you're thinking, "I am not fasting for 40 days, I'll die!" or "I can't even meditate for 5 minutes." Trust me, that's not what I'm suggesting here. Every person is going to find their right combination of practices that elevates them to their highest potential. The point I was trying to make was that there seem to be some practices that are extremely effective and have been used by the highest achievers of enlightenment to heighten their senses and connect with God. Eventually, they got to the point where they could live a life fulfilled by the eternal light within rather than having to constantly chase the temporary lights of life.

I'm also not saying that our goal is to achieve what they have achieved. No matter how much I dribble and shoot, I will not be Michael Jordan. So, I'm not saying that doing these things exactly the way the prophets did will make us one. But by actively using these tools in a way that is intuitively right for us as individuals, we will discover that we have our own unique and special connection and, with that, gifts to share with the world. However, we won't know what those gifts are unless we strengthen our connection to where those gifts come from.

Although spirituality is becoming more known, because many still have not walked this path, it can seem bizarre, extreme, and unobtainable. Ignoring these limitations is the first step to learning how to follow our own instincts and will.

Towards the end of our marriage, I asked my ex:

"Why can't you be unconditionally loving and forgiving like Jesus*"?

[For reference, my ex was a very spiritual Christian. His father was a devout man who was born Jewish but had converted to Christianity and lived for some time in an Egyptian monastery before getting married and having kids. He loved telling the story of the night he went out to the desert to meditate with a fellow monk. When they found their spot, the monk drew a protective circle around them with his staff, making a shallow dent in the sand. The next morning, when they woke up, they found snakes lining the border of the circle, but none of them had pierced the invisible seal. Experiences like this were normal to him, so his knowledge of the spiritual side of religion was vast, and he passed that knowledge down to his son.]

My ex responded: "Jesus* was a demigod, no one can be as unconditionally loving as him."

But that didn't feel right, all the pain, growth, and lessons I learned by the end of our relationship taught me that unconditional love was a choice, not an ability. I still loved him despite everything that had happened between us, and I was not a demigod. He had put a limit on his ability to love and forgive, assigning it to the realms of God and not bringing it here for humanity to share in. I assumed that this was a Christian thing, and that is the reason Muslims and Christians deviate from each other. In Islam, there is no intermediary or hierarchy between any born person and God; we all have a direct connection as it is our indestructible birthright. But I learned shortly after the divorce and moving back home with my mom and stepdad that these limitations are everywhere, regardless of religion.

One night, while having dinner with my mom and stepdad, I was telling them not to count me in for dinner for the next month, as I was planning to start intermittent fasting, and their first reaction to me skipping dinner was:

"That is too extreme."

I said, "But the Prophet* used to only eat 1 – 2 meals a day."

My stepdad responded: "But you are not a prophet."

Again, this limitation presented itself, although instead of ascribing him the title of demigod, he assigned the title of prophet, as if that made him less man and more of something else - It stunned me. They acted as if these great teachers were born with these gifts and that they didn't have to fast, meditate, pray, suffer, sacrifice, and fight their own demons and ego to obtain the enlightenment, wisdom, and connection they worked so hard for. As if they just sat home eating, drinking, and watching TV, and not committing their lives to strengthening this connection, which they knew was the only real purpose of living.

It felt lazy for them to say it was because they were demigods and prophets as if that somehow absolved them from ever having to try and made me feel blasphemous for trying. I wasn't trying to be a prophet; I was trying to discover what I was born to be and do by finding MY connection, whatever that looked like. I would never know the role I was supposed to play until I went inside to find it, and I didn't make excuses; I just followed their formula.

"Truly, truly, I say to you, he who believes in Me,
the works that I do, he will do also;
and greater works than these he will do."
-John 14:12

The Million-Dollar Question: How Do We Find And Strengthen Our Own Connection?

What I was looking for was right under my nose the entire time. The majority of our body is made of water, which takes on different forms: Solid, liquid, and gas. So, just like rain has the ability to pass from Earth to the heavens and back again, our body also has a messenger that travels back and forth.

If our body is solid,
and our spirit is gas,
then our <u>feelings</u> are liquid, the medium between.

One substance, expressed in a trinity of ways.

The body is too dull to understand the messages of the spirit. The spirit is too subtle to get anything through to the body. They need senses and feelings so that everything that is not subdued can pass freely from one aspect to the other - allowing true communication to happen, which strengthens our connection.

Because feelings are the way spirit communicates with us, when I shut mine off to protect myself as a child, I also accidentally cut off my ability to receive love and guidance internally and kept seeking external experiences and achievements to fill and direct me instead. It wasn't until the second explosion of pain that led to my divorce that this method of communication was forced open for me again, and with it, I realized what I had been missing in life. After that, nothing I gained externally would ever truly fill me again, and I knew I needed to adapt if I wanted to live rather than just survive.

It was scary, not just because of the pain, but because all of my coping mechanisms were built from my experiences in an external seeking environment. If I wanted to live a life that received everything I needed from within, I had to throw away all of that knowledge and learn a completely new way of living – where instead of looking out for what I needed, I had to feel in.

We are relearning this ancient concept that feelings are divine revelation after years of negative conditioning to believe the opposite. Although no one can deny the truth behind a gut feeling, at some point in our upbringing, feelings were deemed too childish and not okay to be freely expressed, so we were taught to suppress them. Boys were ridiculed and called 'babies' if they cried or showed any emotion other than anger. Girls, on the other hand, were allowed to express emotion, but because of our huge capacity to hold this sacred communication without guidance on how to manage it, we were labeled "too emotional" and, therefore, unstable. These negative judgments caused many of us to dissociate from our feelings at a very young age in order to not be labeled as crazy or weak, but this disconnection was an absolute robbery.

As an adult, when I learned that this secret communication was hidden in our feelings, I tried to meditate to hear what they were trying to tell me, but I ended up running into two big obstacles. The first problem was that I had created a wall between me and my feelings as a form of protection, and undoing it to open my heart felt vulnerable and wrong like I was opening myself up to be easily attacked. I got past this by weighing my options and seeing that I had no choice. It was either stay on the external seeking path I was already on and be certain that another blow to the heart would occur if I ever allowed myself to love anything external/temporary ever again, or start the scary journey, where I would have to revisit every emotion ever suppressed with an open heart and decipher what it was trying to communicate to me. Neither option was ideal, but one was a dead end, and I didn't know it at the start, but the other path would reward me in ways I never could've imagined.

After getting past that first bump and allowing all of my messy emotions to come up to the surface so that I could face them, my second problem arose, and I started to understand why we were instructed to alienate our feelings as children. Although I was giving my best effort to silently meditate and translate this internal communication, I wasn't able to confidently hear or understand what my feelings were conveying. There were so many other competing voices inside of me that it made it impossible to discern what was true guidance and what was noise. So, at first, it felt like I was reopening old, painful wounds for no reason, and that was not fun.

That's when I discovered how polluted my inner and outer worlds were with distractions. I was so overstimulated I couldn't sit still long enough to properly meditate, nor could I differentiate between feelings that were truly mine versus those that were artificially induced by my environment and what I was consuming. After a few fruitless tries, I knew that in order to hear properly, I had to eliminate as much noise as possible. I needed to see which voices disappeared when they weren't evoked with stimulants, which ones stayed, and what they had to say. I was learning to develop the superpowers of silence and discernment to strengthen my connection to my inner world.

After trial and error with meditation and fasting for a few months, I was able to tell how different foods affected the silence in my body, and I found that caffeine and sugar were the loudest and biggest troublemakers. They absolutely fried my nervous system and gave me false and erratic signals that would scatter my attention so much I wasn't able to focus on my inner communication. Also, they gave me so much excess energy that I wanted to jump out of my skin and go for a run rather than sit silently to listen. Once I reduced those foods, I immediately noticed how much more relaxed and calm my nerves had become, making it so much easier to sit silently long enough to pick up the more subtle communication.

Prior to that, I had only given my attention to the loudest noises in my body because when they got loud enough if I still ignored them, they would cause physical pain to get my attention. There was a time at the end of my marriage when I started getting a sharp stabbing pain on the left side of my breast every time my husband and I fought. It was so loud that it would forcefully pull my attention in to concentrate on its internal signal, and every time, the exact same distinct thought would accompany it, getting louder and louder, 'If you don't leave this relationship, this is going to become cancer.' After following that guidance and getting a divorce, the pain disappeared completely.

I didn't even know how to decipher the language of feelings yet, but the really loud communication came in clear, even when I was deaf to it, as it does for everyone. Everyone who experiences tremendous amounts of pain always comes out the other end wiser for it. It is only because we are distracted that the urgent messages have to come in so loud and painfully to tell us that we are in disease. When I stopped subduing these messages and started learning how to translate them, receiving and obeying their internal communication became the biggest priority in my life, as I learned that its purpose wasn't to scare me or cause me more pain but to save me from it.

In order to make connecting with my feelings a daily ritual, I would take time each morning to sit in silence and do a body scan from head to toe, noting any tension in my body and silently sensing its communication. Many times, it would tell me that I was pushing myself too hard and that I needed more rest, and even though I hated to hear that because I love pushing myself to my limits, I respected the wisdom now, and my body rewarded me for it with the best health of my life.

After having this tactile experience of inner sensations and the way they communicate with me, I started reading work by new-age teachers like Louise Hay, who taught about the relationship between illness and communication from spirit. During her years as a religious science practitioner, she compiled a list of common emotions that her clients consistently experienced when they had similar diseases, which put spiritual ailments on a scientific map in the West (this knowledge has been around for centuries in the East). As most healthcare revolves around research of the physical mind/body aspects of our existence because they can be seen and measured, Louise found a way to scientifically acknowledge that we are made up of a mind, body, and spirit.

I've had conversations with people who have asked me to prove that the spirit exists, and obviously, there is no way for me to prove this in the physical world, but I always ask them (very sincerely) if they have ever seen a dead body. I was young the first time I lost a family member, and since then, every funeral I have ever attended, there is always one stark visual that never leaves my mind when I see someone in their casket - they look like all the lights have gone out of their body. I remember at my dad's funeral in particular, I picked up his hand, perhaps searching for warmth or light still hidden somewhere, and for some reason, I fixated on the tips of his fingers, but the light was gone even from there. It was during those experiences that I saw the most profound difference a soul can make in a physical existence.

Although there are many factors that affect our health, with the rise of spiritual healing and other eastern established medical modalities in the West, we are starting to see holistic strategies that acknowledge both our physical and spiritual illnesses. In Louise Hay's book *You Can Heal Your Life*, she provides examples of emotions that are common in top illnesses and how to address the spiritual as well as the physical symptoms:

- <u>Heart Attack</u>: Squeezing all the joy out of the heart in favor of money or position. Feeling alone and scared. "I'm not good enough. I don't do enough. I'll never make it."
- <u>Cancer</u>: Deep hurt. Longstanding resentment. Deep secret or grief eating away at the self. Carrying hatreds.
- <u>Stroke</u>: Giving up. Resistance. Rather die than change. Rejection of life.
- <u>Lung disease</u>: The ability to take in life. Depression. Grief. Not feeling worthy of living life fully.
- <u>Diabetes</u>: Longing for what might have been. A great need to control. Deep sorrow. No sweetness left.

We might ask why Spirit would use our health and loud pain to communicate with us? An Indian proverb immediately comes to mind:

"A healthy person has a thousand wishes,
but a sick person only has one wish."

Health has a way of focusing our attention on nothing else in life other than what's going on inside of us. We are normally so distracted, but as soon as a health issue comes up, we are laser-focused, and depending on how intense it is, it can actually force us to sit down with no choice but to go within. This is why so many ancient spiritual teachers were also healers; they were well-versed in the language of feelings and could translate the most subtle communication planted in the roots of our feelings and beliefs.

Although poor health and pain seemed to be the most common communication from spirit in my early days of learning how to meditate and translate messages, it was only because of my distracted state. Once I got started using my spiritual discernment tools to silence the noise and amplify the instructions, I realized there was an opposite end of the spectrum, where my feelings weren't just communicating what was wrong but also how to reach my highest potential in life. After I cleaned out enough of the noise, I was able to listen to the bliss in my body, which became a siren whose sound I couldn't evade. I became addicted to hearing the directions that led me to my greatest joys in life, making me want to tune my body even more so that I could hear the instructions loud and clear.

The Five Pillars Sharpen Our Hearing and Focus

Our connection to Source and the communication that passes between us is a birthright – EVERYONE has it. But in order to hear it clearly, we MUST: 1) Heighten our senses, and 2) Reduce noise. This book covers in depth the physical and spiritual ways to use the five universal tools prescribed to us by God and used by everyone who has ever achieved enlightenment to gain a heightened state of sense perception. The five pillars are:

1. **Intention** - teaches us how to focus our attention inward. This allows the internal light and vision to grow and become more tangible so that we can make our dreams a reality.

2. **<u>Prayer</u>** - teaches us how to communicate back and forth with our Source, but first, we must learn the true language of 'Ask and Receive.' I thought it was straightforward, but after enough prayers went unanswered or getting the opposite of what I asked for, I realized I needed to revise my understanding. There is a saying:

"I asked for wisdom, and God gave me problems to solve. I asked for strength, and God gave me difficulties to overcome. I asked for courage, and God gave me danger to overcome. I asked for love, and God gave me troubled people to help. All my prayers were answered."[6]

3. **<u>Fasting</u>** - is the most powerful tool for hearing God. When our energy is free from digestion, we become silent inside, which heightens our senses, heals our body, and stimulates our higher energy centers.

4. **<u>Charity</u>** - teaches us how to balance true giving and receiving so that when we prioritize filling ourselves first with Source energy, we become so full that our presence alone becomes a charity that spills out of us.

5. **<u>Pilgrimage</u>** - teaches us how to strengthen the everlasting commitment we make to follow our heart, the carrier of our light, and the only sun we ever revolve around again.

<u>Please Remember: It Is A Practice!</u>

"We prefer the devil we know over the devil we don't know." My friend from Louisiana used to say this all the time, and it seemed true, but I didn't understand its depth until it came time for me to change my life. I was an extreme perfectionist, and when I first started experimenting with the five pillars, I applied them with a feast/famine mentality, either jumping into the deep end and doing everything right or quitting and allowing the floodgates to open. When I initially tried fasting, I started too intensely, and although my senses felt more heightened than ever before, I was starving and weak. Then, my body's natural reflex for homeostasis kicked in, causing me to go on weeklong binges to make up for the starvation. Although it felt amazing to eat, my senses were completely numbed, cutting off my ability to sense my connection. Just like Buddha*, I learned that too much of a good thing can hurt.

It was a painful lesson, but it confirmed to me that the tools worked; I just needed to learn how to use them effectively, and in order to make them my foundation, I had to learn to go slow and be consistent, something I had never done before. I am unable to count the number of times I went on an extreme diet to lose weight quickly, only to gain it all back again, but I desperately needed to find my true self, and that need caused me to finally change my old extreme ways. I knew that in order to see this journey of self-discovery to the end, I had to commit to the middle way; I couldn't feverishly and haphazardly apply the tools; I had to live them. They had to define me and become as normal a part of my existence as showering or brushing my teeth every day because the devil is in the details, and so to succeed, the pillars had to become my automatic habits.

Good Small Habits

Everyone talks about the benefits of good small habits, but Tim Ferris has done the world a favor and documented all the habits of the world's healthiest, wealthiest, and wisest people in his book *Tools of Titans*. Even though each person is uniquely talented, their habits follow some combination of the same ancient formula:

Intention, fasting, and meditation, with the added wisdom of how to apply them - by setting goals so small they could trip over them and succeed.

Every time we feel successful, no matter how small the achievement, our bodies naturally produce a dose of dopamine, which is highly addictive. What successful people have figured out is that if they prioritize those little internal shots of success, with enough consistent practice, their external success would be inevitable. I had been doing it wrong because I wouldn't allow myself to feel successful with each small achievement; I would wait until I accomplished something huge to feel proud of myself. However, what they were teaching me was how to enjoy the road rather than the destination. Also, after learning how to translate my feelings, I learned that those tiny hits of bliss were God's way of lighting the path to my highest destiny; they guided me by saying: 'keep doing more of that.'

However, it was difficult to get started because I didn't understand how to flip my perspective to prioritize my inward experience of life or translate that guidance. I was paying so much attention to my external achievements that I completely disregarded what I was feeling inside, and so when things didn't quickly change outside, I would give up.

I realized that the difference between me and someone successful was that they were as addicted to cultivating success as I was to carbs and social media, one giving me a quick hit of love and the other numbing the pain of knowing I wasn't living to my potential. I thought that to get to the next level in my enlightenment, I would have to make harsh changes and sacrifice things I loved cold turkey, but that was only because I had tried to change so quickly and drastically before. I was learning now that going slowly was the only way to make real, lasting change and that I had to learn how to shift my focus from the pain of sacrifice to the internal reward, no matter how small.

Early on in the surrendering process, I experienced the pain of having to sell my favorite car. I go into it in more detail in the next chapter, but immediately after experiencing the pain of selling it, I got to experience the excitement of getting a new one. One old experience exiting to usher in the new, and even though I perceived my old car as a symbol of my accomplishment to that point in my life, the new car was even more of an upgrade. I had to get used to how it was handled, its bigger dimensions, and that it was higher off the ground. But once I settled into it, I felt like I was safer, I could see more, and the sunroof felt luxurious. The paint color, Midnight Sky, was a beautiful collage of glittering emerald, sapphire, and amethyst pixels. When I stepped back from the car to take it all in, the colors mimicked Indigo to the eyes. It was art hidden in plain sight and a stark contrast to the dark grey I was used to on my old car.

Knowing that something amazing was waiting for me on the other side of my food and social media addictions enticed me to move forward. However, my early attempts at change quickly revealed to me how much my current habits had control over me. If I was bored or anxious, I would immediately reach for my phone, and without even thinking about it, an hour could disappear while I was scrolling, and I would have no clue where the time went.

My body moved and took action without my conscious consent, and my attempts to stop this automatic, unconscious process felt futile, like fighting against a tsunami. Also, the thought of giving up my bad habits filled me with dread inside. They were my coping mechanisms for surviving life for so long that I didn't know who I was without them. It took months of trial and error for Tim's wisdom to finally dawn on me; I had to stop wasting my time trying to change bad habits and instead slowly refocus my attention on my small, successful habits. As Tony Robbins says, "Where focus goes, energy grows," so by focusing on those tiny internal doses of success, eventually, they would gain enough momentum that they would create an uplifting presence within, like a good tidal wave that would at first balance my good and bad habits out and then overtake the ones that no longer served me.

Momentum

"God Said:
I am with my servant when he thinks of me.
I am with him when he remembers me.
If he remembers me in himself,
I will remember him in myself.
If he remembers me in company,
I will remember him in a company better than his.
If he draws nearer to me by one inch,
I will draw nearer to him by one cubit.
If he draws nearer to me by one cubit,
I will draw nearer to him by one fathom,
and when he comes to me walking,
I come to him running."[7]
-Muhammad*

This is exactly what the momentum of good small habits felt like in my life. When I ignored what I was doing wrong and started focusing on even the smallest thing I was doing right, the explosions of success kept feeling exponentially better with each achievement, causing my body to naturally want to refocus on the better feeling addiction. Because I was no longer looking for external success, I didn't measure my smaller goals as a means to an end anymore, and when that mental shift happened, I just looked up one day and found that the wave had tipped in my favor, and my bad habits fell away on their own. I never had to fight; I just had to stop being a slave to my bad habits and learn how to let my good habits serve me. By the end of a year of being completely committed to my new practices, I was unrecognizable and not just physically changed, but as if God turned up the brightness of the light inside of me.

The Phoenix Only Rises After Willingly Burning Alive

When I began my journey of changing my habits, the mountain of diet, exercise, focus, sacrifice, and discipline not only seemed too high and intimidating to climb, but I also knew it would require me to become a completely different person - a devil I didn't know. Because the only way to become new is to kill the old.

Abraham* woke up from a horrific dream once, and in that dream, he believed that he was being asked to sacrifice his son. The idea that he could trust and want to move forward with something like that, I think, for many of us, would not only be horrific but, by today's standards, would definitely qualify us for a lifetime in a psych ward or prison. It is beyond our comprehension that a dream could have that much conviction over us, but because he was so connected, he knew that this wasn't just a dream; it was a command.

He didn't gaily run up the mountain with his son in one hand and a knife in the other, enthusiastically ready for the slaughter. It was, without a doubt, a heavy weight knowing what he had been commanded to do. His fear of forever losing something temporary was being tested, and with that, the jihad - internal struggle - begins.

His first instinct was to tell his son about his dream and ask him what he thinks. His son, without hesitation, responded:

"O my father, do as you are commanded; if God pleases, you will find me patient."[8]

Miraculously, his son complied; he didn't resist his father, call him crazy, or try to run away. He surrendered immediately, which amplified Abraham's* conviction because he knew how to recognize signs. The sorrow of having to sacrifice his son muted under his ultimate conviction to succeed at doing whatever God commands, which propelled him forward with a level of such intensity that he unleashed the most powerful force for change in the world: evolution.

Savagely, in order to evolve into my highest self, I had to kill off the old parts that weighed me down with my own hands. Initially, I felt like I was betraying myself until, like Abraham's* son, I complied and surrendered. It wasn't hard, like fighting an enemy; it was the agony of intentionally hurting someone I loved. I had to leave behind the part of me that protected, guided, and helped me survive to this point in my life. Like a booster on a rocket, it is critical to get into space, but once there, it becomes a burden that must be released.

Surrendering isn't just a technical process of changing small habits until we accomplish greatness. It's emotional and painful to prune ourselves. That's why we don't like change; no matter how small, it's still death. That's why the pillars are best used slowly with compassion. With every small success, we refocus from death to being reborn, and eventually, the feelings of death inform those of life, collapsing the darkness and light into one… Craving our own annihilation and leaving us fearless.

There is infinite potential within us, and each step forward rewards us with gifts of talents gained, wisdom ingrained, unconditional love, and confidence in our unwavering connection to God. However, the ultimate benefit is 'Knowing Thyself'; there is no person that set off to become better or do something great that didn't learn who they were and what they were made of during the process. But without surrendering old experiences, we will never make the space necessary to experience this growth. The only way to heighten our senses and make new experiences our new normal is by evolving and changing our habits with balance and consistency.

Consequences of Enlightenment Without Practice

Prior to understanding how to apply the five pillars through consistent habits to experience evolution and enlightenment, I experienced my first awakening the good old-fashioned way - through tremendous pain. It blasted me through so many veils and to such a heightened vantage point that the way I saw the world from there completely blew my mind. I was so shocked at how blind I was before that I immediately wanted to see how much more there was to know. Incredibly, as soon as I started looking for ways to quickly achieve enlightenment, something I had never heard of before appeared: plant medicines. Many religions prohibit their use, while many spiritual communities promote them. I do not speak with any authority or bias on this, but I will tell you about my experience to perhaps open some minds and to caution others.

Four months after discovering such a quick method for enlightenment existed, I found myself in the mountains of Ecuador at an Ayahuasca retreat. 'Aya' means soul, and 'waska' means vine; together, it becomes 'Vine of the Soul.' The Andean natives drink this plant medicine in the form of a brew during their spiritual rituals to experience deep, introspective journeys and to heighten their perspective of reality. The chemical within this brew, DMT – scientifically dubbed as the 'Spirit molecule' occurs naturally in our bodies and is released at the highest levels when we are born, when we sleep, and when we die. Interestingly, in many cultures, sleep is described as a temporary death, and one of the reasons why meditation asks us to fall into a deeply relaxed (sleep-like) state is so that we can naturally release this chemical.

DMT is used to pierce the veil between the physical and spiritual world so that we can perceive the other side of life. In small natural doses at night, when we sleep, we get vivid dreams, but in large doses, like at the retreat, we go on a journey that words are insufficient to describe. All I can say is that I was 33 years old the first time I saw my true self. I recognized who I AM immediately, like what someone waking up from amnesia might feel like, causing me to erupt into a feeling that, at the time, I described as "full body laughing while orgasming."

It wasn't even in the seeing of who I was; it was specifically the recognition that made it so euphoric. There was something in the oldness of it that made remembering who I AM the ultimate feeling. Like those videos of soldiers surprising their families after coming back from duty, there is an element of 'a piece of my heart is missing' and 'I hoped but feared that I'd never see you again.' The pain of separation from oneness caused me to bury this feeling so deeply within that I forgot about it, and from a nostalgic distance, I mistranslated it as 'I'm missing something' for 33 years. But no matter how deeply I buried it, with it was the undying impulse to find it, and with a sigh of relief, I finally had.

As wonderful as that might sound, when I came back from my journey, life was full of magic… for a few weeks, and then it became absolutely dreadful. Because I had not developed the physical habits to prime my body to maintain and ground those high spiritual levels, I plummeted back to this state of darkness, which is not that it was bad or evil; it was my normal everyday life. But it seemed so dark now without the light spilling in from the other side; it lost the richness, colors, taste, and music of the other world; life was now black, white, and flat in comparison.

In a desperate attempt to regain that magic, I would go on crash diets and meditate for hours, only to fail to be able to maintain the intensity of such rigorous new activity; then my willpower would weaken from all the effort, and whiplash me back to my old habits of binge eating and hating myself for knowing what was at stake and being too weak to fight for it. For two years, I lived in that miserable existence until I finally overcame my addictions and started to truly embody my practice, and I can confidently say that this was the darkest time of my life. Nothing seemed to matter other than remembering this connection, and every time I failed, I lost all my confidence in myself and felt lost.

There was a period of time in Muhammad's* life where, on a few occasions, he almost committed suicide. It took two years after the first time Angel Gabriel initiated contact with him to connect with him again, and this waiting period was wretched. I speculate that perhaps he thought the lack of contact was a punishment for not reacting well to the initial encounter or that he felt he had lost his mind, but whatever his true reason, twice he went to the top of a mountain with the intention of throwing himself off and ending his misery. With each attempt, Gabriel would descend and whisper to him, "O Muhammad*, you are truly the messenger of God"[9], easing his distress and calming him down enough to return home and wait patiently despite his efforts.

As I mentioned before, DMT is naturally released when we die, but a near-death experience can also stimulate its release. When we think we are about to die, our body releases a super cocktail of hormones that heightens our senses and makes our mind silent and laser-focused, which enables us to experience with acute clarity our connection to Source. This is the reason why many people are addicted to extreme and dangerous activities; however, luckily, there are gentler ways of achieving this level of connection without drinking medicine or jumping out of planes, but it takes time and consistency to achieve it.

The hardest part is the waiting period in the middle because, after the initial excitement of changing our habits, it takes what feels like forever to see the benefits of all our consistent hard work. This time can feel like a punishment, but really, it is a critical part of the journey. It is the time and distance that create a need so strong that it forces out any remaining distractions we used to have and allows us to laser focus on accomplishing our true, deepest intentions. Dr. Eric Thomas says:

"When you want to succeed, as bad as you wanna breathe, then you will be successful."

I could never relate to this statement because, for the vast majority of my life, there was nothing I wanted more than to breathe, but during this waiting period, I felt the power in his words. I was ready to give up anything to feel that unity again. Also, to go from the highest high of feeling truly alive and then plunging back into the dark emptiness... the word wretched from the song *Amazing Grace* immediately comes to mind.

"Amazing grace,
How sweet the sound.
That saved a wretch like me.
I once was lost,
but now I'm found.
Was blind but now I see"[10]

I tell these stories to relay my experiences of unfathomable highs and equally demoralizing lows, only to show that when trying to reach enlightenment without a plan or practice, we can just as quickly fly as we can crash and burn, but the feeling definitely won't last. The greatest benefit to going that far that fast was the inspiration it gave me of what life could be if I worked hard enough, but it also made the journey from where I was to where I wanted to be that much harder. It was my first time understanding the true wisdom that ignorance IS bliss.

Purpose Of The Remainder Of This Book

The remainder of this book is divided into five chapters, and each will explore in depth one of the five pillars of surrender: Intention, Prayer, Fasting, Charity, and Pilgrimage.

Each chapter has three sections, explaining:

1. What the pillar is,
2. It's spiritual meaning, and
3. I provide real-life examples of:
    a. How I failed at it.
    b. What I learned, and
    c. What success looked like.

I share my stories in hopes that they will act as a guide, helping others fast-track through my successes, avoid the pitfalls on my journey, and give them signposts to reassure them when they feel lost.

My ultimate goal when I set out on this spiritual path was to deepen my connection with God, making my communion so strong and constant I could tap into the rightly guided wisdom any time rather than experience it as a temporary one-time whim. I wrote this book intending the same for the reader. For people like me, who have known of God but have never known Him. Having been estranged for whatever reasons life has presented, my hope is that if you have gotten this far, you are already aware of the deep intention within you to find home and that this book helps light the way.

Since keeping an OPEN mind will be critical on this journey, I present an English translation of The Opening (Al-Fatiha). It is the first chapter of the *Quran* and is composed of **7** verses.

<u>**The Opening**</u>[11]

(I swear) In God's name of Compassion and Mercy.

That through God's most praiseworthy qualities,
he raised existence.
With Compassion and Mercy.
Reign over our daily decisions.
It is You (in our heart) we obey, and Your wisdom we seek.
Guide us on the path of the middle way,
The path walked by the blessed,
Not the path that is too rigid, nor that is too loose.

Ameen.

Once, I was on a first date with a Harvard grad, and we were having a deep conversation about spirituality and whether the spirit 'exists.' He was skeptically interested but didn't know much about the subject. He had focused all his time on business pursuits, so understandably, he didn't have much left to dive deep into the non-physical. He was a nice guy, but even the nice ones get weird in unknown territory. I don't know if it's because he's a man or an Ivy Leaguer, but he really wanted to convey to me on a subliminal level that he felt superior to me intellectually. He had a very straight posture, and his chin stayed up the entire conversation, listening from up high. He was mildly amused and invested just enough effort to see if there was anything in it for him later. I, on the other hand, was really open and hoping he would eventually drop his guard so that I could get to know him deeper. My sister says I have Golden Retriever energy.

As a way to bridge our worlds and help him understand where I was coming from, I tried using science to translate the mystical to him. While I was explaining the spiritual relationship between nothing and everything via the Big Bang Theory, he interrupted and asked expectantly:

"So then, if everything came from nothing, what is nothing?"

He was baiting me, but after a calm, measured beat, I answered:

"Nothing is infinite potential." I punctuated with a pause to give him a breath to let it sink in. "When you become something, that's it. You're defined and limited to only be that thing. But when you are nothing, you can be anything."

It deeply satisfied me to see his eyes squint to hood their widening surprise, and his brows try not to narrow. He tried to hurry the conversation along to distract me from noticing that he had to focus his attention to understand my response.

We didn't stay at the restaurant for long after that, and he never did open up. So, needless to say, there was no second date. While at home alone that night, my mind did what it always does. I kept replaying the conversation over and over, analyzing and wondering how I could've said something better or whether I should've said anything at all. I had this deep feeling that something was missing or left unsaid. It almost felt like he had asked me the wrong question, and then all of a sudden, out of nothing, I watched the question he should've asked me explode to life:

'When you become something,
how do you access the infinite potential of nothing?'

Chapter 1: Intention

"We have created man and know what his soul whispers within him, for We are closer to him than his jugular vein."
-Quran 50:16

Every single person I have ever admired, whether they are an Athlete, Political Leader, Prophet, or CEO, always starts any piece of advice by talking about intention. It is the first pillar on which everything stands, and nothing else matters if it is not firmly defined.

So critical yet so elusive, I was never taught how to perceive the energy that pushes people toward their goals or pulls them to their luck. It was like my concept of God; I couldn't ever see the intention itself, only knowing it based on seeing the thoughts, words, and actions it created.

What is Intention?

Intention is living with our attention turned inwards.

Many of us make the mistake of thinking that our Intentions are something that we make or wish for, but it's the opposite. It is a direction that has been sent to us that we receive via an idea, dream, or deep desire for something. That is Spirit initiating contact with us and showing us a picture of the next step in our journey of evolution. Embedded within these desires are the steps for how to raise our energy levels and attracting it into our existence. We understand these instructions with our 6th sense called Intuition.

"As soon as you truly commit to making something happen, the 'how' will reveal itself." - Tony Robbins

<u>Intuition has four clairvoyant ways of communicating with us:</u>

1. <u>Clairsentience</u> – is a feeling and is the most common form intuition takes. Everyone has had a gut instinct at some point. I especially experience it when I sense that someone is not being genuine with me, but we constantly use it subconsciously.

    - Jacob* had a feeling that if he let Joseph* go with his brothers, 'a wolf might eat him'[1].

2. <u>Clairvoyance</u> – is an image/scene that appears in our mind and usually comes as a metaphor that we have to decipher. I know I am getting very stressed when I start having vivid dreams of myself drowning, meaning it's time to relax a little and let go of so much responsibility.

    - Joseph* demonstrated this when he accurately interpreted the Egyptian King's dream regarding 7 lean cows devouring 7 healthy cows. He explained that the 7 fat cows represented 7 years of plenty, and the skinny cows represented 7 years of extreme famine. He used that intuitive information to advise the Pharaoh to harvest and store as much grain as possible for the first 7 years so that the Egyptians have food to eat when the 7 years of famine arrive.[2]

3. <u>Clairaudience</u> – is a voice/sound in our mind like someone is talking. Although we hear many sounds in our minds, this one is calm and straightforward. It can also be used to communicate with animals or nature.

    - This describes Solomon's* ability to hear the ants speak as he walked over them: "O ye ants, get into your dwellings, lest Solomon and his hosts crush you without knowing it."[3]

4. <u>Claircognizance</u>– is a subtle knowing without understanding how we know, and can also feel like a download of information.

- When Muhammad* would receive downloads of the *Quran*, his body would tremble, and he would sweat from the intensity of it. Afterwards, he described the recitations as being engraved in his heart.[4]

We naturally have each of these abilities, and there are other ways to sense things through our scent and taste. Once, after a medicine circle, one of the participants confessed that during the ceremony, she was so disturbed because it smelt like someone was passing gas the entire time, until the end when the realization popped into her mind that it was the stench of her negative thoughts. As soon as she understood what the smell was trying to teach her, it completely went away.

Long ago, these abilities were considered miraculous and only obtainable by the most righteous of people, but as humans have evolved past survival mode, our intuition has been prioritized and strengthened. There are some clairs that we are inclined towards. I am personally strongest with claircognizance, but like any other muscle, we can develop them to make them stronger – which is the whole point of this book - to improve our ability to hear the internal guidance we receive.

These forms of subtle communication are as necessary to us as our actual hearing and sight because they are the direct way we hear internal communication from Source. Without them, our journey toward our dreams feels like walking alone in the dark, but with them, we receive the guidance attached to our intentions. These intuitive pictures and feelings serve as a northern star, guiding the three wise men – our mind, body, and spirit, to follow the light of inspiration to our destiny.

Common Pitfalls When Understanding Intention

The first pitfall I fell into was getting attached to the pictures and dreams in my mind, which made them mental idols rather than tools for communication. Desires or inspiration come in an unmanifested state as feelings, and in order for us to process them in a way we understand, our mind turns them into pictures. The pictures we generate are normally pulled from our past experiences as a quick way to translate the feeling, but by doing that, we can inaccurately translate new information.

For example, there were many times when I would feel a surge of love within me, and then after, I would see a picture in my mind of someone I loved, causing me to miss them. In that, I made two wrong assumptions: one was that I was the originator of the love, and two was that it was aimed at the specific person I had pictured. Once I learned how to properly translate clairvoyant communication, I understood that I was not the originator but the receiver of love coming from Source and that I wasn't missing anyone, but it was God that was missing me.

What I should've done was rather than get attached to the mental images of the incredible life waiting for me in the future, I should've deeply felt into the feelings of excitement the pictures were evoking within me, because that is where the instructions are hidden. This is one of the reasons why all prophets caution us to break all idols. It's not just the physical ones we worship but the mental ones we hold within, that can cause us to misunderstand God's guidance through our inspirations and intuition. If we get too attached we also get stuck in expecting to receive that exact mistranslated image, and when we don't get it, we become confused or disheartened.

So surrendering assumptions and expectations, and focusing on the feelings behind the mental images is the first key to becoming unstuck. Because although feelings are more vague than pictures, they carry the unfiltered steps we must take on the path to bringing our dreams to life, and we know we are going the right way when the step we physically take resonates with the feeling embedded within the picture inside of us.

This led to my second pitfall, which was that when I became so intensely attached to the specific pictures in my mind, I elevated them, causing a separation between us. So, rather than allowing happiness to unfold from within me, I found myself falling back into that cycle of reaching externally for a happiness that was far away. But the inner world works the opposite way, in that we must feel good first so that our intrinsic happiness spills out of us, rather than be a feeling we are chasing to acquire.

For example, when my very active kids are home all day on the weekends, I can either feel like the best mom ever, or like a huge walking bruise based on only two criteria: did I exercise and feed myself a good healthy meal first thing in the morning. If I do, they get a happy, energetic mom who can outplay and exhaust them. If I don't, I feel lethargic all day and nag them more to pick their things up. Our day goes completely differently just because of the way I feel. My intention is to be a good mom, but in my definition of goodness it isn't just the finality of providing for them that makes me good; it's the things I do to connect with them on a daily basis that inform that definition. I was doing things to be a good mom, without feeling like a good mom, until I realized the only way to feel like a good mom, was to feel good.

Before I awakened to prioritizing my internal state, I never valued how much the way I felt dictated my day. I used to believe that feelings come second to survival, and would go through the motions of my day getting things done, without any regard for how I felt about it, which can actually be helpful to a certain degree, but detrimental in other ways. I was working harder to get the things I wanted so that I could be happy, but because I wasn't cultivating the happiness internally, when I would finally acquire my physical achievements, the happiness that came with them would only last a moment until I was back on the hamster wheel again.

This is why it is critical to toe the line between making our internal feelings our main focus, while not getting attached to the pictures those feelings usher in. The same images that motivate us on this path can become pitfalls that delay our progress if we fall back into our old habit of externalizing or projecting out our happiness.

Living In Intention

Falling in love with connecting to our intentions is by far the most important lesson on this journey, even through to the very end when we have materialized our dreams. By prioritizing the reality of our inner world, we find that the job, car, or money we desired was only for the opportunities of love and respect that came with them. They have no true intrinsic value on their own as we never sit in our house kissing our money or hugging our car, maybe once when we first get them, but after that, they don't fill us anymore. So it's critical that we learn to cultivate the love within ourselves first. Otherwise, we get stuck in the karmic cycle of constant consumption.

The Buddha* used to call these unquenchable desires 'hungry ghosts,' because they never get full no matter how much we feed them. The ghost I was forever feeding was the financial instability I felt within my childhood home. No matter how much money I made as an adult, inside, I was still a little girl eating plain, off-brand *Cheerios* because WIC considers honey a luxury. My child-self decided the solution to our problem was to collect as much money as possible so that we could buy the better cereal, but what she really craved was the stability of knowing someone out there was watching out for her, a feeling neither money nor honey could fulfill.

Once I realized that no amount of money could fill that hole, I knew it would be insane to keep doing the same thing and expecting to get a different result. So, after years of having an acquisition mindset, I shifted my attention to my inner world, but initially had the same problem, my dreams felt far away like I had to reach for them – I was still chasing. It wasn't until I learned how to bypass the images to connect with Source that I found the light inside filled me with the safety I had always been chasing. It provided the direct, unconditional, and unlimited access to all the guidance and assurance I ever needed, constantly reminding me that everything was going as planned, and that no one could ever take this wisdom away from me.

Having security didn't mean I would never get hurt or be hungry again, it meant knowing I would be safely guided through the pain so that I could understand it and appreciate it, rather than fear it. Also, no matter where I got in life, my intentions never stopped getting bigger, and I realized this is natural. Our dreams always exceed our current limitations because they must shine brighter than where we are, so we know where to go. We are like moths to its flame, unable to resist its allure because intentions express our deep spiritual need for creation and evolution. However, now I knew how to fill myself up when I felt that hunger.

> "At the center of your being, you have the answer,
> you know who you are, and you know what you want."
> -Lao Tzu

Without my connection to Source, I could only rely on myself to ensure my safety and security, and so it felt like I was throwing darts in the dark when I turned 18, started college, and had to decide what I wanted to do for the rest of my life. I didn't know anything about myself or the power I carried within me. All I knew was that I was roughly aiming for the fastest and easiest way to feel stable and make lots of money, so I became an accountant.

I picked a profession before I knew what truly made me feel alive and poured so much of my life into cultivating that skill rather than strengthening my connection to the only form of true nourishment, believing that money and a husband would patch that hole. But after achieving all my goals of graduating, getting my CPA license, a good job, and married, I discovered that all the magic was slowly being drained out of my life instead, and I didn't know how to replenish it. My life didn't become better after having money and stability; I just started surviving more comfortably, but I wasn't thriving or living life the way it's supposed to be lived.

After a lifetime of survival, making the switch to prioritize love and living our dreams can initially feel like a risk because the price of chasing our dreams is directly correlated to how much discomfort we can handle. This is a standard part of the journey for a few reasons: 1) Changing our habits always feels uncomfortable, but once we do, it empowers us to adapt to a new, richer path, and 2) Having faith in the light inside of us feels the same as having faith in ourselves, and that level of confidence and trust in ourselves is mandatory to bring our dreams to life.

We are all born with the ability to directly connect and communicate with our Inner Genius, and by living with our attention focused inward, we allow that feeling of what we love and enjoy to guide us to our true purpose in life. It Isn't always a pleasant path, but neither was the path to becoming an accountant, I still had to spend years in an expensive college, pull all-nighters studying exceptions to tax rules, and take exams that made grown-ups cry. Had I known then about the power I had within me to obtain unlimited guidance toward my highest good, there is no telling where I would be in life now, but I also know that I had to have that experience of getting lost so that I could tell my story now of how to be found.

The main takeaway is that our ability to take directions from our Inner Guidance depends on how often we look at it, and how much we trust it to guide our actions. When I didn't obey this internal guidance, I ended up doing something I didn't enjoy for the sake of security and eventually, I woke up one day and realized so much of my life had passed, and I couldn't remember the last time I did something for the fun of it. Which is the mark of true wealth, being able to afford the time to do what we love. Intention is our treasure map that sends us on an epic journey to find the wealth within, and eventually, when we live in intention, we become like Midas, turning everything we touch into gold.

<u>Mysticism of Intention</u>

This next section is composed of ideas that came to me during deep meditative states. I jump from one idea to the next, so please allow your imagination to be flexible and play with me for a few pages.

<u>Declaration of Faith</u>

To set the Intention of Surrender, there is a sacred oath that believers declare:

'There is no God but God, and Muhammad is his messenger.'

To decipher this, I ask 'What is God?', and although this concept is undefinable, the closest way we as humans can conceptualize it, no matter who we talk to, in any race, religion, or creed, in any part of the world, the definition above all else is that:

'God is Love'.

So then I ask, 'Who is Muhammad*?' and it was revealed that:

"We have sent you forth (O Muhammad) as nothing but mercy to people of the whole world"[5]

So, at its core, the meaning of this pledge is that:

'There is no love but Love, and Mercy is its messenger.'

The initial part of this statement, 'no love, but Love,' negates itself. God is flirting with nothingness and everything, and in only four words, revealing the elegance of the Big Bang theory. Because this negated affirmation leaves us in a collapsed state of pregnant nothingness, we gather that there is a portal to infinite potential through nothing.

That's why when we meditate or pray to contact God, we go to that dark, empty space inside of us so that we can access its potential in the form of thoughts and feelings. It's one step away, all we have to do is close our eyes, and we are there. We ask a question to the black screen of our mind, and magically, a picture, word, or sound appears. It's so natural we don't appreciate the miraculous nature of it. Our connection to God is so normal, it is hidden in plain sight.

We never deeply ponder: 'Where do thoughts come from?' We just mindlessly think and believe the thoughts are our own. Is it truly possible that our communication with God could be that direct and accessible to anyone? Chef Gusteau tried telling us long ago that "Anyone can cook."

Acoustics and Affirmations

When the first part of the oath: 'There is no God but God,' is said in the ancient language of Arabic. It allows the sacred sounds to come to life:

'La Ilaha IL Allah'

When you hit the IL hard and stretch the last Lah, the acoustics of the words serve as heart openers. Similar to saying Hallelujah – which has similar acoustics.

If you would like to try out the effects of these acoustics, say it like this out loud a couple of times and see how it pierces and then expands your chest:

La Ilaha IL (Hard) Allaaaaaaaaaaahhhhhhhhh (long and deep vibrating exhale from lungs/chest).

When performed for long periods of constant recitation (33 or 99 times for beginners, 30 minutes to an hour for adepts), afterwards, a reverberation occurs in your heart space where the cells in your body have taken on the rhythm. It feels like the heart portal has been stimulated, and for those who practice consistently, eventually, they detect a lightness afterwards, almost as if they are flying.

Now, to take this game of ideas to a different level. Flip your mind and imagine that in order for us to say this statement, because all thoughts come from God, that God had to think it first.

Inspired thoughts are different from noise, distractions, and an overstimulated nervous system. They have an electric quality to them, which many people have experienced, when they hear something that feels so true, they get goosebumps or chills. The deeper the thought, the more power and effect it has on us.
So, traveling to those depths now, we imagine the place this sacred oath originated from. When said from God's point of view, as if He were saying it to Himself, that 'there is no other than me.' The name Allah has no other that it can be externalized to. The concept of two collapses and Al Lah becomes 'The One,' or I AM.

'No i am, but I AM'
– when held long and deeply enough evolves to –
i am that I AM.

I cannot go very deeply into that statement because it would cause the length and scope of this book to become another million pages, but I do strongly encourage anyone interested to look into it. It is an English translation of a Hebrew phase, which is also translated as "I am who I am," "I will become what I choose to become," "I will be what I will be," "I create what I create."

It is a self-affirming statement, which, not coincidentally, all of the strongest Intentions are also stated as I AM affirmations. The words spoken after 'I AM' exude externally what we are internally, and that thought/word becomes the first physical creation that our intention has given birth to. Each time it is repeated it enlivens it and serves as a reminder of who we are.

Because I AM is infinite, what we put behind those words may feel huge to us, but it actually limits it, so we have to be careful and intentional with what we limit ourselves to become. But with that said, everything in creation is made in His image, and so although we may never be able to see the totality of infinite possibilities within our lifetime, we are privileged with seeing the limited aspects of it that we can bring into existence.

I Am Loving.
I Am Compassionate.
I Am Powerful.

Even deeper, we ask: What if we didn't put anything after I AM? Allowing existing to be sufficient, without needing it to be defined. We become one with the In in intention, and thoughts at this depth become briefer but more energetically loaded:

Our Intention is to love. Intention is love. To is love.
To experience, exude, embody, and emanate it.

Fishing for pearls at this depth reveals the deeply hidden 'why' at the root of every intention ever made. No matter what shape the intention takes - our deepest desire is to be love and mercy for ourselves and for all. So when we take our sacred oath, we say out loud that there is no God, but God, and Muhammad is his messenger, but the energy carried within it (at different levels of depth) declares:

I worship the One Love and Mercy for all.
I serve the One Love and Mercy for all.
I AM Love and Mercy for all.

The Light Within

In the *Quran*, there is a chapter called "an-Noor" (The Light), where God is explaining the mysticism of the light within:

"Allah is the Light of the heavens and the earth.
A likeness of His Light is a niche in which there is a lamp,
the lamp is within a glass,
the glass is like a pearly white star lit from the oil of a blessed tree,
an olive tree – neither of the East nor of the West,
whose oil all but glows though no fire touches it.
Light upon light,
Allah guides to His Light who He chooses.
And sets forth examples for the people.
And Allah is the Knower of all things."
-Quran 24:35

In *The Reality of Gnosis* by Muhammad Said al-Jamal, he explains that the lamp is a metaphor for our heart, and like a white pearly star (or a northern star), it is our First Intellect, which I translate as our intuition via our clairvoyance.

By fleshing out this understanding further, the heart – which is where intentions emanate from, receives inspiration (or light) from within itself. This light then glows like a northern star, which guides us to our highest and best destiny and encoded within it are the steps we must intuitively take to get there. Our heart uses its own light from within to guide itself to love.

Light guiding light.

How I Failed at Intention

I was 37 the first time I experienced a deeply inspired intention - I felt that I had to write a book. Before that, my intentions were focused on things I needed to get: a college degree, a better body, husband, job, home, kids, etc., and although they fulfilled varying needs, none ever filled my deepest need to feel whole. They were the shallower intentions whose value was in the getting of it and not in the having of it, the children being the closest exception to this rule.

I could say the desire to write was an inspired dream, but it was more of an obsession, and the unclarity of it was eating me alive. I thought about it constantly and tried to imagine the chapters and words, but all that came was a vague idea about the universal experience of surrender, accompanied with chills that electrocuted my entire body. But no matter how badly I wanted it, the feeling also scared me because I knew that in order to be qualified to write about surrender, I had to experience it completely. So I did exactly what Jonah* did and tried to run away from it.

I had painfully given up plenty of things before love, money, friendships, and with each one, all the beliefs I had wrapped up into them. When I had to sell my car a few years after the divorce, I was gutted, it was the last relic tied to my old life, which I dedicated 15 years to 'getting.' It was the first car I bought after getting a job as a CPA, and it represented me making it in life - I had money for something more than survival. It was rare, the last stick shift of its series, standards weren't being made anymore because everyone wanted automatics, and no one could drive a stick. I remember pulling up to the valet and watching them take a look into the car, then walk away to hand the keys to a more senior teammate. They would look away from me as I walked past the stand, and it would chuckle something deep in me.

But even deeper than that, it was the car I brought my kids home from the hospital in, and I had a lot of dreams tied up in that home. Dreams of growing old, family dinners, wholeness, and so much love. The car was attached to a life that I had already let go of, and yet I was still holding on to the dream of it. In selling the car, the last item I had from my old life, I not only grieved it but also the feeling of completeness tied to it when I had my family whole under one roof, a wholeness my kids would never get to know. All of that meaning was stored in a car, and letting go of it was so painful, it shook me to my core when I imagined what I would have to let go of to experience ultimate surrender.

It felt crazy to desire my own ego's death, but I didn't really have a choice. It was either fully surrender (and allow my ego to die) so that I could achieve my highest potential and write about the experience, or live a stagnant and meaningless life in a job I hated but needed so that I could buy things that would give me a moment of happiness. Both options would kill me; one would slowly drain the life out of me over a long period of time, and the other would swiftly slice me in half, but at least that option came with the promise of resurrection. I had to kill the only person I have ever been, to become the person that resonated with the light inside of me, because in order to write about feelings so big, I had to become bigger.

Since we are defined by our habits, in order to change into the best version of myself, I had to end my old destructive habits of overeating, oversleeping, *TikTok*, and TV, and build new healthy habits that would raise my vibration, which meant upgrading my physical and mental health. But that was hard because I had developed these coping mechanisms over a lifetime, and I needed them now more than ever because of the newly added pressure to start writing.

My body buzzed with anxiety at the thought of writing something so huge, which I had never done before because I was an accountant, not a writer. But the more I procrastinated working on it, the more I needed something to numb the pain of the intensity growing inside of me. Just thinking about how much I had to change overwhelmed me, like attempting to climb Mount Everest while ten months pregnant, but no matter what I did to avoid it, its intensity kept gaining momentum to remind me that this task was coming due.

Added to the pressure was my internal turmoil. I thought there was nothing more that I wanted than to serve God. I had thrown my entire old life away in pursuit of only Him, and even with that level of commitment, I was scared when it came time to truly give myself to Him entirely. My feelings during this time were complex. I was paralyzed by the fear of surrendering even more, and on top of that, I felt ashamed for having that fear, like I was a coward for being scared and not trusting God. I consoled myself with thoughts like, 'Perhaps this fear is normal, like being afraid of dying.' But it didn't matter; even with all that crippling fear and shame accumulating within me, it couldn't stop the intensity of the impulse urging me to change from within.

I was being called to God in a way He had never contacted me before, and although I knew how to listen to my feelings, this was too big, but He gave me no choice. To ease me into surrender, He not only sent me the all-consuming urge to write, but He also bombarded the dark screen of my mind with blindingly bright pictures of a new future. The more I saw this dream, the more my fears gradually transformed from fear to excitement, amplifying my level of commitment to it. I thought I was pursuing God, but truly, He chased me so relentlessly that I couldn't run away from His call anymore. The moment I realized that the only way through this pressure was to start writing, I was propelled forward by a force so intense it was as if I had been spit back out on shore, and my journey began.

Taking The First Step Through Chaos

The energy to start writing came in the strangest form. After a year of avoiding my intention, one day, I woke up and couldn't stand my life anymore. It was hard to get out of bed because there was nothing waiting for me, no purpose, no job, no kids (I had a 50/50 custody split with their dad)… nothing needed me. Also, I had gained a lot of weight, my belly was bigger than ever, apart from when I was pregnant. It made it hard to sit up, so I would have to roll onto my side first and then slowly lift myself up so that I wouldn't get vertigo, it was demoralizing, having spent most of my life a slave to fitness. When I got to the bathroom and looked in the mirror, my eyes focused on the worst parts of me, and I was disgusted.

I knew that living like this wasn't right, and that I needed to make changes, but I felt helpless to break my habits, even though I could clearly see that they were not keeping my vibration high enough to fulfill my purpose. I kept hoping a sudden inspiration would fill me with so much energy it would take over, and I would easily fall into good habits of success to execute my mission quickly. But I also knew that if God had granted my wish, my body would've shattered from trying to download that high of an energy frequency into the current density of my body, like trying to run an ultra-marathon in one hour without any training.

I knew the road ahead of me was long, and I dreaded it. Beyond being out of shape, since my first awakening, I was having a really hard time controlling my emotions. I had suppressed them for so long that when I woke up to the value of their communication, it caused decades of feelings to surge to the surface, making me feel completely destabilized in my inner world for a long time before my emotions ran their course and settled down. During that time, I probably spent more time on my couch hiding under covers and absorbing pain than I did anything else that I would've classified as constructive before.

So, it was incredibly hard to change my habits and accomplish goals in the beginning, not only because of all the inner chaos but also because I didn't know how much energy an empathetic mindset can drain from you. Before, while in survival mode, when I used to get up early in the morning to exercise and felt the pang of 'sleepy' or 'exhausted,' I just ignored it like I did all my feelings, and because I was numb to them they were easy to resist. But now that I was more sensitive to them, it was harder to resist them when they spoke so vividly to me, 'Let's go back to our warm bed and put our head on the soft pillow until the sleepy feeling goes away.'

Also, I wasn't just drained from my emotions but from others as well – something I definitely never had before! It was such a foreign ability to be able to empathetically sense other people's feelings that, at first, I didn't know how to protect myself from the negativity around me. So, for a little over a year, at the start of my spiritual endeavor, I went from trying to survive my external world to my inner world and realized that I never left the mentality of survival behind.

Intuitively, I knew that in order to fulfill my intention to write my book, my inner world needed stability, and so the first steps I needed to take were:

1) Find a way to calm the waves of emotion inside of me,
2) Have enough willpower over my feelings to accomplish goals and
3) Exit survival mode mentality for good.

I thought I would have to generate the power to do all this on my own, but God had already started building the momentum to push me towards making these changes. I just couldn't live in my body anymore, and so it was the same chaos and pressure inside of me that I loathed, that I surrendered to when it reached a critical mass and allowed it to move me to change. To guide me, God started streaming images of my future, and I saw visions of my healthy and fit body with glowing skin, no brain fog, and easy and constant access to my intuitive knowledge, which guided me on the path to achieving my dream of becoming a writer. I craved the confidence, abundance, security, and peace that I tasted in these vivid images, giving me the willpower I needed while at rock bottom to slay my fiercest opponent – myself.

<u>What I Learned</u>

<u>Perfectionism and the Art of Failing</u>

I had always known that I had an inner perfectionist, but our relationship became more pronounced when I started doing something that mattered to me. Before, she would hover and whisper words of judgment, but because I wasn't totally invested in what I was doing, it never bothered me. If anything, I thought it was a cute Virgo quirk which helped me be extremely organized, but now that I was working on something I truly cared about, I got to know her on a much more intimate level, and she crippled me with standards that felt impossible to reach:

'This has to be the best book that has ever been written,'
'It needs to open every heart that ever reads it and change the world,'
'The words in it need to make you feel electrocuted.'

It got so severe that during a session with a writing coach, I admitted that I wanted her to feel "punched" by my words. She asked me: "Why do you want to punch people?" I honestly didn't have an answer for her, it was just an overwhelming feeling inside of me that wanted to have a huge impact on people's lives through my words; my perfectionist was apparently a boxer.

The pressure of producing anything, even something mediocre, was crushing on its own, but this added expectation of perfection choked the words from coming out of me. When I would finally get the courage to write a few words, I would be filled with nausea and dread because it was never up to the perfectionist standards; she felt dirty to be associated with something so beneath her, and embarrassed that I was making a fool of us. She almost took me down, until divine guidance interceded to teach me how to face my fear of failure.

My oldest son, who is nine and normally obsessed with technology, developed an equal obsession with Dav Pilkey books, which I happily fed. As I started writing this book, Dav came out with a new series called *Cat Kid Comic Club,* which my son had been massively anticipating, and so we would rush to the store to buy them as soon as they came out. This series wasn't so different from his other books, which were mostly really fun to read and also a little educational, but reading this specific series felt like every star in the sky aligned and conspired to make Dav write the book I needed to read, exactly when I needed it.

It innocently appears to be about a family of silly, unruly tadpoles that join a writing club taught by a cat, to learn how to write comics. But what it actually is, is a review of the entire creative process, with coaching from a published author (Dav in the form of the cat teacher), to help get artists through all of the hiccups along the way. The very first lesson the club addressed was the fundamental stress felt by all writers – writer's block. To teach them how to get past it in a fun way, he made his first assignment a challenge: 'Write the worst comic in the world.'

By eliminating their fear of failure, and instead making it their goal, the tadpole's imaginations exploded. The stories started out silly and undeveloped, but as the series goes on, we watch how the books transform from simple ideas and outlines, to creating drafts, and then continually adding detail until they develop into full stories. All while staying true to his initial message - that the goal is to fail while having fun. By keeping their standards low, and making sure they continued to enjoy the process, by the end of it, their stories became so good, they were selling them to publishers.

Tim Ferris came back to haunt me, he knew I was still focusing on what I was doing wrong, and wasn't focusing enough on what I was doing right, so he sent Dav and my son to remind me. Each night, we read stories about children blowing up the Earth to save a stolen free toothpick, or grilled muenster cheese sandwiches that turned into monsters and ate kids instead, and it truly loosened something in me. I felt myself unraveling from the perfectionists hold, and set a new small goal for myself: To write like an 8-year-old and to fail. In sticking to that principle when I wrote, my standards would be so low I would always meet them, and I couldn't be judgmental anymore, because who would judge an 8-year-old? I learned an incredible lesson about the power of mediocrity, having feared being mediocre for so long, I realized just how much courage it takes to create something that sucks, and how proud of myself I should be for it.

After massively lowering my expectations and allowing myself to fail, I focused on just having fun with my ideas, and words started to flow. What used to be demoralizing, felt like a release now, but after months of practicing, I hit another speed bump in that I was still writing journal style. I knew that in order to write the specific book in my heart, I needed to refine my writing and take it from random thoughts, to coherently organized wisdom that I was confident in. Because I had been gentle with myself for so long, my perfectionism also transformed from an enemy that tried to destroy my creativity, to a friend who wanted to refine my writing into something we would feel proud of, which was exactly what I wanted. I knew that in order to write something I felt confident in, I had to feel confident first, and that would make me feel proud, no matter what I produced.

So I asked myself, "What can I do to make myself feel more confident?"

The answer that came back surprised me: '*Be consistent.*'

I thought the answer would be to take more writing classes, work your skill to death, get 10,000 hours of practice in. But instead, I was being taught that confidence doesn't come from what I am able to do, it comes from how deeply I trust my inner light, and how consistently I follow it. Just like I had to feel good, to feel like a good mom. In order to feel like a confident writer, I had to gain confidence through consistently showing up and keeping promises to myself in every part of my life because they were all connected, so in order to feel confident in one area, I had to feel it in them all. God was teaching me alignment, and showing me that it wasn't my writing that needed to be improved, but my thoughts, words, and actions that had to align with God's wisdom.

I started where I trusted myself the least - my eating and exercise habits. I could hear my inner guidance say put the chocolate cake down and go for a walk instead, but my hand reached for it without my mind being able to stop it. Not reacting to this impulse would feel like a superpower, and I had no clue at the time how much this willpower over food would spill over into every other part of my life.

Confidence

Years ago, I could wake up at five a.m. and run six miles before the rest of the world was washing the crust out of its eyes. So, when I initially set out on this new venture of getting healthy and fit to gain confidence, I tried to tackle it the way I had in the past - by brute force and perfectionism. I clearly had no clue what moderation or physical limits meant, and because my expectations of myself were so extreme when I attempted to set small goals, they were still too big.

Before, in my 20s, when I had no kids or emotions and could control every aspect of my life, it was so much easier to get up and run or stop myself from over-eating at will. But now I was older, tired, and more in touch with my feelings, so after years of abusing my body with extreme behavior, when I tried to employ my old stoic strategies, I was met with massive inner resistance, and my cravings felt so much stronger than me. Just the idea of cutting carbs made something inside me clench and say: "Eat everything now, she is about to starve us!."

So, at the beginning of this journey to find confidence, there was a lot of experimentation. I had to take the time to know what my new self was capable of, and so I only moved in the general direction of better health and willpower but didn't meet any specific goals. It was agonizing to let so much time pass without 'accomplishing' anything, but I needed to learn how to care for myself.

I cover this topic completely in my chapter on fasting, but ultimately, what I learned was that my body had a natural rhythm for hunger, exercise, and rest, and the key to having enough energy to overcome the emotional forces within me was that instead of working out, I had to 'work in.' My old way of training with high-intensity intervals was too hard on my already exhausted body and caused me too much physical stress now, so I started doing activities that re-energized me instead, like walking and yoga, which made me feel calmer and mentally sharper.

I became gentler with myself, and by doing so, it had a domino effect on the rest of my life. My thoughts became calmer and kinder, I criticized myself less, and so my writing became more confident, and because I felt uplifted all the time, I made better eating decisions. Not only was my internal state of peace spilling out into every area of my life, but most importantly, it uncovered a false idol I didn't know I had.

In becoming gentler with myself, I wondered why I had been so hard on myself to begin with, which is when I realized that before I prioritized my inner world, I defined ultimate health as whoever was on the cover of a fitness magazine. I know it's crazy to compare myself to people in magazines who dedicate their lives to being below 5% body fat, but I did it unconsciously, and when I didn't measure up, I judged myself as lesser and unworthy.

My intuition was making me aware of not only the physical but also the spiritual effects of my lifestyle and beliefs and how they affected the way my body operated as a holistic system, so if I had a harmful mental idol or false belief in one part of my life, it affected all parts negatively (and vice versa). Before, I considered those pictures harmless motivation because I had no clue how deeply they affected the way I viewed myself. I would literally tear myself apart both at the gym and mentally so that I could measure up to their standards, but after years of doing that, all I had was shin splints and insecurities.

By making me aware of how much self-inflicted damage my unconscious expectations could cause me, I woke up to that danger but still struggled to break that idol. I could objectively see that the people in magazines were dehydrated and airbrushed, and that they probably didn't look like that in real life at all. But because I had held the belief that that is beauty for so long, it was difficult to look in the mirror and convince my brain that what it was seeing was also beautiful, I just didn't measure up visually. So again, I had to radically flip the way I viewed myself and remind myself that rather than look out, I had to really embrace the process of feeling in.

For a while, when I first began making changes to my life, I avoided measuring my body, because I knew I would fall back into old habits of criticizing myself for being imperfect. Instead, I only checked inside to see how the changes made me feel, and through that, I developed an entire curriculum on how to care for my body in every aspect of my life. I learned that it loves yoga (which it hated before), fresh green juice is the luxury it is most grateful for, and wearing linen made me feel like I was always on vacation. Even though my body wasn't drastically changing, the way I expected it to when I made big changes to my diet and exercise habits, I felt happier in it, and that happiness eventually became love.

My intuition was teaching me that confidence doesn't come from a beautiful body, or a highly developed writing talent, it comes from trusting that I will kindly keep promises to myself. It also showed me that love and security are our natural state, which become blocked by false beliefs, and the solution to that isn't to cover our insecurities with achievement but to dig deep and uproot the rotten beliefs.

In being flushed with love internally, it spilled out of me, and I started loving the way I physically looked as well, which made me understand the power of surrendering our false beliefs. Before, I took submission to mean whipping my body into shape with no excuses allowed, but what it actually means is to submit to our body's innate ability to regulate itself, which mine did as soon as I got out of its way.

For years, my body was subjected to severe diets to keep my weight down, and when I started taking a more moderate approach, setting smaller goals, and focusing on my inner experience, I made great strides in my energy levels, but my binge eating habits were the most resistant to change. I knew it was because my old survival mode instincts were being triggered by years of forced deprivation, so as an act of good faith to show my metabolism that I trusted it and that I would never starve it again, I set two firm rules:

1. I would never go on a starvation diet again, and
2. I would focus on feeding it success.

It may sound insane to give the car keys to the toddler who has, on more than one occasion, had chips and popcorn for dinner, but when I gave my inner guidance my trust, something happened that I didn't expect. At first, it tested me and kept my appetite and cravings just as strong as ever, but I showed it that if I felt any hunger, I ate, no questions asked and no judgment. I did not limit my cravings in any way, and then after about a month of proving that I was not ever going to starve it, my hunger did something very mature: it became self-accountable.

Because I knew I could have whatever I wanted, whenever I wanted, I no longer felt the need to constantly reach for food. The urgency and desperation went away, and because I was more focused on the after-effects of how the food I was eating made my body feel, I started naturally feeling repelled by foods I used to love. I noticed the way my joints would ache after I ate dairy or how itchy my scalp felt after eating white sugar, and although I had never paid attention to those sensations before, now I couldn't tolerate the way it made me feel inside. Focusing on my inner world made it feel effortless to cut food that made me feel bad, and not because I told myself I couldn't have it, but because I legitimately didn't want it anymore, and that made all the difference in the world. I was no longer being deprived; I felt empowered, and the more amazing I felt in my skin, the more willpower it gave me to elevate my standards.

Over time, the tides of success vs survival had finally turned, and I started craving feeling good way more than I used to crave queso and chips. It was a double win; I not only built myself up by doing things that energized me and made me feel good, but also, the fight went out of the cravings inside of me. Like there used to be a child within me that had to rebel against unfair rules, but now, when I gave it my trust, it just immediately self-regulated. The simple idea of abundance and knowing I could have anything I wanted, put my mind in a new 'full' place, and I didn't feel that clawing need for junk food anymore - my inner war finally ended.

I'm not saying it was completely an easy street after that. Even with more inner peace, as I continued to focus less on what I was eating, and more on building strong habits that made me feel good inside, initially, it felt like I was taking one step forward and two steps back. It took months of diligent, consistent, compassionate practice for these new habits to really become programmed into my life, and when I say I made my goals small, I mean it.

Some habits started as small as just waking up and putting my shoes on. I didn't have to go for a walk, I was just getting used to waking up and putting my shoes on, I could go right back to bed afterwards. I know it sounds insane, and it is the reason why I had absolutely no tangible results in my body after months of practicing better habits, but I was solidifying something within me. I was establishing a rapport and telling my body that it was the law to wake up at a certain time every day. Eventually, it felt so natural for my body to wake up early to put on my running shoes, I found that I didn't even feel like going back to sleep once they were on. Further down the line, this habit grew into me jogging one mile each morning, and then eventually six again. I was working hard, but it felt effortless because I wasn't pushing myself hard or fighting against resistance. I was slowly flowing with success, and at first, I was collecting little drops, but before I knew it, those drops became rivers.

For the first time, I was moving with compassion, ease, and no expectations apart from showing up. When I released all that pressure and started giving myself credit for the steps I was taking, I started feeling success in every step I took, and that programmed in me a new addiction - feeling good all the time. I felt myself breaking out of my old vicious cycles, which drained me, while solidifying this new virtuous cycle that paid abundantly.

The changes I made were so gradual, I barely noticed how much progress I made by the time I got to the end of my journey, mentally I felt like I had just started. Every day felt like Day 1, and even though that is a very powerful thing, it can also be disheartening when you are working so hard and not seeing any results. Even though I wasn't focused on my external progress anymore, I was still aware of it, and during the process, I had to create checkpoints to stop and remind my inner perfectionist that 'Three months ago, I could barely get out of bed, and now I am walking for 10 minutes every day.' Eventually, one day after the tides had turned and I was consistently feeling good on a daily basis, I started completely relying on that feeling to dictate my entire day, and I checked in before making any decisions. When I finally relinquished that control and submitted to obeying the light inside of me, that was when the magic of momentum took over. Like Jesus said: "Seek first the Kingdom of God, and all will be added unto you"[6].

I looked up a year later and had lost twenty pounds, was in the best shape of my life, and had a manuscript with 100,000+ words that I was really proud of. My original intention was not to lose weight, or have my work published; it was to gain confidence and trust in my connection with God, and write the book He asked me to write, but those accomplishments were the realities that were added to me when I focused on my spiritual abundance within. When I cleaned out all the beliefs that held back my innate confidence and refilled that space with consistent positive action, the result was that my natural state of confidence returned and was no longer something I was chasing.

The Straightest Path Isn't Straight

I was about six months into my journey when my new habits started to clumsily click into place, where before a bad decision used to ruin the rest of my day, now I could shrug off having a cookie with breakfast, knowing that I would feel better after a jog and a healthy lunch. I wasn't perfect, and that was the point. I still had so many bad habits, but they just didn't matter anymore, because I had consistent good habits that stabilized my emotions. My feelings of imperfection were still there, and I acknowledged them, but they didn't stop me anymore, and that is when the tests started coming in to strengthen me.

Initially, I started developing my writing skills, thinking I would use them for my thesis paper on the "Mysticism of Islam," but the criteria for writing a thesis was so specific that the writing fell flat and lifeless on the pages - It didn't have the electricity of the feeling inside of me. I was 150 pages in when I sent my work to a writing friend who honestly told me it was "preachy and boring." Sigh, everyone needs a friend like this.

With a heavy heart and many tears, I threw away the 150 pages, and started again from scratch. A few weeks later, a book about spirituality in Islam was suggested to me, and I don't know how I missed it during my research, but my jaw dropped when I read it, it was the book I had just written, we even had word-for-word thoughts on some of the pages. Had I read this book a month before I threw out my own pages, I probably would've gone into a state of deep depression, realizing that what I had set out to do had already been done and was better. But because I was counseled to drop the pages, and push myself harder to write with my more authentic voice, in a miraculous way that saved me.

While following my inner guidance, there were so many moments I thought were dead ends or pit stops along the way, but as time went on, I was coming to find that they were not fruitless. In spending the months to write those 150 pages, although it wasn't the final product, it was invaluable practice. It formulated and organized concepts in my mind that I wanted to present, but it also revealed to me how I didn't want my writing to feel. In knowing that, I found my unique style and what made me feel special, rather than trying to fit myself into a pre-formulated way of doing things.

Although there were points where I felt lost and in the dark, the Light within guided me to see that even getting lost is a part of the journey because without it, I wouldn't have found parts of myself I didn't know I had, and to date, those are the parts of me that I am proudest of.

It was during this time that I learned:

1. God would send people to redirect me when I was lost, and
2. Following my intention wasn't a straight path, it was just the straightest.

How to Fail Harder

There was a point where, even with all my confidence and keeping my expectations low, I still hit writer's block. After months of words flowing and then having to scrap my thesis, I felt I had nothing to say that hasn't been said before, and even if I tried, I didn't know how to say it in a better, more magical way that was less thesis'y. At exactly this time, I was partnered up with a woman in my spiritual healing class who turned out to be a best-selling author and writing coach. She asked Me if I would be interested in having a bartered session with her, where I would coach her through our spiritual healing lessons, and she would coach me on writing. God sent the exact guide I needed, exactly when I needed her. During our sessions together, she taught me how to write with emotion and how to really dive into it rather than make it pretty and palatable. She showed me the power of a raw, simple word rather than a paragraph of polished fluff and taught me to remove limits from writing and allow it to be offensive, hilarious, and free. I thought I knew how to fail before, but she taught me how to fail harder. For my first exercise, she had me write 10 horrible titles for my book, here are the worst ones:

1. The Transformation: Shedding the cocoon.
2. Following the religions of Law and Love, comes the religion of Surrender.
3. Understanding the Truth behind the Veil.
4. God loves everyone, you fucking morons!

I was allowed to be corny, and icky, and an asshole. Because life was that way, and art imitates life. Again, she unlocked another limit within me, releasing compassion for the uglier parts of my human nature. By allowing them to exist, she showed me that kindness creates creativity, and meanness kills it. I had to be kind to all the voices inside of me, not just the ones I deemed worthy. They all needed to have a chance to speak.

She showed me how spiritual writing was. As I wrote, I became more compassionate and kinder towards myself and others, understanding now that their frustrations probably come from their inability to express themselves freely, after years of being told to be polite or to behave. Writing was uninhibited, and in order to work, it had to be completely free. It made me understand and value why, of all our rights, Freedom of Speech is our First Amendment. Listed before voting, taxes, and guns is our right to express ourselves… Living as a writer in Texas, this is almost romantic.

I was working at it like a technical skill, but she understood the mysterious, uncontrollable world that books come from and taught me how to open myself to it by being free of judgment of whatever comes through. She showed me that it was good to get lost, to hit dead ends, and that our triggers were where the good stuff was hidden. My writing completely changed from that point on, it was flagrant and started having the intensity and effect I was originally aiming for. I believe, with all my heart, that my intention attracted her to me to teach me the next step in the writing process, when I was ready to receive it. If she had come to me before I had practiced on my own with those 150 pages, I wouldn't have valued what she had to say as much, but now it was worth its weight in gold, and I fully absorbed everything she offered me.

Writing Is How I Pray

As I got into the swing of writing as a spiritual rather than a technical practice, I wanted to learn how to explore the mystical world the book was coming from. I wanted to connect to it more, and lo and behold, as soon as I asked, I got a newsletter from my spiritual community advertising classes on 'Automatic Writing From The Heart.' God sent another marker to guide me on the trail.

In this class, which was based on the basic writing principles in Natalie Goldberg's book *Writing Down the Bones: Freeing the Writer Within*. She instructed us to time our writing, starting with as little as 10 minutes, and during that time to follow these simple rules:

- Keep your hand moving
- Don't cross out
- Don't worry about spelling, punctuation, or grammar
- Don't think, or get logical

In following the rules, magic happens, words come out in an unexpected flow, that are coherent, raw, and beautiful. Something in me knew how to write, even without me mentally thinking about what I was going to say next. Just sitting at a blank, empty screen and allowing my fingers to be moved by the writer within me produced something, and it was good. My entire Prayer flow section fell out of me in one 20-minute timed session, and when I read it after I wrote it, I got chills, I couldn't believe I could write something so beautiful. I discovered the hand inside my heart doesn't just discipline me, it also writes me love letters.

The Sufis have a saying: "I am just a pen in Allah's hand," but for the first time, I experienced it, and it was everything. It was food, money, sex, vacation, luxury, and the feeling of holding a newborn baby in my arms for the first time after months of anticipating what it's eyes, hair, and nose would look like. Now I see it, covered in muck and squished on the way out, and I'd never seen anything more perfect.

I became a silent student of Natalie's, one of many lives she has touched that she will never meet or know, and her book illuminated for me not how to write but how to get out of the writer's way. Just like when I trusted my appetite to regulate itself, when I trusted my inner voice to write, all I had to do was silence the criticism in my mind so that the real writer could appear. Writing became more than just a skill I was acquiring, it was my active meditation and communion with God, and truly, without a doubt, my gift. I cannot express the amount of joy you have when you discover amazing gifts inside yourself that are effortless to reach for, and that just spills out of you. It is a wealth I have never known before and that nothing else in life has compared to.

This communion with my inner voice was informed by my intuitive clairvoyant abilities. The only way I could write was to translate to words, the meaning of the feelings coming through me, which I did by heightening my senses so I could hear them loudly and clearly. When I was no longer at war with my feelings, they became my writing currency, carrying the connection between me and God. Writing the book used an identical process to how I pray. I would sit silently, listening to my inner voice, and try to translate the unmanifest feeling my heart conveyed to me, into a manifested word. I was giving birth to God's words.

"In the beginning was the Word,
and the Word was with God,
and the Word was God."
-John 1:1

Intentions and Words Connect Us To God

Islamic tradition teaches that all three books in the Abrahamic religious trilogy come from the same 'Mother of books.'

- "The Law – The Torah,"
- "The Good News – The Gospel," and
- "The Recitations - The Quran"

In the Quran, almost every chapter begins with God swearing by His names:

- "ar-Rahman – The Compassionate," and
- "ar-Raheem – The Merciful"

In Arabic, these words come from the root word "Rahm," which means womb.

Whether it is a word, a book, or anything in creation, we see that the greatest power to create is held in the feminine essence, because a mother's womb is the only way to bring anything to life.

I used to take words for granted, not understanding the mysticism in something so common. I never thought about the time in our human existence when words weren't used. Eventually, when we evolved enough to name things and communicate through words, it was very few who could read and write them. So when people were able to write down energetically charged words that came through them (prayers) and recall them from a book later when they needed them, those people were considered magical, and their books were powerful, not because of the word, but because of the feeling the word evoked within the reader.

'Read' is the first word uttered in *The Recitations* conveyed by Angel Gabriel:

"Read, […]
and your Lord is most bountiful,
he who taught by means of the pen,
taught humankind that which they did not know."[7]

In following the path my intention set out for me, I found that what I thought was the simple act of writing words on paper, was actually a winding path to realize my connection to God within me. My intention illuminated the way, and although I was derailed and had to focus on diet, exercise, and perfectionism for a large part at the beginning of the journey, every pitfall and bump on the road was necessary. They caused me to express my need for a solution, which put me in a state of constantly calling out to God for help, more than I ever had before, and in a deep and desperate way. When I did, suddenly, help would arrive, as if it had been patiently sitting there on the path all along, waiting for me to discover the right questions to ask. When I started this journey, I had no clue what the end result

would be of this endeavor, but by the end, I knew more about God,
myself, and the gifts I held within me, than I ever had before.

He sent me on this writing journey,
and taught me by means of becoming His pen,
Him, which I did not know.

Summary of Success

After a year of starting this journey, I was unrecognizable. I was in great shape, my energy was significantly higher, and paradoxically I felt calmer. The act of aligning myself with God's will made me understand that the point was never to control my feelings, it was learning that when I hand control to Him, I can trust that they will automatically self-regulate. I was no longer in survival mode, I had joined the ranks of the rich and starving artists, and now I understood that creativity feeds me and that I couldn't live on bread alone.

My intention to write a book, resulted in not only a book I was proud of, but it led me down a path of compassion, love, mercy, and ultimately, finding myself and giving my life purpose. I had to surrender all the parts of me that were no longer serving me by changing my habits, expectations, and beliefs, like chiseling away at marble so David could appear, and although it was a bit painful, more than anything, I felt set free.

The element that surprised me the most regarding how to accomplish my goals effectively was learning how to relax and let go. I didn't understand how to apply ease while performing actions to write a book, yet incredibly, the majority of my time was spent sitting, breathing, and listening. Just like when I was pregnant with my children, I only carried them, I didn't have a single hand in their construction, and when it came time to give birth to them, my body knew how to break its own water and steadily increase contractions until they were out. My only job was to breathe, and this labor of love was the same, I wasn't responsible for the writing; I was just the vessel, and it was done through me. Even in moments of absolute fear that the words wouldn't come and I would have nothing interesting to say, the voice inside was clear: *'Your only responsibility is to breath, I will do the rest'*.

It was exhilarating and humbling, to realize how insufficient I was, and what a passive role I would be playing in such a massive effort. Yes, I am still 'writing' this book. I have taken the action of sitting at this computer for hours, and typing words onto the screen with my own hands, but the only true effort I put into it was tuning into myself, and getting my senses heightened enough for my heart and mind to coherently communicate with each other. Where the words come from is a mystery, many of the passages surprised me and came the moment I asked for them, suddenly emerging from the dark. It was around the same time that I kept seeing black mold in my external world, and it frightened me, I always considered it a bad omen, but now it was teaching me that some life grows in the dark. It was in this insignificance that I found that no matter how small i am, I always have direct access to the infinite I AM, and there is nothing in the world that comes close to that feeling.

Making something from nothing is the closest act we can perform that aligns us with the creator, but the reward is not just in the accomplishment but in the entire journey, even Day 1. Creating anything, whether a book or a baby, gave me a high that was only sustained while in the process of creating. As soon it was created, it moved into the manifested category, and now it was something that was temporary, as all created things are. So, even in my writing, I learned that I had to fall in love with the act of conveying a book - The art of connecting to the darkness, and bringing it to light. With every big bang of emotion came a word, and in that word, I discovered the part of myself that has no intermediary, it is my birth right to have a direct connection to God, and nothing feels better than Knowing Thyself. My first step in accessing my connection, was simply to look at it and feel it.

To turn my attention inwards.
In attention.
Intention.

Intention Flow

All Intentions ever made, at the root, are one and the same.
In the pursuit of Love and Mercy.
You can receive it and give it in multiple forms and ways, but
There is no love but Love, and Mercy is its messenger.

There is only one Love.
Love cannot be felt unless we feel safe.
Mercy is our safety.

Mercy is blissful ignorance. Already protected from things
unfathomable.
Like a child, oblivious to the countless falls their parents
prevented them from.
So that they can focus on playing.

I had always used intentions unintentionally.
I had intended to be perfect.
Subconsciously believing that if I were perfect, I would deserve
love.
In trying to accomplish this, I kept falling.
Resentful, 'where was the one responsible for catching me'?

But in falling I realized my arrogance.

My Luciferian tendencies to think I am nothing, if I am not perfect.

Every single time I fall short of my perfection I feel the sting of
disappointment, my lack of discipline, my body's inability to do
what my mind wills it to,

and so deeply I felt my humanity, and I hated it.

It's strange to identify so deeply with the Devil. To understand so perfectly his arrogance, and refusal to bow to the feebleness of humanity.

The more perfection I failed to achieve, the more self-hatred would accumulate within me. The opposite of the Love and Mercy I didn't know I was aiming for.

It was in this entanglement with perfection, that I had never felt more disconnected.

Leading me to the Genesis of my understanding,
of why God honored the human.
Honored us with humility.
Honored us with the fall.

In humility we gladly allow ourselves to be shaped and sharpened,
to bend and to bow.
It hurts and can feel sacrificial, but its hidden gem is compassion.
You recognize the fall in all.
It allows you to understand others deeply and completely, to become them.
Two Become One.

Union being the ultimate goal, It takes humility to unify.
If Perfection is the veil that separates us. Humility is the glue that binds us.
Slowly realizing that humility feels so much closer to divinity than perfection.

'In the image of God' takes on a whole new meaning.
Thinking it was just the soul, but now realizing, it encompasses all:
It includes the humanity.
        It includes the humility.
                It includes the fall.
Always thinking of surrendering as something we do to a force
outside of us.
Bowing in defeat. Bowing in worthlessness.
What if we don't surrender to Love. What if Love Is the Surrender.
We don't surrender, we Become Surrendered.
Bowing to reflect the image in which we were created.
Mirroring the Humility of Divinity.

We are told Love is patient, Love is kind.
But Love will also burn you alive, and nail you to a cross.
Misunderstanding the fall, we make Love our enemy, building
walls in our hearts.

In perfection we are climbing a ladder, which feels so much more
powerful,
than the naked vulnerability of tearing down our walls.
You can hear the angry crowd echoing the chanting within:
"Build the wall! Build the wall!"
Allowing ourselves a moment to feel the illusion of safety.
The Devil whispering in our ears – 'Resist the fall'.

Understanding now,
how the road to hell is paved with good intentions.
In intending to be perfect,
To protect our hearts and avoid the flame,
We fall deeper into the fire.
And In the end, no matter what decision we make,

we either burn in agony or in love.

So turn the tables over,
Break your ladders,
Tear down your walls.

Exchange your den for a house.

Love your enemy,
your humanity.
Trust the Mercy you will never see.
Choose to Burn in Love,
Willingly.

My son was six the first time he asked me: "What is God?"

We were having a casual chat while stickering, and because I talk about God a lot at home, this was a normal topic of conversation. He knew the idea of God, but he didn't understand that they were enmeshed.

Too young to explain concepts of consciousness and creation, his question was so simple and yet, undefinable.

So, I said what everyone says, and the closest answer adults have to understanding:

"God is Love."

He asked me if God "lived on the clouds with Angels"?

And I told him, "Yes, he does, but he also lives in our heart."

He looked up at me, distracted from the task at hand by his wondrous confusion at my response. I was his mom, so I had to tell the truth, in his world, I know everything. Then I saw him do something I'd never seen him do before. His focus softened, and I watched him feel inward, into his heart. He was searching for something big and unusual that he might've overlooked before.

When he found nothing out of the ordinary, he snapped right out of it, having spent maybe a breath or two looking. His eyes came back doubtful skeptics, not sure whether he was doing it wrong or if what I told him was wrong. I watched a seed get planted, and didn't know if I would get to see the fruits of it one day, and whether it would grow fruits of doubt or curiosity.

I got a hint based on all the questions that followed his little adventure inside, which he asked while stickering, to keep him entertained:

"How can God be in two places at once?"

"Because he is God, he can be everywhere."

"If he is in my heart, is he in your heart too?"

"yes."

"Is he in everyone's heart?"

"yes."

"How can he be in everybody's heart at the same time?"

Chapter 2: Prayer

"Allah says:
Neither My heavens nor My earth can contain Me.
Only the heart of My faithful slave contains Me."[1]
-Muhammad*

It's crazy how hard it is to describe something all-encompassing and yet so subtle. He only trusted his external senses of touch, taste, sight, smell, and sound, so it was a challenge to describe the Unmanifest, who can only be sensed internally. This is strange for a few reasons: one, because the only thing we ever remember about anything is the way it makes us feel inside, and two because we have the same issue with all our external senses as well, but don't judge them as harshly.

One game of telephone can prove how distorted an externally received message can become just based on our inability to hear or understand it, but we know we can improve the circumstances to enhance what we see and hear to obtain the message more accurately, so we lead with those senses. But when given our full attention, our intuition can also be strengthened, eventually becoming so dependable that we start uncovering the deeper layers of our inner messages and notice that the connection is everywhere. Not just inside us anymore, but inside everything.

"Split a piece of wood; I am there.
Lift up the stone, and you will find me there."
-Gospel of Thomas

In the holy trinity of the mind, body, and soul:

If we are the body, and
the soul is made in God's image,
then the mind is the connection.

We normally think the mind is the brain, but the mind is our attention, our consciousness, and when we pay close enough attention, we can tune to the thoughts in the mind of anything.

In prayer, we discover - the mind of the heart.

What is Prayer?

One night at an Ayahuasca retreat years ago, we all sat with reverence around grandfather fire, and one by one, each of us got the opportunity to sit on the generations-old leopard skin mat to mine the Shaman's wisdom. He believed that if you gazed at the fire long enough, it would transmit knowledge directly into your heart, and so as I patiently waited my turn to ask the Shaman a question, I watched the fire grow from a timid first spark to a passionate flame. By the time it was my turn, my heart was so ablaze it emboldened my ask:

"What is the one truth?"

The Shaman gently laughed and then took a moment, bowing his head to his heart to access the wisdom I asked for; then he looked up knowingly and started telling their story of creation:

"After the world of illusion was created, the Great Spirit debated on where to hide the truth. Spirit said: 'I'll put it in the sun,' but then decided eventually, man would create a rocket to reach the sun. So, then He said: 'I'll bury the truth in the ocean,' but then decided man would build a submarine and would find it too easily there. After thinking of many places to hide it and realizing that those places would be too easy for man to find, He finally decided: 'I'll put the truth in their hearts, they will never think to look there.'"

His response annoyed me. At the time when I asked that question, I didn't know how to look into my heart to find the one truth, and I wanted him to directly tell me how to do it, not just give me another mysterious story to learn from. His story echoed the same one truth found by all of the greatest spiritual teachers in the world, who found it while sitting alone in silence, exploring their own inner depths. When they emerged back to the external world and created systems to relay the knowledge they found within, although they were all so different, their core message was identical, regardless of time, space, or borders: Life should be led with Mercy, Compassion, and Love. They were teaching people to lead their lives with emotions cultivated in their hearts, which is why every religion on the planet instructs us to pray, regardless of whether it is done standing, sitting, facing east, or west, when done sincerely, all prayers are truly directed towards the heart. It is as universal as it is personal.

So if intention asks us to look within our hearts to find God's light and guidance, then prayer teaches us how to communicate with the Light by:

1. *Asking* for what we need, and
2. Being open to *Receive* guidance from it.

Before I understood prayer as either a wish-fulfillment machine, an obligation to the creator for creating me, or as a way to ask for forgiveness for things I didn't necessarily regret doing, it didn't hold a lot of magic for me because I didn't know how to use it properly. I would go in and make desperate demands for things that I never ended up receiving, and because it never seemed to 'work,' I lost interest in it at a very young age. It wasn't until much later that I discovered its purpose and learned to decipher the true language of 'Ask and Receive.'

What Does Prayer Do For Us?

While on our journey of self-discovery, finding God, and our purpose, it is very helpful to be able to ask for what we need and identify when we have actually received it… I didn't know how to do either. Although throughout my life, I had interacted with the wisdom in my heart, it was all subconscious. Pain and joy would pull me into its depths, and when I emerged, I always had some mysterious wisdom to show for it, but I didn't know how to intentionally go in at will and get exactly what I needed until I learned how to pray.

Prayer, I learned, was the subtle mechanism for communicating with my heart, which once again is done through our clairvoyance. It wasn't until I heightened my senses that I was able to distinctly hear my heart's knowledge, which is why, although I always had this ability, I couldn't recognize it. When prayer is done as a consistent meditative practice, it allows our 'mind' or consciousness to relax into a soft dreamlike state, where our attention is so singularly focused on our heart's frequency, it creates a telepathic bridge for communication to travel between our heart and mind called coherence. Once this state is achieved, all the wisdom carried within the frequency of our heart can be translated into thoughts we understand, like our mind is a radio tuning to a specific channel in our heart.

Strengthening this telepathic coherence is the purpose of prayer, and it's actually slightly incorrect to say strengthen. For so long, I believed communing with God was only attainable by the holiest people on Earth, but the truth is that we are all already tuned to His wisdom. Distractions and life experiences cause us to look away from it, but when we learn how to properly ignore those distractions, our attention defaults back to facing our inner light, and once again, we remember what it feels like to be divinely guided on our journey home.

How Does Ask and Receive Actually Work?

1. First, We Connect and Ask:

To become more aware of this connection, we softly focus our attention on our heart, which energizes it… it's that simple. Even just the basic action of putting our hands on our hearts makes us feel it more deeply, but when we make the solid effort to focus our attention entirely on our hearts, it becomes coherent with our minds. This means that our mind has relaxed from its normally distracted or working state to match the safe and loving frequency we find in our hearts. While in that open state, knowledge, guidance, and support is instantly and clearly received.

We experience this in the opposite direction all the time; when our brain perceives danger, it automatically takes on a fight or flight frequency. We don't think, 'Oh, I need to run and survive,' instinctively, we know how to protect ourselves without a second thought. That state is very useful in specific situations, but when our mind gets stuck in that high adrenaline 'protect yourself' mode, it cuts off the coherence to our heart, and we end up trying to get through life based on what we think (which is limited), rather than what we know (which is unlimited). In an effort to encourage ourselves back into an open-loving state, we reconnect to love by petting puppies, painting pictures, and spending late nights catching up with great friends we don't see often enough.

Before, when I thought prayer was something we only did in a holy place, I always felt like a stranger in someone else's building; there were lots of rigid rules I didn't know and eyes that whispered criticisms. But once I understood that prayer was simply the act of connecting to the love in our hearts, and that could be done anywhere, by default, I was intuitively guided to find my true community, where I learned that communal prayer felt like flying. When we worshipped and connected to love as a united group, our hearts amplified each other, and our energies merged from being small individuals to becoming One loud symphony of devotion. It's very similar to the experience of going to a concert, where the entire crowd sings as one, and we lose ourselves in the harmony.

This timeless weightlessness is called the flow state. Sometimes, when I'm writing, I look down, and three hours have passed, and I don't know where the time went. I become so deeply engrossed in how words feel in my body that while playing in the thesaurus, trying to figure out if the word I'm feeling is revival or renewal, I lose track of time. Also, when I'm jogging, once I find my stride, I glide through the hour, lost in the melodic rhythm of my feet hitting the pavement and my breath going in and out.

The more we stimulate our hearts, the stronger the connection becomes and the more communication we receive, and in doing it consistently enough, eventually, we are in such a consistent state of love that anything we do becomes a ceaseless prayer. Every modern spiritual guru on the planet always says – 'follow your bliss,' the old way of saying that is 'pray,' which means connect to your heart. In doing what we love, we switch from chasing love to being absorbed in a love that consumes us, and in that state, wisdom effortlessly pours out of us. Normally, people don't think about dancing, writing, singing, or painting as acts of prayer, and yet who is more in love than someone whose worries are so light and their happiness so intense that they feel like they're spinning in the air - ask a whirling dervish.

Because I was always seeking to experience the ecstatic bliss I saw on their face, I didn't recognize my little doses of daily connection for what they were and thought that euphoria was far away from me, only attainable by monks who renounced the world and meditated all day. Again, certainly, people who commit their entire existence to the path of chasing their bliss will accomplish incredible feats, but just because someone else has baked a really good cake doesn't mean no one else should ever bake a cake again. All cakes taste good, sugar is sugar, and being a connoisseur and having a small taste can be just as good as being chocolate wasted.

I had overlooked my bliss before because it was hidden in the mundane of my daily actions. For example, my mom loves pomegranates but doesn't have the patience to open them. It's not my favorite task either; it's tedious and yields so little for the eight minutes it takes me to open each one, but each week, when they are in season, I open them for her. The whole time I'm picking the little kernels out of their cozy pulp homes, I subconsciously think about how insane it is that she seems so genuinely thankful for this tiny act when she cooks huge elaborate meals for us all the time, yet she always asks God to bless my hands when I do this task that is too annoying for her to do for herself.

I show her love the way of her tradition: no praise, hugs, or kisses, just pomegranates. Some of the most potent acts of love are not the dancing or shouting from the rooftops; it's the calm and quiet things we do every day to let people know their existence matters to us. Because loving ourselves and others uses the same muscles as loving and connecting to God, I would almost go so far as to say each day we should only choose to do what makes us feel love, but I don't want people to think love is contingent on what we are doing, we have the power to infuse anything with magic. Our attention is our love, so anywhere we focus our attention is where we infuse our love; we just never give ourselves credit for how wonderful and loving we are, and that each time we do something for the sake of feeling the love in our hearts, that we are in fact praying. I don't love opening pomegranates, but I love my mom, and I love the way it feels to show her love.

Although joy is the preferred method for connection, anything that causes us to focus deeply into our hearts will be just as effective. Empathy, compassion, and suffering are the first that come to mind, and I go into depth about them later on in the chapter. But regardless of how we connect, whether by praying or playing, it is when we are in this natural state of connection that our Ask comes to life. Instead of being a flat request for something we want, when we ask in a state of deep love, the question is transmitted deeply into our hearts, and it returns in a transmuted form.

As a demonstration of how this works for me, I offer a dialogue of how I communicate with my heart and the types of responses I typically get back. For example, if I were to ask God for more money, I might receive more money, but what usually happens is I receive a response back from my heart inviting me to dig deeper into the root of what I am truly asking for. It looks like this:

1st Ask: God, I need more money.

My heart responds: *Why do you need more money?*

2nd Ask: For writing lessons.

Heart: *Why do you need writing lessons?*

3rd Ask: To improve my writing so I can sell it and get money.

Heart: *That is circular reasoning, so what do you truly need the money for?*

4th Ask: I need money so that I can feel financially secure.

Heart: *What will financial security make you feel?*

5th Ask: I need to feel safe.

Heart: *Does safety come from money or from God?*

After falling deeply into my self-inquiry, I realized that even though I asked for money, all I truly wanted was to feel safe, but money and safety are entangled in my mind. Safety meant being able to ensure my survival by having a skill I could unlimitedly reproduce and sell for money. However, when I finally learned how 'Ask' actually worked, I saw how God used my desires to reveal cracks in my faith at my deepest levels. He was using my logic against me and forcing me to admit to myself that I didn't believe he was the one who provided for me, showing me the kind of false beliefs buried within me so that I could dig them up once and for all.

The next day/week/month, free writing lessons might actually appear in my life, but the difference after digging deep was that I could identify and appreciate when my prayers had been answered. Before, when I would just ask for money in a mindless way, my heart would know what I actually needed – safety through writing lessons to make me feel more self-sufficient. Because of that disconnect, when writing lessons eventually appeared in my life, I would feel disappointed rather than grateful because it wasn't the money I had asked for. Giving me further proof that prayer doesn't work, not realizing that the writing lessons were the true answer to my prayers.

That's why, for a long time, I was impatient and ungrateful and decided to take things into my own hands. God was probably busy taking care of bigger, more important things and didn't have time for my insatiable appetite, but as I walked further along the path and got better at understanding how to properly connect with the wisdom within, I learned that God actually loves our appetites. Many times,

97

He became disappointed in me because I didn't ask Him for enough, and I suffered because I thought I had to be so independent. I had correlated asking God for things as annoying him when, in fact, it was my personification of Him that was ruining our relationship. If my child were to ask me for something, especially something they really wanted, I would move Heaven and Earth to get it for them, and I am just a human. I cannot imagine what God, who created us, would be willing to move for us.

I no longer limit His abilities or desire to care for us, and through my experiences, I now believe that He puts desires within us just so that we can Ask for them because anytime we Ask, we connect to Him.

2. Second, we Listen and Receive through Humility:

What we Ask for and what we Receive are like two ends of a rope, one side in the light and the other side in the dark. When a desire arises within us, it lights us up from within, and attached to it are the instructions on how to attain it, but that guidance is found in the dark, which is why heightening our clairvoyant senses is so critical. We still receive messages no matter how subtle the whisper is, but when we are open and silent inside, and our senses are heightened, the messages come through loud and clear.

In order to become open to receiving messages, many spiritual and religious traditions have a similar concept of humility, atonement, or ego death. For a long time, this was considered one of the main ideas of prayer and was interpreted as us having to beg God for forgiveness for our sinful mistakes. It was echoed recently in my spirituality class when our teacher was explaining that the first step in contacting God through prayer was to ask for forgiveness, which is right but not easily understood. Years of going through the motions of the ancient teachings had diluted the essence of this pivotal step, and one of the new students in the class was slightly offended and defensively asked:

"Why should I have to say sorry when I haven't even done anything wrong?"

Which is understandable, and I will explain the deeper meaning of forgiveness in a few paragraphs, but for now, I'd like to offer the idea of a humble state of mind. Asking for forgiveness can get us there, but it is just a vehicle and not the real point – unless we actually have done something wrong, which then realizing that mistake and making amends for it makes sense. However, when we approach prayer with a humble mindset, it is like a magical key that puts us directly into a quiet, receptive mode, which is exactly the silence that helps us hear God clearly. If gratitude is the magnet that attracts what we Ask for, then **humility is what opens us up to Receive it deeply**.

Imagine the difference between having a conversation with a know-it-all, who is just waiting for you to stop talking so that they can say whatever it was they wanted to say, without any regard for what you've just offered. Now, contrast that with someone who is earnest, humble, a good listener, and eager to hear what you have to say. In the first conversation, no matter how much the teacher explains something to them, they are closed-minded, so even though the wisdom is still offered, it doesn't penetrate their mind because they already have a preconceived notion of what they think is the right answer.

The second person, on the other hand, will absorb not only the words offered but lean deeper into the emotions conveyed and the way the teacher emphasizes different words. Not getting lost in semantics, but instead understanding the essence of the teaching. They find the real gold, learn deeper, appreciate the wisdom, and leave the conversation richer and changed.

"What is meant for you will reach you,
even if it is beneath two mountains.
And what is not meant for you will not reach you,
even if it's between your two lips."
-Ghazali

This level of absorbing wisdom is called Zen, which is a state of inner silence where transmissions of wisdom are received energetically by those quiet enough to listen with their entire being. Buddha* had a famous silent Zen teaching called *The Flower Sermon*. He simply held up a white flower in front of his students and waited for them to receive its transmission. Only one student smiled, signifying he had received the teaching.

I used to be the know-it-all during prayer, I asked for what I wanted and then impatiently waited for it to appear exactly as I dictated it. When I didn't get what I wanted, I thought God was giving me the silent treatment, with no concept that I was the one shutting myself off from receiving deeply. My arrogance and independence HATED admitting that I needed help and that I wasn't self-sufficient, and so if I had to ask for something, I wanted it to be done my way like a lost man who refused to ask for directions, trying to retain my last shred of dignity and preferring to be lost over being demeaned.

It wasn't just with God that I was arrogant and unskilled at listening. I was the same at home, at work, and with friends. I didn't know how destructive always wanting to be the one who knew everything was to my relationships. Having been humiliated so much as a child, I believed knowledge was power, and I never wanted to be dominated again. I confused humiliation and humility, believing they were the same, and I did everything to avoid them. I had no idea that there was a very significant nuance and that having a humble mindset was a superpower.

"Stay Humble and Hungry" is a mantra I hear Tony Robbins use to motivate high achievers the world over, and yet this was exactly the formula of the prophets years ago - Prayer and Fasting. By staying humble, we stay open for endless amounts of knowledge to come through us rather than cutting ourselves off by believing we have hit the highest limit of wisdom. When I finally got to the point of my journey where I had to throw my hands up in defeat and admit I didn't know everything, a hungry silence was created within me, like a vacuum, drawing unlimited knowledge from my bottomless depths.

Each time before I prayed, I used the ancient formula and made a humble admission, using humility as a key to unlock my conversations with God:

'I don't know how to properly connect with you.'

'I don't know how to understand the messages you are trying to communicate with me.'

'I don't know how to become enlightened.'

The point of making these admissions was to deflate my ego, which by nature is in a closed-off defensive state, so it doesn't like being vulnerable or admitting defeat. The ego is assigned to us at birth in order to ensure our survival while on Earth. One way it does this is by inflating our 'self' so that we seem bigger and more intimidating than we actually are, which is very helpful for survival, but to access the deeper workings of our heart, the opposite muscle is necessary. Our overinflated thoughts must become small and quiet enough to hear our inner knowledge, so reducing our ego is truly the first step in that process.

When I approached prayer with a humble state of mind, had no expectations, and just stayed open to anything that I received, my inner flow turned on like a spout. Very similar to the writing process, where when approached with expectations of being perfect, I developed horrible writer's block, but when I approached with the mindset that it's okay to fail and make mistakes, my creative ideas started flowing. Prayer follows this exact same creative principle, but instead of saying it's our goal to fail, we say it's our goal to stay humble because it is in that soft openness that we are no longer critical of what wants to come through and so we can take in much more. I used to think humility made me small, but now I know it's the opposite; it makes my ability to grow unlimited.

As we go through the self-inquiry process of humbly falling deeper into our Ask, we find our root need was always to connect to the light inside of us. What started out as wanting money turns into needing safety, which, when we get to the deepest level of connection, becomes a reminder that I AM the light within me, and that light is eternal and safe. In sensing that safety so deeply, it becomes my new core belief that I am safe, and the desire for money becomes superfluous. As I look into the world with that mindset, I recognize all the safety already around me; I've never been so poor that I didn't have a roof over my head, clothes on my back, or food to eat. I've actually lived a very comfortable life, and instead of focusing on all I had and showing gratitude for it, I only focused on what I wanted that I didn't have.

This is the seed we talked about at the very beginning, of why teachers of the old traditions guide us to begin prayer by asking for forgiveness. Because by directly embodying that essence, we can skip through several layers of self-inquiry and dive straight into the main source of all our misery and also our redemption - Our ability, or lack thereof, to see the abundance all around us. While I was busy being disappointed that I wasn't getting my caviar wishes and champagne dreams, I forgot to be thankful for having everything I needed. So now I respect and honor the wisdom of the traditions,

and I start prayer with a bowed and humble head and initiate contact
with my heart by saying: 'I know there have been things you have
done for me that I haven't realized or appreciated, forgive me and
teach me.' Which eventually becomes a natural state where no words
are required.

It is in that state that the gift is the gratitude. Truly feeling deep
appreciation for what we have fills us and satisfies us in a way no
material wealth can, and from there, we realize that what instigated
the entire journey from humility to satisfaction was an initial desire
sent to us from God. He does this because when we desire
something, we Ask Him for it, and so every desire is an invitation
from God to connect so He can show us how much of it we already
have. Which is a self-fulfilling cycle because it leaves us in a state
of contentment with our inner kingdom, and once that is the focus
of our lives, all physical things are added to it.

Prayer, for me, is no longer a matter of getting what I asked for.
Not to say that it doesn't work like that sometimes, but its true value
is in having a direct connection to unlimited love and wisdom at any
point in time. Imagine how lucky we would feel if we had a top-
performing mentor in our field that we could reach out to with even
our smallest problems, anytime, day or night. With prayer, we have
access to that and so much more.

Finding the Mystical in the Technical of Prayer

Prayer

I used to meditate for three hours every morning and another hour before bed at night. After my divorce, I wanted a do-over in life, so I threw everything that defined me away, including my religion, and completely wiped my hard drive clean as if I were born again. All the beliefs, expectations, hopes, and dreams about how life is or should be were gone. I was starting fresh and decided I would only operate from love, joy, and fun, ready to accept whatever God had in store for me on this new journey. I dedicated my life to 'study, worship, and serve' Him, and like all new converts to spirituality, I was committed and enthusiastic, so it became my life.

I didn't leave Islam because I was angry with it, it just didn't serve me. I had no real connection to it or the practices apart from being born into it. Also, I felt the teachings of a man who lived in the desert 1400 years ago didn't apply anymore to an American girl in the modern world. So, it was easy to relinquish the title of 'Muslim' and just be open to whatever life had to offer; little did I know that God was very intentional in the life and title He had endowed me with.

One day, my spiritual guru commented on the intensity of my meditations and offered his wisdom on how to practice with the most efficiency and effectiveness. He said meditation is meant to be a natural waking, peaceful state, not only something we do alone in the dark. He explained that during meditation, we ignite our pineal gland, a small pinecone-shaped gland that sits in a cozy nook at the top of the spine in the middle of our brain. This gland is the one responsible for secreting DMT, the spirit molecule that, among other things, enhances our intuitive connection with spirit and is dubbed the 'Seat of the soul.'

It's naturally ignited through a piezoelectric effect in our bodies, meaning all you have to do is apply pressure to it through concentrated breathing, visualization, or postures that encourage our spinal fluid to travel up our spine, allowing us to connect with spirit using built-in methods. Once our gland is ignited, it continues to reignite itself until the charge eventually fades. So, he advised me to meditate many times a day in short spurts to keep recharging this current rather than sit for hour-long sessions. He recommended five - 10-minute meditations per day.

My jaw hit the ground.

I had lived in a Muslim household my entire life. I had seen my mom going back and forth five times to that spot in her room each day, and growing up, I thought it was excessive. But now, when I compared it to my monster three-hour-long sessions, it seemed too easy.

So, I started praying the traditional five prayers a day, but rather than focus on whether I was doing it right, I just allowed myself to go through the postures while enjoying the acoustics and rhythm of the recitations. There was no judgment or expectations; my only goal was to silence my mind and feel into my heart peacefully. I didn't see a tangible difference between my three-hour session and this new practice of smaller check-ins, which I suppose was the point he was trying to make. Less was the same as more, and when in doubt, always do less.

Wadu

After some time, my mom noticed my commitment to praying five times and asked if I was doing the obligatory water purification process prior to it. It's a simple washing technique done if we have any natural discharge, slept, or touched someone of the opposite sex. It goes like this:

3 times each - we wash our hands to our elbows, swish water in our mouth, take a shallow amount of water into the bottom of our nostrils and wash our face.

1 time each - we wet the top of our head, wash in and around our ears, and the back of our neck.

3 times - we wash our feet up to our ankles.

Except if we have sex – then we have to take a full-body shower.

It sounds easy and straightforward enough, but I hated wetting myself all day, especially my curly hair. She explained that washing before prayer was the "key" that unlocked the prayer but couldn't explain further the purpose of it, so I argued with her. I told her that it was an old tradition and that we have to think about why rules are put in place and actively try to modernize them for the current day instead of being stuck in the past.

I imagined that this practice probably originated from the fact that the religion was established by desert-dwelling people with no A/C or irrigation. So, it made sense that they had to wash all the time because they were probably always covered in sand and sweat. Whereas now I shower daily, then sit in A/C all day. Our lives are so different, even living in Texas, which during the summer could feel like the largest open-air sauna in the world, I never broke a sweat. I went straight from my air-conditioned house to my air-conditioned car to my air-conditioned job. I still felt freshly showered by the time I got home at night, needing to bring a jacket with me to work because of how cold they keep the A/C during the summer.

So, I went on, stubbornly doing my prayers without the purification process, and then the opportunity came for me to attend a seven-day meditation retreat held by one of the top experts in the field that merges science with spirituality. He opened the retreat with a lecture explaining what happens chemically and electrically to the body during meditation. Summed up, when we meditate, our body measurably goes into the same state of consciousness that we are in during deep sleep. As our body starts accessing these deeper sleep states, it ignites our pineal gland and the release of melatonin, which has the same parent molecule as DMT, and our bodies develop a subtle energetic charge. During this process, our body starts retaining our water reserves because water is an excellent conductor of energy, and in order to access higher states of consciousness, our energy has to move freely throughout our body.

Energy mainly enters and exits the body in two ways:

1. Energy can enter up through our feet, going all the way up and exiting out of the top of our heads, or the other way around, entering down through our heads and exiting through the bottom of our feet. It does so in a non-stop cycle that creates an energy field around our bodies, resembling the shape of an eggshell.

2. The energy can also accumulate in our heart, which acts like a motor that releases the energy by sending it through our arms and out of our hands. Presumably, this is why, in the old days, healers could heal people just by putting their hands on them. It also explained to me why Muslims put their hands over their hearts when they pray. We are recycling this healing energy back into ourselves, healing our own hearts.

After he explained that the head, hands, and feet were the entry and exit points for energy in our body and that the body naturally retains its water during our meditation activation process, a marriage of thoughts occurred in my mind. When we do purification/washing rituals, it is not only for the sake of cleanliness but also because we are washing these entry and exit points so that energy can more easily travel through our body – the 'key' that unlocked the prayer.

When I got back from the retreat, I was excited to share this confirmation of my mom's wisdom with her. Her "I told you so" was followed with pride, that I was open to learning, which took the sting out of it. Luckily, growing up, she allowed me to ask questions, make mistakes, and figure things out on my own. There was never a compulsion of religion in our household. My dad always used to tell me that I liked learning things the hard way, but I always said it was the organic way. I could never take instructions or rules at face value; I needed to understand what purpose they served if I were to follow them. During the Golden Age of Islam, believers were encouraged to challenge the religion because they knew that each challenge would result in believers that no longer had doubts.

The more I discovered about the benefits of the postures and cleanliness of traditional prayer, the more I fell in love. I saw how far ahead of its time it was during the pandemic when the entire world started washing its hands as much as the Muslims naturally do every day to prevent the spreading of disease. Then, while practicing yoga, I learned the magical effects of the bending and prostrating postures, which open the pathways of our body's energy centers and encourage the movement of our spinal fluid up our spine, stimulating our pineal gland at the top, and effectively 'turning the lights on' inside of me.

After unwittingly leaving the religion, it was abundantly clear that God was calling me back. Not from a position of adhering to rules, so I don't go to hell. From that organic position, of understanding the energetic value and wisdom of it. He was silently guiding me to the knowledge I was seeking that would affirm my voluntary dedication to it. There was never any anger or judgment for leaving; God welcomed me back home with open arms and a warm embrace, reminding me that in His eyes, it was never too late to come back, and now I was grateful for what I had.

<u>How I Failed</u>

If you remember from way back in the introduction chapter, before I awakened, praying was the one thing that always made me feel like a fraud. I instinctively knew I should be feeling some sort of bliss or connection, but instead, it felt empty. Just a series of standing and bending postures and saying words I didn't know the meaning of, I felt nothing. At best, I was observant and faithful, and even though I was seeking that ecstatic elation, I had never personally seen anyone have it, so I figured feeling nothing but duty was normal while praying. I went about my life going through the motions, appeasing mom and God, with whom I had a very distant relationship.

I acknowledged that He existed and was taught to blindly worship Him, but never how to connect with Him, and when I would talk to Him, I never expected to hear back. I mistakenly thought His voice would sound different than mine, so I was expecting supernatural contact as He was always explained as something outside of me to pray to; no one ever told me He was in my heart. So when an alien didn't appear in my living room with tons of money, I assumed He was just a mysterious, silent watcher who never intervened with free will.

I say He never intervened because I used to pray a lot as a kid. My dad was a really interesting teacher in my life. He was an unwilling refugee and had a lot of buried anger, and as a kid, I was an easy target. I didn't know anything about mirrors or teachers back then; all I knew was that he had an iron fist and a concrete heart when it was time for discipline, and because I was so extroverted and uninhibited, I was on the receiving end of it a lot. I remember the pain, but mostly the disproportionate rage in his eyes; the punishments never fit the crime. When we were alone together in my room, his pupils would sharpen like knives, and the air in the room would thicken with the stench of blood on fire. His anger drove him far into the darkness, relishing in his own release and having no mercy. It was loud, so I know everyone heard, but no one ever came. Not the people alive who heard it, and not God, whom I prayed to with all my heart to stop it. No. One. Ever. Came.

I was eight. I never thought to myself, 'I will never pray again because it's a waste of time.' I just accepted it; it was a piece of information I didn't know about this world, and now buried deeply within my knowing, it was saved as law. Gravity. Momentum. Inertia. Relativity. No one ever comes. Which gave birth to my subconscious program that I only have myself to rely on because no one ever comes. We collect these false beliefs over our lifetime that create a cocoon of veils around us, making the world feel smaller and safer because we know and can predict how it works. Deducing the world to our size immediately makes us feel more powerful and in control; it is a handy survival skill for a child.

I never had a fighting chance to connect with God through prayer; being stripped at such a young age of my belief that contacting Him was possible made the next 25 years of my life consumed with only one goal – wanting to control everything because I believed that was the only way to survive this world alone. If the people who were supposed to care for and protect me could do this to me, what would the rest of the world do? Believing there was Nothing outside to catch me if I fell, I made up for all the control I didn't have as a kid by controlling everything as an adult, and I'm a Virgo, so that's a scary amount of control. Gym 5 am. MMA classes in the evening. Master's degree. No debt ever. Husband, house, and kids before 30. Management before 35. Controlling goals made me feel powerful, especially because I thought I had done it all alone, without help from anyone else.

So it's not that I didn't know how to pray; it's that I tried before and found nothing, so it didn't seem necessary to try again. My innocent beliefs, cultivated at such a tender age, unknowingly and unintentionally blinded me from being able to perceive God's communication, which I would come to find much later, was there all along. But it was a long journey to get there, and I still had many more obstacles to overcome, which came in the strangest form, spirituality and manifestation.

Controlled Manifestation

The Law of Attraction seemed like what I thought prayer was supposed to be, but with the ability to control it, so I was immediately drawn to it. The elements are similar; both require us to go within and ask for what we want, but for the first time, I was taught how to use visions and feelings to communicate what I want, talking to 'the universe' in its language.

The process was easy:

1. Close your eyes and imagine what you want. Make the image vivid, as if it's already happening in real life.

2. Feel gratitude as if you already have it - gratitude being the energy frequency that magnetically pulls what we ask for towards us.

3. Then, end by surrendering any expectation of a specific outcome and wait – which was also similar to praying.

Visualization and manifestation were the prayers I was always looking for, and because my efforts resulted in tangible results, I felt empowered and like I finally understood the mechanics of the world I lived in. I was finally able to reduce praying to being a wish-fulfillment machine like I always wanted, and I discovered that I was pretty good at it.

It really boosted my confidence in myself, finally seeing both big and small things I asked for come to life. The biggest happened after my divorce when I moved in with my mom for a while. After about a year, she started hinting that I was meditating too much and needed to get my own house and a job; within a week, I had both contracts in my hand. Then there was the silliest one. At a meditation retreat, they asked us to think about something to manifest by the end of the day to prove 'this stuff really works,' even on a deadline. Since we were at a beach resort, I picked something easy and probable but that I hadn't seen before - a dolphin. I didn't want the test to be too hard because it was on a 12-hour deadline, but I did want it to make me feel special when it did happen.

All day, I thought about a dolphin, visualizing and feeling grateful for seeing it. Our last meditation of the evening was on the beach. It was dark as we all silently laid down and absorbed the elements. The soft sand and gentle breeze enveloped us while the sounds of the waves crashed against us, mimicking the sounds and carefree feeling of our mother's womb. The day ended silently, and although I still hadn't seen my dolphin, I was at peace. Before I left the beach to go back to my room, I hopefully looked out one last time, and although there was not a single dolphin in sight, I was mesmerized. Looking far out, I saw the full moon clearly reflected on the ocean's calm surface. Instead of getting a dolphin, I got two moons.

I walked back to my room completely satisfied, nothing in life was missing, and while in that state, I passed by the centerpiece of the hotel, its huge posh pool. I appreciated its beauty and display of luxury and noticed there was something in the middle of it that didn't fit the picture; its gaudiness captured my attention, begging for a closer look. Someone had abandoned their massive plastic floaty, big enough for six people to sit on, and lo and behold, it was in the shape of a dolphin. I laughed all the way back to my room at this epic inside joke. Someone had an amazing sense of humor and perfect timing.

Eventually, after just a year or two of attracting what I needed at my whim, the weirdest thing in the world happened - I stopped enjoying manifesting.

I was back to that feeling of emptiness, even with all my new stuff. None of it filled me the way I thought it would, and I felt like I had reduced a really holy thing to being a pony trick. Like Solomon*, when he had everything available at his fingertips, all he kept saying was "meaningless. meaningless."[2]. Manifesting a job and house in a week was awesome, only to realize I hated the work but had to do it to pay the bills, and since I spent most of my waking hours in the office, I never really got to spend time in the home I was slaving away for. Apart from the feeling of control, it gave me, manifesting only made me happy the second something arrived, and then it quickly turned into an energetic burden. 'Be careful what you wish for' became my truth.

With both praying and manifestation, there was an element missing, a key I hadn't gathered yet because the things I was looking to get were external, and I was trying to control the world around me. My focus hadn't shifted to my inner world yet, so although I was using spiritual manifestation rather than physical effort to get things, I was still stuck in the cheap joy of getting things, which veiled me from experiencing true inner joy and contentment. I knew that something was wrong because even though I was successful at manipulating energy, my intuition was calling me back to remember something I had learned long ago but forgotten about.

I still didn't know it was possible to hear back from God; my old programming convinced me it was impossible, so I ignored my disappointment in manifestation and decided it was good enough, or at least better than what I had before, which was nothing. Eventually, I got to a point where my manifestation skills worked so often I deduced that Jesus* was right, 'If you ask, it must be given'[3]. I was finally the master of my universe, and in elevating visualization over prayer, rather than wishing for, I dreamt my world into place. I believed in my power to manifest anything I wanted to such an extent that I even believed I could literally raise Lazarus from the dead, and I tried, nearly killing myself in the process…

Elon Noor Medina

It was an unusually beautiful day, 70 and sunny, with the perfect amount of crispness in the air. I don't remember anything else about it or even what I was doing when I got the call. It was my younger sister, and when her face popped up on my screen, she didn't have to say a word; the adrenaline instantly spiked my mind into laser focus, seeing the panic too big for her eyes to contain.

"They can't find the heartbeat."

She was 38 weeks pregnant. She was full-term. It was any day now. This was just a routine doctor's visit on a beautiful, sunny, crisp day. We didn't know that soon, beautiful days would become our trigger.

My mom, youngest sister and I immediately went to the hospital, and even though there were strict Covid precautions that only allowed one other person in the room at a time, the staff allowed us all to come up, knowing what we were there for.

As soon as I walked into the room, I immediately went into default survival mode and tried to control the damage. With the force of a savior, I asked everyone in the room to focus; even the nurses slowed their frantic movements, bowed their heads, and tuned in. I put my hands on her stomach and focused, visualized, and prayed with every cell in my being:

"God, I know everything is in your power and that there is nothing in this world that is beyond your reach. If you will it, it will be. You love us, have mercy on us, don't give us more than we can bear. You have done this before, and I believe with every cell in my being that it can be done again. He is not so far gone from us that you can't bring him back now. Please feel and know my belief in you and your power. I KNOW nothing is above or beneath you. Please show us Your mercy. Let this baby live."

Time passed in a void, watching her in the throes of labor, all of us silently praying for a miracle. When it was time to push, they ushered us out to the empty room next door. We sat for 30 minutes in absolute silence, broken by the sound of their hallowed screams.

He was stillborn.

9/9/2020

When they let us back in the room, my sister would jerk up anytime someone came near her, and her eyes would jump out at us as if we might have an answer that would make the world make sense again. She needed an explanation, a way to understand what she did to deserve this. I saw the storm of thoughts spiraling in her grieving mind:

'How could he be perfectly healthy one week and gone the next?

Is this my fault for going to a midwife instead of a hospital?

Would they have done more ultrasounds and taken more tests?

Would they have noticed something earlier?

Could they have saved him?

Is this my fault?

This is my fault.'

Needing something, anything, to fill the gaping hole inside of her, she poured guilt on top of the pain. A primal instinct to prevent us from feeling the depth of our emptiness.

Each of us got a turn to hold him, his mouth slack and diluted blood running down from the corners of his eyes and mouth; he looked like a beautiful, melted strawberry. We had to wrap him with an icepack to keep him from atrophying while we met and mourned him.

Losing him was bad enough, but giving my beloved sister false hope left me shaking in my own humility. Beyond feelings of nausea and dread, it was the silence. The hero within me was dead. My savior complex, no matter how well-intentioned, made worse the worst thing that could ever happen to a mother. It wasn't a matter of guilt or forgiveness; it was so far beyond that, making those states seem trivial in their distance. It was one coffin, but in it, we buried so many souls. Humbled to the point of resting in peace.

In Islam, there is a belief that when we die, if we have done more good than bad, then we are granted entry to heaven, but as a part of clearing any last karma before entering, on the way, we must walk across a bridge. Below this bridge, we see all the people, including our loved ones whose scales didn't weigh in the right direction, being burned alive beneath us. Our punishment is that we aren't able to help them; we can only helplessly watch while we walk above them. This is how this experience felt for me.

Noor is a special sister to me. She was the embodiment of pure, undiluted light. When she was born, the doctor said she was the most perfect baby he had ever seen. The way she looked at me made me feel elevated in her presence, seeing the good in me, even when I couldn't see it myself. But the world was always so hard for her; she could never understand why a creator would make so much darkness when she was no God, and yet she had so much light to share. The world didn't make sense from her vantage point, and although I understood the lesson she was learning now, seeing her suffer was more painful than anything I had experienced to this point in my life.

In the wake of the death of the false messiah within me, helplessness was born. I didn't think there was anything worse than giving her the false hope that he could be saved until I learned the pain of having no hope at all. All I could do was stand back and watch her suffer. I had nothing to give her, not even a word.

We buried him on 9/11/2020. The date, a coffin that already contained so much, became 5 pounds and 14 ounces heavier.

When we talk about life now, our timeline is Before Elon and After Elon. In this new era, reality flipped, the external world magnified what was happening for us personally, people were dying out of order, it wasn't natural. We didn't understand this new world we were living in. For a year, we existed together in upside-down, pitch-black darkness, only having each other to keep her alive.

She gave me purpose during the day, helping her. But at night, when I was home alone, I couldn't escape how lost I felt, the deaf leading the blind. I was desperate to find the light, but after so many failed attempts with prayer, visualization, and manifestation, I was defeated in every fathomable way. It had been two years since my mystical Ayahuasca experience in the mountains of Ecuador, and the truth haunted me. Before I felt that I knew the truth, I knew who I was, I knew God. Now, I had no clue who I was, and I didn't have the faintest idea of how to reach God.

That day in the hospital, I focused all my energy and all my might into my heart to the point that it could've burst from the amount of Ask I put into it. I thought, surely, there was no way I would not get a response with the sheer amount of energy I had brutally forced into this plea, and yet the silence was deafening. It was in that destabilized state that I started self-medicating with food and TV. I was escaping the humility, the helplessness, and the fact that I was constantly being reminded that I knew nothing and had no control. I couldn't beat the darkness anymore, so I joined it.

There is a saying, "When you are in hell, don't look up and take pictures."[4] So, for a year, a month, and 13 days, as a family, we collectively put our heads down and held our breath until our rainbow baby was born. Once my sister had an alive, healthy baby to hold in her once empty arms, we finally exhaled. The release was cathartic. With him, the world slowly started to stabilize, and we could bear the sunshine again.

I hadn't looked up during that entire year, and when I finally did, I didn't recognize myself anymore. I was different. Insecure. Unsure. Desperate. Depressed. I had never been to any of these things before. I was always so independent, confident, and powerful.

It was at this lowest, humblest, neediest point of my life that I was finally broken enough and admitted, 'I need help.' As if it were received through a direct link to the entire universe, I was thrown a lifeline. A northern star appeared in my mind. I received an intention.

Rest in peace to all our dreams of love that die unfulfilled.

May they carve a hole in us so deep,

we can carry an Ocean of Noor,

without drowning.

Learning the True Meaning of Prayer

Solitude speaks

While in middle school, I was grounded for three years.

I had lots of friends at the time, and naturally, we always wanted to hang out, but my dad was very traditional. He believed that boys and girls shouldn't be friends and that girls should stay home and dress and act very modestly. So the idea of me going to the mall with a mixed group of boys and girls and buying the latest fashion of sleeveless shirts and summer shorts sent him completely over the edge. There were so many differences between my American lifestyle that was completely opposite from his traditional Middle Eastern expectations, and instead of accepting those differences, he believed my friends were a bad influence on me. So, although at the time I didn't understand this, I now believe that in order to protect me, he decided to ground me until my friends and I outgrew each other.

At the time, I felt like I was being raised by a tyrannical dictator; his unjust punishments were so disproportionate to my innocent crimes of just wanting to fit in with the society around me. Because I would rebel against his rules, I was considered the bad child who constantly needed to be disciplined, and because he had a lot of repressed anger from his childhood and was always disappointed that he never had a son, I was often the receiver of his pain.

For three years, I was only allowed to go to school, then immediately after, I would come home and go straight to my room. I wasn't even allowed to sit in the living room with my family, and when my mom's pleas to allow me to eat dinner with them were seldomly granted, there was always this awkward tension between me and my dad at the table. He made every effort not to make eye contact with me and would go out of his way to praise my sisters, making it obvious that he was ignoring me, which made me feel worthless to him. He used dinner as another passive-aggressive punishment; it was a mind game to show the others what happens when you question his law. Also, in not acknowledging me, he was sadistically demonstrating that he controlled my small existence effortlessly. Perhaps, in a way, he wished he had control over his own life.

Sometimes, I would try humbly approaching him and asking him to hug me and forgive me, my arms open in anticipation of his embrace. When he wouldn't respond, I'd make the first move and hug him, and as if I were a leper, he would claw my hands off of him in disgust.

"No! Go back to your room now!"

No matter how well I behaved or how much I tried to reconcile with him, I was always met with the same cold rejection. He knew that if he accepted my apology, he would have to relent and let me out of the house at some point and that if he showed my sisters signs of weakness with me, they might also get ideas. So, although I was persistent in my pursuit of his good favor, I never let go of the hope that one day, his answer would change, and he would finally have mercy on me and free me. That all came to an end one day when I overheard my mom fighting with him to let me out. He shouted at her, "I wish she was never born!"

I don't even remember how many days it took me to get out of bed after that. After not eating for a few days, he came home with a cookie from his deli, offering it to me as an apology. He must've realized he had finally gone too far and succeeded in breaking me. Eventually, I did get out of bed and resigned to my fate; I finally gave up all hope. I was forced to surrender to aloneness.

This was the time before the internet, so there wasn't any social media for me to keep up with the outside world, which, in a way, may have been a blessing. While all of my peers were out learning to socialize, I was alone, unconsciously trying to find ways to escape reality. At first, always missing out felt like a death sentence, I know that's dramatic, but I was 12. The more I missed out, the less friends expected to see me, and something about that alleviated my desire for company as well. Life was teaching me deep solitude. Not just sitting alone, existing alone.

Beyond the boredom, the most painful part of it was being confined to such a small space at an age when I was bursting with energy. I had to find ways to get it out in order to not lose my mind, so I would punish my body with a prisoner's workout: 100's of push-ups, crunches, squats, as fast as I could, until absolute failure. Afterwards, I would collapse onto the floor, too exhausted to even open my eyes, and just listen to my heartbeat while my body tingled. The endorphins made my blood sing in my veins, and I would get lost after a few breaths in that high, and without thinking about it, I was able to clearly translate an internal dialogue that was occurring in my heart that wasn't spoken but felt.

I didn't realize this at the time, but now that I think back, that state was very similar to the exhausted high I would get after a physical punishment from my dad. The beatings hurt more, which increased the intensity and depth I could drop into my heart, and by the same equivalent, it also amplified the internal dialogue. It was during that height of pain that I heard the voice inside of me speak loud and clear as if speaking in front of an audience. Somehow, it balanced the experience; moment by moment, the pain fueled the volume of the inner voice, which was different from the thoughts I had in my head. It wasn't angry or unjust; it was compassionate, loving, and understanding, putting all my worries at ease.

While alone in my room, after my dad would leave me to lick my own wounds, I would lay there numb. Exhausted from the screaming and crying, but mainly from the energy it took to absorb all the pain. The cocktail of hormones swam through me, and I remember pictures would appear in my mind of my dad's life. I knew his stories. How severe his father was to him. I met him when I was much younger, and all I remember about him was the candy cigarettes he would give us and his reptilian eyes. My dad, in comparison, felt like a warm angel. He became a teddy bear when he talked about his mom, who died too young of breast cancer, and just the mention of Palestine would cause him to fall apart. A big, angry man reduced to a sobbing, heartbroken, helpless boy. It took him back to their escape from the war, bombs exploding beside their car, wetting himself. What hurt him more was that he didn't want to leave; his father forced him to, so when he would think of all the people who were left behind, it gave him survivor's remorse.

At that time, people didn't really acknowledge PTSD, and being raised by a dad who survived war skewed his own understanding of mercy. He never apologized to me for what he did to me as a kid. I'm certain it's because to him, in comparison, I must've appeared so coddled. Perhaps it was an elaborate form of Stockholm syndrome, but despite his lack of awareness and everything that he did, when I would enter that state, by the time it wore off, I would feel sorry for him. Somehow, during those moments when his pupils would black out in rage, I would simultaneously reach beyond my limit to absorb pain, and a sort of Zen state would descend on me, merging his pain with mine. Connecting us in a way that felt like we were the only ones in the world who could understand each other. Trench brothers.

It was bizarre; on one level, my hope that someone would come to save me had died, but then, on another, this internal connection with my heart was blown so far open that I would swim in love, forgiveness, and compassion. It was such a natural experience within my body that I didn't think it was special at all, let alone miraculous. It felt good, but in no way did I attribute it to my connection to God; if anything, I thought God was completely absent from it. I assumed that such moments of darkness and pain couldn't exist in His presence, that He would be separate from me, and that when He arrived to save me, order and justice would immediately prevail. I had written the entire experience off as a normal effect of a body high and assumed everyone knew they had this ability. It wasn't until much later in life that I discovered most people have never had the privilege of spending a significant amount of time alone with themselves.

Looking back now, knowing more about spirituality and the way physical lessons inform our spiritual growth, I realized so many things during those years of solitude and suffering:

- I was being pre-cleansed of my arrogant expectations and demands of life. Cured of thinking it should go my way or that I knew better than the creator. Although I would still have deeper lessons to learn about control as an adult, this humiliation and pain I experienced as a child plowed and softened the ground so that instead of a tree of arrogance growing, only a weed could grow, making it easier for me to rip it out of the ground later on.

- I learned that the world wasn't about me and my pain and that I had the power to look past the pain inflicted on me and forgive those who caused me pain unconditionally.

- That pain, rejection, and loneliness weren't things to be feared, which gave me unlimited courage to reach higher toward my dreams as an adult.

- That life had a natural balance, and although at times it felt harsh, with that pain came the wisdom that altered and armed me.

- I learned how heavy emotions like bitterness, resentment, and anger felt in my stomach, throat, and breasts and that at the end of the day, even though I had no free will to control any other aspect of my life, my only true free will was my choice: to either see my experiences through the bitter lens of my head, or through the humility in my heart.

I chose forgiveness and empathy, not only because I knew I couldn't survive under the crushing weight of resentment but because it was my single act of rebellion. Life could control every aspect of my existence, take anything it wanted from me: my freedom, my dreams, my hope. But it could never control the way I felt inside, to love in spite of everything. Choosing to align with love was my only true sovereignty; the world could enslave me externally, but internally, love set me free.

Those years in isolation were both hell and the greatest education I have yet to receive about the nature of life. That time alone allowed me to grow a relationship with my true self, something many people have yet to discover, and while my peers were developing relationships with others' masks, I learned to 'Know Thyself.' By the end of this era, socially, I was sheltered and stunted, but internally, I was royalty within my kingdom.

Strangely enough, I knew myself and had all of this knowledge, but perhaps because I gained it when I was so young, I didn't realize its worth. There isn't a time in my life when I don't remember having this voice, so I mistook it for my own. I had no clue that in those silent moments of pain when I lost myself in the feelings and wisdom emanating from my heart, that I was experiencing what old men used to sit alone in caves to achieve… I was successfully praying and communing with God. It wasn't until almost three decades later, in the process of following my intention to write this book, that I discovered this gift for what it actually was and how to utilize it to create magic in my life.

<u>Focus and Embodiment</u>

Through my deep desire to write this book, God was reminding me of the gift of communion that I had all along, but with the added bonus of showing me how to use that power and share it with others rather than just enjoy it alone in the dark. As I went through the process of heightening my senses with dieting, exercising, and silencing my inner noise, the crucial next lesson about prayer revealed itself - that it is an active practice.

Prayer may start with a silent request, but it was the actions I took on a daily basis to obey the guidance of my heart that ground the prayer into reality. Through repetition, God was teaching me to embody my ability to commune with Him to such an extent that even when I think I am lost and cannot find the light within me, there are infallible steps I can take to bring me back to it every single time. Each step taken with the intention of returning to the light within when we have lost our way is a prayer in and of itself, which is why active prayer - focus and embodiment - are the pivotal next steps to usher our prayers to life.

As I explained in the first chapter about intention, once I hit rock bottom and made the firm decision to stop running away from my purpose in life, I had to finally face myself. I had to acknowledge all the damage that had been done to me and that I had done to myself and admitted that I couldn't carry the physical or emotional weight alone anymore. I looked in the mirror, and as if for the first time, I realized all along I was looking at my adult self through the eyes of my inner child. If I was going to make it on this journey, I needed to learn how to ask for the help that my inner child thought would never come and believe that it would come. My reflection looked lost and distorted, but it had nothing left to lose. So I took a leap of faith, challenged everything I knew, and said my first honest prayer:

"God, I have no clue what I'm doing, and I can't do this alone anymore. I need your help."

The ask was simple and humble. With vulnerability, I admitted defeat and that I needed Him to come, even though I felt betrayed that He never came before. Also, there was a silent admission that I must've misunderstood something about Him and His nature along the way and that perhaps He was there, but I couldn't perceive Him. I needed Him to teach me how to see because I obviously had a blind spot, and instead of training myself to see, I blamed Him for not revealing Himself in a way I could understand.

By limiting God's infinite potential and making Him something small enough my mind could understand, I brought the error of expectation upon myself, and after years of deeply misunderstanding God's nature, I realized that feeling lost and blind were not states of being, but side effects of false beliefs. It was by becoming aware of this unintentional arrogance that I was able to finally alter the energy of my prayer so that rather than being tainted with indignation, it hummed with humility and an undertone of requesting forgiveness. Knowing it was my own wrong that needed to be righted and that the only thing I had control over was myself, I felt empowered to know I could change myself and repair my error now.

I started fixing mistakes by no longer defining what help meant to me, nor holding any more expectations, allowing it to be truly felt and not just lip service when I humbly admitted that I didn't know what I needed or how to fix myself. After that surrender, I put my head down and got to work. As the months went by of gently disciplining myself daily through diet and exercise and gaining the benefits of heightened senses and reduced noise that came with them, I added prayer as a daily practice.

As a recap, to this point, these were the things I had already learned about prayer:

1. Prayer is like meditation in that it is a peaceful state I walked in all day, and that there was a greater benefit in five recharges per day rather than one several-hour-long session.

    a. I maintained that state of connection to God throughout the day by doing anything I loved.

2. The way to communicate my Ask to God was through a sincere evoking of heightened loving emotions.

    a. To illustrate this using old teachings, there is a story about the Prophet*, where he left his house in the morning and saw his wife sitting down praying. When he returned home later, she was still sitting in the same position. He asked if she had been praying that whole time, and she responded in the affirmative. He offered her the advice that if she cried (shown heightened emotions), her prayer would've been better.

3. My ultimate goal was to connect with God with no other expectations, even though there were many Law Of Attraction benefits that came with maintaining that heightened state of connection.

Prior to making prayer a daily practice, I had only flirted with it. Praying when I felt like it or when I was in deep sorrow and needed solace, but just like any other habit, in order for it to be solidified, it had to be grounded in routine. Before, I made the mistake of becoming apathetic to it because I thought I never gained any real benefit from it, but that was the crux of my misdirection and inability to perceive my connection to God; I was looking externally for a blessing rather than internally for the connection. God was constantly trying to reach me via the calling in my heart, but for so long, I ignored it, allowing it to become diluted with distractions and disappear in the background. But just like with exercise, writing, or loving someone, prayer only flourishes with a consistent commitment, the same way romance dies in a marriage when one partner stops trying.

When I started paying attention to the way God communicated with me, I started to see that He used any means to reach me. He gave me a sharp wake-up call one day when my son was telling me a story while I was looking at my phone. It was common for me to unconsciously placate him with canned responses when I was distracted, but after saying them so often, at only five years old, he had enough one day and exasperatedly said to me, "Stop saying 'that's crazy!'"

He called me out in such a way that I snapped out of my scrolling trance, all at once realizing that I wasn't present with him at all, that he was old enough to know I wasn't listening, and that my lack of attention hurt him. It was like a little rubber band snapping in my heart, bringing me back to what was really important. I had to change not only my behavior with him but with God as well. I couldn't count the number of times I went to pray, and instead of focusing on my heart, I was distracted and thinking about what I should eat afterward, causing me to miscount and shorten postures.

I was being painfully taught the gift of focus, which hurt when I realized how much of the good stuff in life I was missing because I wanted to escape the hard reality around me. My life was flipped outside in, and instead of the things that truly mattered being my main focus, my distractions were center stage. I needed to regain the ability to direct my thoughts at all times, not just when I was sitting down and meditating.

That was when my journey got an up-leveling boost; something in me snapped, and I realized that if I was serious about this, I had to go to the next level. I stacked deep solitude on top of my diet, exercise, praying, and writing habits, meaning that I cut all distractions for several months: I deleted social media accounts, turned off the TV, and rejected invitations from friends to hang out. By simplifying my day, I made my inner voice the center of my life, and the effects of that, without exaggeration, gave me the ability to bring my dreams to life.

The more I embodied this focused energy within me, the clearer the book became, giving me full-body chills but, this time, in a good way. I finally caught on to what exactly the book would be, its true message, and even what the passages sounded like. Each day, the inner guidance clarified that I was to write a book explaining surrender/Islam in a universal, practical, and entertaining way. So that anyone could enjoy and access their innate and personal connection to God rather than relying on anyone else's interpretation or teaching. The book's purpose would be to explain the mysterious internal process of relinquishing control to the intelligence built within us so that we could reclaim our power and never walk in fear or be controlled by something external ever again. Because "If God is with us, who can stand against us?"[5]

The power of receiving this level of clarity caused me to shake uncontrollably at times. My sister saw me while I was writing once and asked if I was shaking because I was scared, and I honestly told her, "No, it's the greatness," she immediately understood.

Five times a day, after every traditional prayer, I would sit and focus with all my concentration on my heart and thank God for choosing me to give birth to this intention. After about nine months of patiently developing these consistent habits, I found that because my inner lights were so consistently turned on, chapter and content ideas would pop into my head all throughout the day, not just when I was meditating and praying but also when I was jogging, playing with my kids, reading a book, or journaling.

Visions started coming to me whether I was sitting down to intentionally visualize or not, and not just about the book. In one of my visions, I saw myself radiating with the confidence of someone born into royalty. I could physically feel the difference between how I felt about myself now versus how God was signaling to me I should value myself. I immediately recognized I was vibrating at the same level as the book, as I had been feeling it for so long that its energetic signature was unmistakable to me, but instead of coming to me in the form of a book, it came as a vision of my future self. The vision didn't speak using words, but it clearly conveyed to me that the only way to write the book would be to become it. It demonstrated to me how to embody that level of energy and that I should keep going because I would need to raise my default vibration even higher so that the book could come through me.

My visions were showing me that I still had too much density, and when my energy would dip, the vibration of the book trying to come through me would knock against my physical density, frying my nervous system and sending shock waves of anxiety through me. It felt like I was trying to give birth to a mountain in one push. Every setback now hurt so much more, not because I would get angry with myself, but because I wanted it so bad I could see and taste it, which is when I discovered the most radical part of this journey of evolution, that the habits and consistency that got me to one level were just steppingstones that I would have to relax, in order to step into the next level.

After about a year of burning myself at both ends to remove as much density as possible and heighten my senses, I now had to move into a completely different station that was the opposite of effort. Incredibly, it was my intense amount of effort that was causing me to increase my density rather than reduce it, and the final element of praying that I had completely misunderstood all along was that I needed to learn how to toe the line between action and ease in order to receive.

To do this, I had to follow the guidance from my vision and take my future self's lead. Any time I needed to make a choice, I would envision my future self and embody her energy, then allow her to make the decisions for me. For example, before eating anything, I would ask, "Would you eat this?" and if she said no, I wouldn't eat it. I would know whether she would say yes or no because I would tune into my heart.

"Would you eat this bag of chips, or would you eat this banana?"

Instinctively, the answer would come, and surprisingly, it wasn't always what I predicted. Sometimes, she would say yes to the chips, proving to me that I could still eat anything that I wanted and that even this late in the game, we still weren't on any kind of diet. We focused on eating things that raised my vibration, but it was equally important for my mind to feel abundant and free and never resort to starvation mode or lack.

There were weeks when I felt like she was taking it too easy on me. I knew I could do so much more, but she was reminding me of the part of the lesson I kept forgetting. In the practice of going slow, I learned to respect my body (the temple that housed the Light) and that recovery time was just as important as effort. Most importantly, she was nailing into me the point that this was not a race toward a finish line; it was a journey to be enjoyed.

In my eagerness to vibrate at her level, I assumed that I would have to become more extreme, cut carbs, do harder workouts, and meditate with more focus. Even though I had accomplished so much, I felt that because the book wasn't in my hands already, that I wasn't reaping the fruits of my labor, and I needed to push harder. The vision was trying to show me that I was still too heavily reliant on my masculine energy, which goes out and gets things, and in order to give birth to the book, I had to tap into my feminine energy, which receives from within.

I had spent so much of my life in my masculine energy that I didn't know how to be more feminine. So, the book came in the form of a regal woman, not to encourage me to push harder but to demonstrate how to relax and embody the nobility of patience. For so long, I had been acting like a desperate peasant, rushing through life collecting crumbs, and in order to break this nasty habit, I had to learn how to trust my inner connection and value and respect myself. I thought by working hard, I was showing gratitude for the guidance I was being given, but God was illuminating to me that false belief within me that was holding me back. That although hard work was important, effort and faith had to be balanced. It was at this part of the journey that he was testing my trust and belief in His plan and will. It was as if He was asking me:

'If you truly believe that my royal throne dwells within you,
and you have unlimited and direct access to it,
then why would you ever chase anything?'

I was being taught how to balance embodying my power while also taking external steps to bring my prayers to life. It was an all-encompassing experience, and I could no longer segregate my internal wishes from my external steps; everything had to be aligned and work together in perfect harmony to bring the symphony to life, but I only knew how to work harder. I didn't know how to relax deeper. However, because I was open now to receiving guidance in any form it came without any preconceived notions, God sent two teachers to show me how, and they took on the most unconventional forms.

<u>Childlike Trust and Patience</u>

Even though I knew it should be about the journey and not the destination, years of being impatient made it a constant companion while trying to write, and although God was using that impatience to teach me how to trust His will, it was such a painful lesson.

At one point, I was still trying to control the results and prayed for more willpower so that I could quickly achieve more, thinking God would suddenly fill me with a power so intense I never craved another carb again and could work 18 hours a day without needing a break. After not getting an immediate internal response, I accepted the silence and went back to slowly chiseling away at the book. Shortly after, my sister called me and told me she had a friend who was struggling to lose weight and was feeling very helpless. She had seen me making progress on my health and fitness journey and asked if I might be able to coach him.

I am always happy to help others, so I agreed, and she gave me his number. I gave him a call, and he started telling me about his experiences with being really 'good' for a week or two and then rebounding and finding himself elbow-deep in a bag of chips and not even knowing how he got there. He talked to me about how angry he would get at his lack of willpower and that it would cause him so much stress he would just quit altogether, he resigned to the fact that he would always be that way. As I started advising him, I almost bit my tongue from the realization that all the advice I was giving him was what I should be telling myself. I gave him the basic commandments for making a real, everlasting change:

- Go slow.
- Make goals that are so easy to achieve you could trip over them and succeed.
- Become addicted to the taste of success, which eventually drowns out the taste of anything you could ever put in your mouth.
- Be kind and gentle with yourself, and
- **Trust the process.** Because eventually, with consistency, the tides have to turn in your favor. It's an energetic law.

We hung up, and I don't know if I helped him or he helped me. Rather than sending a teacher to guide me, God placed me in a situation where I was the teacher to show me how to reflect on how far I had come and how much I already knew about solving my own problems. If someone else had come to me to relay their guidance or wisdom to me, it wouldn't have penetrated as deeply as me having to say it myself, out loud. Once again, I was humbled by God's ability to reach me so deeply when I needed Him and in the exact way I needed Him to. It energized me to refocus and take my own advice to trust God and the process, which I thought I did, but I would soon come to find that my trust was only lip service compared to how much more He was about to teach me about real trust.

I was getting closer to what I mentally defined as the end of my writing journey. I had been diligently practicing my writing for a year, but it had been two years since I had an income, and I knew I couldn't go on much longer without some cold, hard cash. The book was nowhere near fully formed, and If I didn't complete it soon, I would be forced to get an accounting job - the only profession I am qualified in. My heart dropped at the thought of it, not only because it would delay my progress, but even worse, I couldn't palate the idea of working with spreadsheets again. I prayed for financial assistance, and when it didn't come, I became anxious. It was a few days later, in my spiritual healing class, that my next unexpected teacher would shake me to my core.

As part of our training, the students in the class had to practice doing healings on each other. The teachers would randomly pair us up and then place us in private breakout rooms on Zoom. There, we would intuit each other's spiritual ailments and guide each other through our emotions until we received the wisdom the feeling was trying to reveal. On this day, I was more stressed than usual. I had to pay some large year-end bills, and when I opened my banking app and saw my balance, it felt like a sharp knife stabbed through my stomach. I hadn't seen numbers that low in my account since I was 16 years old. It took me back to my hustling days, working night shifts after school and on the weekends to help my mom pay bills, that feeling of you must do whatever you have to do to survive. But now I was being tested. I had to ignore that stabbing feeling and trust that if I did what I believed I was meant to do, that number going up would be God's business and not mine. It was a level of trust that hit me right where it hurt the most because I thought He had never shown up for me financially before.

I was surprised to realize that I was paired with the youngest student in our class. Coincidentally, he was 16 and came from a family of healers. He was starting his spiritual education early while also taking his regular high school courses. I felt silly initially, asking for advice and healing from a teenager, but we started anyway. He asked what I needed to be healed, and I told him that I had financial fears and I didn't know how to trust God to provide for me. He asked me more questions about my situation, and I got him up to speed about my experience in writing the book and the difficult position I was in now. He asked me if I felt that God had asked me to write this book, and I said:

"I don't feel like he has asked, I feel that he has commanded me to do it."

He responded with the innocence and certainty of a child who had never had a dashed hope:

"Well, If he has commanded you to do it, then he **must** provide for you."

It was as if he was teaching me that 1+1=2. He said it with such a pure and obvious conviction that it penetrated me. Without a single doubt, concern, or reason to even second guess his belief, it was just a fact in his eyes. It was how the universe worked like he was explaining gravity. It's just the law that what goes up must come down. Because I was doing what God asked, the laws of nature said that if He provided for the birds, He had to provide for me, too; having placed a burden on me, He had to help me carry it.

It wasn't just what he said, but the fact that it was coming from him, a child the same age as me, when I started working and stopped trusting God to provide for me. I wonder if I was paired with someone older, and they said the same thing to me, but differently, perhaps with compassion, instead of certainty and innocence, would it have reached me the way it did now? There was something pure about it. It had to be him. It had to be the way he said it.

In being exposed to his trusting energy and the words of absolute truth that he spoke, it evoked in me a deeply buried memory of trusting like that at one point in time - long ago. It was as if he transmitted to me the frequency required to trust like a child - the way a Zen sermon is received. It's not just that I had to trust; I had to get my **childlike** trust back. At this point in my life, that specific childlike feeling of trust in God was a speck, buried away so long ago that it felt like a distant memory from a past life, and now I was being asked to resurrect it. No wonder my current efforts to trust God were inadequate; I completely forgot that level of innocence existed. Having been hardened by life at such a young age, I had to relearn how to trust without reason and yet with complete certainty.

The more I surrendered to not knowing or understanding how my prayers for the book, financial help, or even how to trust God more would be answered, the deeper the lessons of trust that surfaced.

The Depths Of Our Trust Are Hidden In Our Core Beliefs

After being on the journey of raising my vibration for so long, my understanding of prayer evolved from being done while sitting in silence to becoming an active practice to balancing action and faith. But now I reached a station on this path that was teaching me that a part of praying required me to walk in blind faith - Purposefully - not because I was doing something wrong and couldn't sense my connection to God, but because it was just another step on the path of surrender that we must all take. In order to do this, my trust had to be ironclad, and because I had built such a deep rapport over the year, I was confident in our connection now, even when it was silent. God had sent me enough messages that I received deeply and exactly when I needed them, that I knew He was in control, and so I finally relaxed a little bit.

Although the cash I needed didn't suddenly appear, I didn't worry about money or getting a job anymore. I knew I needed to walk in faith and rely on God's timing, so I got rid of my artificial deadline and decided that if push came to shove, I would just sell some jewelry or cash out my 401(k) and buy myself more time. By releasing that mental pressure, I no longer stressed about how slowly it was taking my book to manifest. Instead, I focused on enjoying how it felt when I was in my flow state and playing with the words trying to form within me. Also, because I had never stopped to take a breath before, I could now take time to reflect on how far I'd come and rejoice at the tangible results of all my hard work in refining my habits.

I was so distracted with my intention that I never took the time to appreciate that I was at the physical peak of my life. In a year, I lost weight by eating moderately and not bingeing, fasting the first three days of the month and every Monday and Thursday, and walking/jogging six miles a day. I was feeling more confident in myself and in my willpower and ability to stick to new habits than I ever had before, but when I reached the height of pride in myself, I attracted an experience in life to humble me. Because pride always comes before the fall, and humility is the first step in ascension, in order to rise to a higher place than I had ever been before, I had to fall harder than ever before.

I thought I was in a great place and that I had really relaxed into my surrender, and was completely trusting God. I was even relinquishing my monk mode, and casually reintroduced socializing, which I had completely cut out. It was my cousin's birthday, and he invited me and my sister to come celebrate, and for the first time that year, I agreed to go do something not intention related. He felt like dancing, and so we went to his favorite club. On the dance floor, I was really letting loose, subconsciously releasing all the pressure I had put on myself for the last year, when the most unbelievable thing happened - My hip snapped.

I felt my leg pop out and then right back into my hip socket, creating a loud knocking sound, followed by absolute weakness. The pain was so bad, I couldn't stand straight anymore or put any weight on that leg. In an instant, I went from dancing queen, to limping my way out of the club, putting all my weight on one leg and my sister's shoulder. In an attempt to make me feel better, my sister joked: "Limping to your car is the only appropriate way to leave a club."

Beyond the pain and embarrassment of ruining everyone's night, I was the oldest in the group at 38, and snapping my hip wasn't even in my top 100 things I imagined could bring me down. I thought that was something that only happened to the elderly, and right then, I felt old and more vulnerable physically than I ever had before. ALL my perceived stability had been chopped down like a tree from right underneath me. I couldn't trust my body anymore – the only thing in the world I had ever given my true, full, and complete trust to take care of me up to this point. I felt old, fragile, and out of control, and I could not reconcile that with the fact that I was at the peak of my physical health in life.

I had been training at an MMA dojo for a year and had to call my Sensei to let him know why I wouldn't be coming in for a while. He was shocked; being my trainer, he knew what my strength and abilities were, and he also couldn't understand how, after a year of watching me spar and grapple with real opponents, it was dancing that took me down. He asked if I thought I had been spiritually attacked, and I did believe it was spiritual, but not an attack, a lesson.

I spent that night in bed reading every article about 'snapping hip syndrome' on page one and two of *Google* when I came across the most incredible story that I had never heard before about Jacob's* limp[6].

Jacob*, the son of Isaac*, was trying to buy his older brother, Esau's, forgiveness years after deceiving his father into giving him the blessing that was supposed to be Esau's birthright. After years of separation, he finally had to face him and sent caravans of gifts and even his family ahead of him, hoping this intelligent tactic would soften his brother's anger toward him before he arrived.

While Jacob* was camping alone, before his trip to see his brother the next day, a stranger appeared in his camp who he started wrestling with. The stranger is believed to be a metaphor for an angel, or even God, and right when Jacob* feels most confident that his own strength will allow him to win the fight, God 'puts out his hip joint,' causing him to limp.

The interpretation of this story is that Jacob* was relying on his own strength and intellect to defeat his perceived opponent (whether it was his brother, or the stranger he tangles with), but by dislocating his hip joint, God teaches Jacob* that he has no strength of his own and should only rely on God.

After reading it, I was stunned. The lesson was so relevant; it was as if God was speaking directly to me through the same injury inflicted on a prophet from thousands of years ago. I knew I was relying on my own strength and intellect to write this book, when I should've relied on God, but I didn't understand what I was doing wrong. I didn't know how to fix the problem, or what the root cause of it was. I was praying consistently, relaxing more, trusting more, and diligently following the steps as I received the intuitive guidance. I didn't know what more I could do.

Because of the pain of the injury, I sat home for a week, unable to do anything at all. I couldn't write because sitting at my desk hurt too much, I could barely walk, and I had to use my son's baseball bat as a crutch to get me from the couch to the bathroom. All I could do was lie down and feel sorry for myself. I begged God to show me what I was doing wrong and how to fix it and move forward.

Coincidentally, a few days prior to snapping my hip, I had scheduled a meeting for the following week with a colleague from school to practice our spiritual healing techniques with each other. His title at work just so happens to be 'Miraculous Healing Intuitive,' so, after only a day of sitting on my couch, I gave him a call at our appointed time, and told him everything that had transpired since we last spoke. I apologized for not being able to work on him due to my condition, but he didn't mind at all, and was happy to help me out. He is very gifted in understanding the language of feelings and emotions, and when he intuitively sensed into my hip, he noticed some anxiety buried in there and asked me what I was anxious about. I told him I had been divorced for five years, and I had not worked in two, and I was feeling some financial and personal instability. He asked if this was the first time I had felt this way, and BAM, the memory blew open.

In my mind's eye, I saw the exact moment I stopped trusting my dad. I was 16 and had asked him to come car shopping with me so that the salesmen wouldn't swindle me. He asked if I had money for a down payment, and I told him I had $1,800. He said he would hold it for me, and we would go next week so that the salesmen would think it was him buying the car and not me. I excitedly handed him the cash, and a week later, I approached him while he was lying down on the couch watching TV and asked if he was ready to go.

"Go where?" he asked.

Thinking he was playing, I said: "Car Shopping!!" With the excitement of a child blowing a thousand bubbles. "Come on, Dad, go get the money, and let's go! You promised you would take me this week."

He didn't break eye contact with the TV when he casually said:

"I already spent it."

I went numb with shock and felt the hair on the back of my spine stand straight up, like a porcupine to protect myself. He went on to lecture me that since I was an adult and making money, I needed to learn responsibility and start paying bills around the house and that he used the money on the electricity bill, which was unexpectedly high that month. No apology. No eye contact. Just a lecture about becoming more responsible. It felt like someone had sucker punched the wind out of me. My mind was completely silent, trying to comprehend how the person I was entrusting to protect me from some sleazy car salesman, ended up being worse than them.

I had learned from him long before that 'no one ever comes,' but this really nailed the lesson to – Trust no one but yourself. If your dad can steal from you, anyone can steal from you. I had worked an entire year at *Cici's Pizza* to make all that money, and one second after putting it in my dad's hands, it was gone. For all his talk about responsibility, shortly after that, he abandoned my mom and two younger sisters. Leaving me, the oldest sibling still in the house, to step up and support them, as if he had been grooming me for this role my entire life. I immediately stepped into his shoes and got night and weekend jobs to help my mom pay the bills and care for my sisters, and became her stability and savior. If no one was going to come save me, then I was going to show the world how it's supposed to be done.

Instead of praying for stability, I became it, and for many years of my life, that worked - until 20 years later, when my hip snapped. With a simple dance step, God taught me the same lesson He taught Jacob* long ago - That I had no true strength and stability of my own, that I was fragile, and that God gifted me with the illusion of strength when I was a child as a mercy, to help me survive some really tough times. I had taken that gift for granted, thinking I was using my own willpower to save myself and that God had forgotten about me. Not knowing that at 16 years old, my physical strength to work and mental strength to put my needs aside and provide for my family, were holy virtues of fortitude that some grown men and fathers do not even have.

Blowing this memory open, and being able to look at it with 20 years of hindsight, made the pain of snapping my hip a small price to pay, for the wisdom it brought to the surface.

I had made the mistake of making a mental idol out of my own physical strength, which I glorified and trusted more than God, the one who created my body. In doing that, I didn't acknowledge that my strength was the blessing, and the answer to my prayers all along. Instead, I lived foolishly believing that God didn't answer prayers, and I had to do everything myself because he didn't solve my problem the way I expected him to – by handing me a huge bag of money, or bringing my father back and forcing him to take responsibility for his family. It was my assumptions and expectations that led me to believe I was alone in a world full of hardship and betrayal. I couldn't see the bigger picture, that by giving me strength instead of money, He was empowering me from within, rather than weakening me with dependence on the material world. Having this realization now makes me weep with humility at my ungrateful arrogance while also being in complete awe of how He perfectly orchestrated this lesson to reach me in perfect timing.

In absolute awestruck humility, I accepted that my Core Beliefs, were false: That I could only trust and rely on myself and my strength, that prayers were never answered, and that no one ever comes. False. False. False.

The world as I knew it was an illusion, and I never would've known that unless God, in all his mercy, took my hip out. By causing that temporary pain and disillusionment, He revealed to me all the false beliefs that I had buried in my childhood and that now formed the unconscious foundation that I was building my life on as an adult. It was the reason I couldn't move forward on my journey, because in order to fully surrender, I had to be a true believer. But at this point, God was showing me that I only truly believed in myself, and not in the truth of all that God had done for me.

Each false belief accumulated one on top of the other, and formed a thick, tangled web that became almost impossible to escape from. It affected not only my mind, but the way I physically saw the world, and blinded me from the truth that was right in front of me all along.

We are Never alone.
Everything that happens to us is either a blessing, or a teaching,
benefiting our constant evolution.

There were so many new beliefs that my new perspective brought to my awareness, but the one that mattered the most to me was that God had truly been there all along; He never left or abandoned me. I believed it unflinchingly now, and I felt that belief stabilize me to the core.

After making this new belief my truth, I became even more aware of the different voices within me, and could distinguish between thoughts that came from my new beliefs, and ones that came from old false beliefs. Before, I had prayed so ardently that God show me what my next step was, and how to overcome the obstacles I was facing in my finances and writing, only to learn now that: <u>The one asking Him that question, was the one in the way.</u>

There was a personality within me who always wanted to know what she could 'do,' not maliciously, but sweetly and innocently, because she believed that no one ever comes, and she has to do everything herself. I thought she was a corpse I had left behind long ago, only to realize she could shapeshift. She took on the role of the false messiah, the perfectionist, the hero, and the overachiever. She was a weed I thought I was pulling out of the ground, but what I was actually doing was pruning her. Destabilizing her temporarily, but eventually, she would grow back, and take on a new, 'more helpful' form. I didn't recognize that all these personalities grew out of the same root of false belief - and in all honesty, I loved that root.

Before this part of the surrendering journey, I was leaving behind parts of me addicted to comfort and distractions, and although they were hard to get rid of, it was easier in the sense that I didn't want them. They enjoyed cheap thrills and didn't really serve me, but her, she had been with me since I was a child. She was the only one who had ever protected me, and provided for me. When I thought the rest of the world deserted me, she stepped in and saved me, sharing my highest highs and lowest lows with me. I loved every part of her, even her flaws. Her perfectionism and judgment came from a place of tough love; she just wanted me to be the best. I didn't know who I was without her, but as soon as I had that thought, the light of my consciousness guided me to my heart, saying: 'Remember the truth of who you are.' If I want to experience a different kind of love, one that wasn't tough or critical, that didn't feel like I had to earn, but rather be given love freely and unconditionally, I knew what I had to do.

It only seemed right, that it had to be me, to take her by my own hand up the mountain. I didn't know if she was a sacrifice or a martyr, but I understood what I was being commanded to do, and luckily, she complied willingly. She understood what I needed to do, and supported me to her end. If she had to die, she would do it with honor, nothing giving her more pleasure than seeing me succeed.

I was at a level of understanding and connection now where the idea of worshipping anyone other than God nauseated me to the core. I atoned for my sin (which, from its origin, directly translates as 'missing the mark') in my misunderstanding. I humiliated myself by spending years unknowingly elevating myself over my Creator, and my ignorance of that made me shudder in fear at what else I was doing unconsciously, but God forgave me before I even made my first plea. As soon as I acknowledged my ignorant state for what it was, I found that He wasn't angry or disappointed in me at all. He was proud of me.

Despite years of being an arrogant hypocrite, calling myself a believer to Him and others, but only truly believing in myself - He loved me, and waited patiently with open arms for me to come back to Him. In finally understanding what was in the way between me and my prayers being answered and rectifying that internal error, I got to the next step in my journey only to realize it wasn't a step; It was a threshold that I could not walk across, I had to be carried just like a bride is carried by her groom.

I wasn't used to being carried, for so long I believed I had to run myself into the ground to prove my worth and survive, but God was teaching me the opposite now. That He wanted to carry me, but in order to do that, I had to allow Him, because He honored my free will.

At every step, I was asked to let go deeper.

Now, I had to let go of the idea that I was writing a book, and instead, I had to trust that God would write it through me. I didn't know how or when He would come, I just had to trust that He would.

I was just a pen, waiting for Allah to pick me up.

Success in Prayer

Within a week of snapping my hip, I was feeling better and able to sit at my laptop to continue writing again, but this time, it was very different. I felt renewed and as if everything I had done to prepare myself for this moment had finally converged harmoniously within me. All of my new habits had sufficiently heightened my senses enough that when my new beliefs solidified my trust and ability to receive, they automatically aligned with my intention. Causing a force of confident inspiration so strong to course through me, that it actually felt like a holy ghost had taken over me.

I had so much energy running through me that each day I would sit at my desk, and make a simple admission: "I'm not able to do this, only you are." Then, time would seem to disappear as I took a step back and allowed God to write through me. It's difficult to truly describe the state I would go into, but it would start with me sitting there feeling deeply into my silent reverence. Then, when I felt completely relaxed, I would ask a question like "What is prayer," and then a feeling would arise, and I would trust that what I received in response was the right answer and translate it to the best of my ability. I felt the tenets of Ask and Receive come alive within me in real-time, and if prayer is communication with God, then every word of this book was a prayer.

For three months, I stayed in this intense state of divine inspiration. On days I didn't have the kids, I worked 16 hours, taking breaks only to eat, sleep, or do restorative yoga for my hip. Because as soon as I started writing, the words (in the form of feelings) would come so intensely that I couldn't steal myself away from my computer, and I didn't want to miss a moment of this momentum.

That's not to say this task became easy by any stretch of the imagination. I still had moments of fear, doubt, and burnout. I was actually amazed that I could simultaneously have so much confidence and inspiration, and still be so terrified. But instead of stopping, I just allowed myself to be small and scared, to cry when I needed to, to doubt myself and be terrified that I was doing it all wrong or that it wasn't any good, and then to keep going anyway. I had been throwing these little stones of fear and doubt at myself for so long that before, I had convinced myself these stones were tough love, but I knew now that they were remnants of an old belief system that would take time to work its way out of me.

Jesus* said: "Let he with no sin, cast the first stone,"[7] and with those nine words, he conveyed the core depth of everything I had learned on my long journey to succeed in prayer and to find what had been standing in the way between God and me all along. He understood that judgment is born from false beliefs and that although it is important to uproot those false beliefs, it is also just as important to acknowledge the beauty in our shared humanity in that we are all prone to misunderstanding (sinning). So it's not just that we shouldn't throw stones of judgment at others, but not even at ourselves.

In order to truly reach the elevation required to walk with God in prayer and purpose, I aligned with the depths of truth within and offered myself compassion instead. Without this key element, it didn't matter how much I observed prayer times or balanced work and ease because until I addressed the cracks in my core foundational beliefs, anything I built upon them would eventually fall. For so long, I thought I needed to work furiously to cultivate enough love to reach God, but what truly served me was a gentler love born from a foundation of child-like trust.

It took this massive adventure inside for me to finally be at peace with how holy my imperfect humanity was and to realize it is because of our fragile nature that prayer comes to life. Before, I believed that perfection and self-sufficiency were superior, but now I know there is nothing to admire about perfection achieving perfection because it is expected and can only work within limits. However, there is something that leaves us in awe when we see an underdog transformed by their light within into a winner that succeeds against all odds. Their light shines so bright it lights up everyone around them who witnesses the transformation as well, and the effect of that on the world is immeasurable. It inspires us to believe, in the deepest parts of us, that perhaps we could do that too if we chose to follow the light inside of us. Light guiding light.

The week before I finished getting the entire first draft of my book out, I kept having a dream that I was giving birth to twins. I knew one was the book, but I didn't know what the other baby signified. On 12/8/22 at 2:22 am, I saved my completed first draft and sat back, surprised by the time and stunned by what had just come through me. I was shocked at how similar this feeling of completion was to when I gave birth to my actual children. They were also born in the wee hours of the morning, after hours of labor, leaving me in a drowsy, semi-unconscious state of feeling like I was floating between two worlds while bursting with pride and a sense of relieved accomplishment. The difference was that with the children, although I felt this same pride, I projected it out to them, making them my greatest pride and joy. This time, there was no one to externalize it to, and so I internalized it as a new-found pride, not in myself, but in my ability to deeply trust and follow God's lead. Just like my children anchor me to the world, this feeling anchored within me the belief that when I did what was my responsibility and then surrendered the rest to God, He would truly come and carry me to the finish line. This new belief elevated me so high I felt like a completely different person - I was reborn.

Listening to my heart was a gift I always had. I never had to earn it, I only had to realize it, and shortly after this experience, this wisdom came to me during a meditation:

I could've given you gifts, but I wanted you to find them for yourself. I didn't want you to feel crippled with the uncertainty of talents unearned. I wanted you to feel the confidence of trusting your inner guidance developed over time, with perseverance and patience. Only granted to those who are the most committed. Who want it the most.

Fake gifts can be given and taken. The real gift can only be found within yourself.

A Summary Of My Lessons About Prayer

When I started down the path of learning about how prayer informed surrender, I put the cart before the horse and thought that with enough recitation and prostration that eventually, a holy ghost would come to take over me, and forevermore safely guide me through life. That ghost did eventually show up, but not in the way I thought it would, and not until after I was led so deep into the torrential emotions within me, that I had to learn how to trade my little tugboat for Noah's* ark to traverse the surging waves.

Surrendering, I confirmed, was a constant cyclical journey of trading up. I was continually being asked to trust that when I let go of the old tools that served me, better ones would be provided. As the levels got more intense, I needed vehicles that were equipped to travel the terrain, and where the hero could only get me so far, I would need humility to carry me up the next step of the way. In order to make this trade, I had to fight against my better judgment, based on all the evidence of my past experiences, and blindly accept that by weakening myself and relinquishing my strong and independent nature, I would be elevated with humility and patience. The Knight in shining armor no longer served me, and now I had to take on my truer form as a barefoot Queen.

This process is necessary for us to evolve into the greatest version of ourselves, but it would've saved me so much time if, at the beginning of my journey, I had the foresight and awareness to ask one critical question: **Who is the one that is praying?**

Had I taken the time to ask that question, it would've given me the opportunity to study the nature of what I was asking for in my prayers. Where the Knight is my masculine energy and focuses on pushing force out and getting external materials, the Queen is my feminine energy and focuses on taking support in, so that she can be properly served. Noting this difference would've clued me in that I was still focusing on going and getting, rather than receiving, which should be balanced.

But I overlooked it completely, because the Knight has no self-awareness, which is what this surrendering process was teaching me – how to know thyself, by becoming aware of the unconscious programs that run me, and how to elegantly elevate them with grace. For so long, I busied myself with becoming the best Knight I could be, only to learn that, in the end, it was the Knight himself who was the problem. He kept himself busy slaying dragons, and even when there were none left, he would find ways to conjure them out of nothing, because that was all he knew how to do, and in order to stay alive, he had to make himself appear useful.

Every time I prayed, I flirted with the opportunity to gain that awareness, but it never clicked until it was time to take the next step. I knew in prayer I went in humble, and waited for the Queen of my heart to speak, but it never once occurred to me that in order to commune ceaselessly, I had to become the Queen. My entire life, I was programmed to believe I was unworthy of her and that I had to approach her as a beggar and ask her to put a drop of light in my bucket. Yet the whole time, she was trying to tell me that I didn't have to ask; it was already my light to begin with. All I had to do was take my power back from the beggar.

This loss of power didn't just affect my spiritual ascension but my physical experiences as well. I can't count the number of times I gave my power away to men who used my kind, helpful nature for their advantage and then disrespected or rejected me after. It felt impossible to find a good romantic relationship, and I thought it was because there were no good men, only to realize they were just picking up on and reacting to the desperate energy I was emitting. My desire to help and be helped attracted everyone within the vicinity who needed help, and the vicious self-fulfilling cycle of toxic relationships went on until I discovered self-accountability.

Although I very easily could've walked away from this path, holding on to my justifiable pain for the rest of my life, always blaming my dad for making me feel worthless or God for not saving me when I needed Him. I knew that would just be self-sabotage, like cutting off my nose to spite my face, and it would just keep me forever trapped in suffering one way or another.

Bashar, a modern spiritual teacher, illustrates this too common and illogical application of self-imposed suffering by explaining that life is a mirror. Since we attract what we are, then someone who continues to willingly suffer is like a person pointing at their reflection in a mirror and saying: "I'm not going to smile until they smile first."

It was while in this position of self-sabotage and the beggar mentality that I decided I had no choice but to take my chances and throw the Knight off the cliff because I knew there had to be a better way to live, but I would never find it if I held on to the baggage that held me back. When I let my beggar mentality go, it gave me the inner space to allow the wisdom in my heart to take the newly vacated throne, which I realized had been with me ever since I was a child. But because I considered it so normal then, I didn't value it (or myself), and so an illusion of distance had to be created so that I could experience life as a beggar in order to understand my value when I was reacquainted with the Queen. The entire journey boiled down to a long lesson in relativity, and appreciation.

<u>If I were guiding myself down this path, I would remind myself that:</u>

1. Connecting with my heart as often as possible is prayer.

2. The more I pray, the quicker I remember who I am.

3. Life is like an elaborate game of peek-a-boo. Do not punish yourself while you are in the dark, or have forgotten who you are, it is a vital part of the game.

4. Don't believe that you can control ANY of it. Just find the joy in it right now. Don't delay. Even if you are squeezing drops out of rocks, start Now.

<u>These are truths about prayer I will live by:</u>

- In making prayer and connecting to my heart a constant practice, I learned to prioritize love for love's sake. Just to feel it and exude it, with no agenda.

- Prayer's purpose wasn't to prevent or protect me from experiencing pain. It walked through it with me, showing me that darkness wasn't my enemy; it was my teacher, evolving and empowering me. All of my most awful experiences are married to my deepest prayers, and it was in those moments that the connections I needed were built and guides were born.

- Pain and pleasure are two sides of the same coin. Darkness and light. Nothing and everything. I couldn't be saved from the pain because suffering was salvation. Understanding duality, and collapsing it into unity, is the golden ticket out. This is what they all did, Buddha*, Jesus*, and Muhammad*. Oneness is the only exit from duality. No god, but God.

- Pain doesn't last forever, but I could choose to hold on to it forever. My internal state was my only free will. In a world where most people choose anger, love is an act of rebellion.

- God is in my heart. He speaks to me with my own voice, and feelings. Prayer gives me direct access to him.

- There is a beautiful, well-intentioned reptile within me, responsible for my survival. When I accidentally mistook it for God, it ended up running around in circles, chasing its own tail forever. In order to ascend this spiraling in my mind, I had to admit I was wrong, with compassion. Then, reestablish my heart on its throne.

- I learned more and reached deeper into myself when I observed the things I asked for and why, than I did when I just visualized and received things shallowly.

If we are lucky, moments will come in life when we receive an Ask so big and beautiful, it terrifies us. I thought if I truly believed, I would have no fear, and yet so much of my prayer was done while terrified of both my potential failure and greatness.

After playing small for so long, being in the presence of our greatness can cause us to tremble. Prayer, at its core, being the union of lovers, holds our hand, and gazes into our eyes as we merge with our highest potential. Strengthening us through the pain and pressure that all rocks must experience, before shining like diamonds of enlightenment.

Prayer Flow

Pray. Worship. Play. Create.
Each word can be used interchangeably.
In an attempt to feel the connection.
To something we sense but cannot see.

A wake in the walk of silence.
He says: 'Ask and Receive.'
A game of Forgetting and Remembering,
A never-ending cycle of torment and ecstasy.

I chant His sacred name.
My lips become plump, and the tip of my tongue starts to tingle.
Like passionately kissing your true love.
You pause to breathe in the sweet essence.

The oral fixation of Allaaaaahhhhh.

My mind wonders, and begins to ponder
The primal wisdom,
Of why at climax, we scream 'Oh my God.'
It's strange to think about something so holy,
While doing something that is so base.
But I suppose it makes perfect sense.
What could be more holy than union?
Two becoming one.

Eventually wanderlust sets in, we want something new.
So we willingly fall away and forget,
to make the remembering stronger.

The primordial wisdom of distance and desire.
We fall deep asleep, and dream of unrequited love.
The pain is unbearably severe.
The only way to awaken is the killing of desire.
The murder of desire.
The annihilation of desire.
Eliminating the desire, eliminates the distance.
Time and space collapse.

But you have to do it with finesse.
You can't shut the door on it,
because then you build a wall to everything else.

Instead, you have to dance with desire,
you have to dance around it,
you have to dance away from it.

Only on reunion day,
Being able to look back and understand the wisdom in the pain.
Saying Thank you,
For teaching me.
For breaking me, so that I could be built back stronger.
For sacrificing yourself, so that I could become me.

Knowing that one day I will play that role for someone else.
Knowing we are all playing.
Playing with each other, playing for each other,
playing the main character, playing the extra.

It's all fun and games until you get hurt, then it feels real.
Back in the forgetting.
The good part is ahead.

The forgetting comes before the remembering.

I used to hate the forgetting part.
I'd always feel so disconnected and useless and sad and depressed
and ugly and stupid and uninteresting and useless.
I couldn't witness life's magic and it drove me INSANE.

But only in utter empty darkness, do you hear the sound:

'Be.'

Be fun. Be healthy. Be interesting.
Slowly I follow it.
One step.
Baby steps.

I follow it to places that shine and to dark alleys.
I follow it to places I've never been and never thought I'd go.
I just follow. It leads me from the inside.
It pushes and pulls me to my new favorite things.
Becoming so consumed in the newness,
I forget about my sadness, and depression, and without realizing it,
I remember.

I remember again what having a purpose, and passion, and love
feels like.
The confidence drowns me.
I remember I can trust myself, or whatever it is inside of me that
leads me.
I am happier, brighter, lighter.
I am home again.

The old slips away.
I barely notice.
No longer compatible with my new way of life.

Alone I walk, but I never end up alone.
We all always manage to find each other on the open road home.
New best friends. New loves. New adventures.
My only responsibility is to learn and grow and play.

As a child I played with toys.
Now I play with words and ideas.
I play with my mind and I play with depth,
seeing how long I can hold my breath at the bottom of the ocean.
Playing quietly in the dark.

I play with sounds of words on my tongue and in my throat.
I play with my breath going in and out.
I play with all the aches and pains in my body.
I play with the light and the tingles.
I play with the love. Then it plays me.
We play together... until we forget.
Who is playing with who.
The Forgetting leading us to Remember.

Jesus* of Nazareth

It is impossible to talk about connecting to our hearts without acknowledging the greatest teacher of love who ever lived.

If Muhammad* was a mercy for the whole world, Jesus* was our gift of unconditional love.

He stood in radical conviction to love, despite all odds, and in so, demonstrated his brilliant understanding of the laws and how they truly applied to the world.

The 10 Commandments[8]:
- You shall have no other gods before Me.
- You shall make no idols.
- You shall not take the name of the Lord your God in vain.
- Remember the Sabbath day and keep it Holy.
- Honor your father and mother.
- You shall not murder.
- You shall not commit adultery.
- You shall not steal.
- You shall not bear false witness against your neighbor.
- You shall not covet your neighbor.

Long ago, Jesus* discovered that the world was a reflection machine - a mirror - and that the 10 commandments weren't just rules, they were words of caution from the spiritual world:

These are the 10 worst things that can happen to you.
Don't do them, otherwise karmically, they must happen back to you.

The majority of people at the time, understood the rules in their most obvious application, as the Law of Return: Eye for an eye. But Jesus* understood the implication of the root law, that the 10 commandments were derived from – which is what you do will be reflected back to you. When he flipped their application around, and looked in the mirror of life from an elevated perspective. He realized that by focusing on what he should do, instead of what not to do, he could unlock the power to cultivate infinite amounts of the only thing of true value in the world - Love.

Taking the lesson even deeper, he understood that not only did the external world abide by this law, but our internal world did as well, as the external was only a reflection of the internal "on Earth, as it is in Heaven"[9]. So regardless of what he was experiencing (internally or externally), as long as he perceived it with eyes of love, his senses had to reflect love back to him. Love was the exit from suffering.

By becoming flexible enough with the tools of meekness and humility, he could easily alter his perspective to always find ways to love any situation, and in doing so, he figured out how to instantly transmute pain into pleasure - transcending duality completely.

Demonstrating in real life, that through the alchemy released into our bodies when our heart and mind are in coherence, we experience divine union, even while living in a world of separation.

It wasn't just the simple idea of the Law of Attraction, where if you feel love, you get love. It's translate everything you experience as love - "Love your enemy."

His ethos is beautifully captured in the biblical account of his crucifixion.

When the angry crowd came to deliver his fate, he didn't run away, and he didn't express gratitude for it either. He just surrendered to God's will, with the conviction that no matter what happened, Love could not fail him.

While on the cross, he prayed, not for a hero to come save him, but for God to:

"Forgive them, they know not what they do."[10]

This simple statement carried the totality of his entire teaching to the world. He knew that The Law, embedded in the fabric of our universe, would have to repay this pain to the ones that caused it, and when it did, if they didn't understand yet how to apply the principle of universal love, they would suffer gravely. Not understanding that the wraths we bring upon ourselves can only serve two purposes: To bless us, or to teach us a lesson about the nature of our reality.

In this final plea of love and forgiveness, Jesus* used the only power in the world that he knew could walk him through this tribulation – Prayer. Culminating in a final demonstration of how to align our heart and soul to become a bridge, that allows our highest divine essence to express itself on Earth. He taught us not only how to love, but how to Be surrendered love.

With this act, Jesus* paved the way and passed the torch on to Muhammad*, who picked it up 500 years later to solidify and finalize the most powerful tenant of the Abrahamic* faith:

If God is in our heart,
then Islam is the religion of surrendering to our own heart.

My mom couldn't understand that I wasn't hungry because I was Full. In our culture, food is love, and even when we are full, we eat.

"What do you mean you're not hungry, just taste one bite?"

"Literally, if I were hungry, I would eat, but I'm not hungry."

"What did you eat before?"

"Not much."

"Ntt. This isn't right."

"The Prophet used to only eat one meal a day."

"You aren't the prophet."

We had the same conversation every week for an entire year. She never accepted that I was full when I hadn't eaten and that my metabolism had changed. Honestly, it surprised me, too. It was the most interesting side effect of following my dreams - feeling so full all the time. It was as if I were pregnant, and I had been, twice. It's remarkable how similar the experiences were. The nausea, lack of appetite, pressure on the bladder, and up the throat, there was something big sitting inside of me.

I never blamed my mom for not getting on board; it is rare for a person to actually change, and breaking character can be really shocking to ourselves and others. Trying to make changes internally while my external environment kept trying to reinforce old habits was a vulnerable process. I found that instead of food, I craved solitude, naturally wanting to cocoon and protect myself while I made big changes, so I silently retreated to my cave of wonders.

For so long, I feared sitting quietly to meditate while fasting, believing it would be hard, hungry, and miserable. It never occurred to me that by focusing my attention inward on my intention, I would become spiritually full, and in that fullness, I could feel no hunger. My body without food silenced naturally, making daily life a waking meditation.

Essentially, I didn't try to fast, my intention fasted me.

It knew what I wanted, and it knew how to organize my energy levels to achieve it, replacing food with something much more satisfying.

<u>God placed five things in five different places:</u>[1]

1. Greatness in obedience.
2. Humiliation in disobedience.
3. Awe in the night vigil.
4. Wisdom in an empty stomach.
5. Wealth in contentment.

Chapter 3: Fasting

"The most beloved deed to Allah,
is that which is performed consistently, even if it is small'.[2]
-Muhammad*

Fasting is either loved or dreaded. People either rant and rave about it, or they dread every second of it and make up for their hours of scarcity with hours of bingeing. I have seen grown men break their fast with a cigarette, and I have seen others almost faint from weakness, and still refuse to break their fast.

Fasting brings out an extreme within us, feast or famine, and when I was initially exploring this tool, I fell into that same hole. I didn't know how to find balance in such an opposing state, and with my background in yo-yo dieting, it was like a recipe for disaster. I was never taught that my body had natural mechanisms for self-regulation, so I did what nutritionists, personal trainers, doctors, and mainly my family told me to do with it for years. I never once thought to listen to it, despite it being so near me.

It wasn't until my intention taught me the purpose of fasting that I realized it was not useful if I was constantly weak and starving, and at the same time, I learned eating was not useful if I was always heavy, lethargic, and had brain fog. I had to learn how to balance food as fuel and enjoyment, and the lack of it as a natural state that healed and heightened my senses.

What is Fasting?

Fasting is silencing the body.

The voice we are trying to connect to deep within our hearts is subtle and sophisticated. It never raises its voice over a whisper, so in order to hear it, we must be silent. A true mark of a person who knows their power is that they never raise their voice, knowing that when they speak, the room silences.

There is a tremendous amount of noise outside and inside of us: Addictions, hunger, worries, infatuations, dreams, expectations, TV, and my mom's stuffed grape leaves – which are to die for. All these distractions are so loud that they pull our attention toward them, making it harder for us to control ourselves.

"In Arabic, the letter *nun* of the word hawan (humiliation)
is stolen from the word hawa (desire).
Therefore, he who succumbs to every passion
is subject to humiliation!"[3]

The first way to feel stable and in control in a world with endless desires is to have the power to silence our thoughts. This is why it is scary when we can't sit still for five minutes to meditate; it makes us realize we cannot direct our own minds. Our best bet is to distract it with something we perceive as productive, but getting it to heel seems like a power only possessed by monks.

The mind jumps and whips our emotions around with it. All it takes is the musty scent of mold, and I am five years old again in my grandpa's dark creaky house with crystal doorknobs and his dusty collection of music tapes that filled an entire bookshelf.

A moment later, The Band Perry's song *If I Die Young* can come on, and slingshot me 20 years later, remembering how often and bittersweet it felt to turn my radio off after hearing the first four lines:

"If I die young, bury me in satin,
Lay me down on a bed of roses,

Sink me in the river at dawn,
Send me away with the words of a love song."

It was a lovely song, but it came out right when my dad passed away. He was only 56 years old, and every time it came on the radio, my stomach would clench, and my eyes would immediately well up with tears.

With the world using its best effort to keep us distracted and destabilized emotionally, it can feel like a herculean effort to silence our minds and refocus our attention on our hearts. Our ultimate goal is constant communion with our hearts, but it's hard to make that connection with a whisper when the world is screaming for our attention, and everyone knows the squeaky wheel gets the grease.

Luckily, with fasting, one silence leads to the other. If intention is what causes us to look in, and prayer is what allows us to communicate back and forth, then fasting AMPLIFIES the effects of both of them. So, we get PULLED into ourselves and hear instructions LOUD and CLEAR.

Ok, I know those caps were loud and sudden when I was trying to emphasize silence, but I did it to illustrate the power of fasting; it is literally and exactly like that. What was once a whisper or a vague inclination becomes a resounding boom or a 4D cinematic experience. In the quiet state of fasting, our internal senses are most heightened, like when we are trying to sleep at night, and everything is silent, but then all the little noises in the house get louder. With fasting, we become an empty castle where we can hear all the whispered wisdom inside.

Mysticism of Fasting

Physical Effects

Fasting traditionally is abstaining from food and water, but we also fast from sex, smoking, gossiping, and anger. In doing so, we silence experiences that evoke huge chemical and hormonal productions in our body, making us feel calm, balanced, and at peace.

Fasting is just as mystical for the physical effects on our body as it is for the spiritual effects. Just a tiny fraction of the physical benefits are that it[4]:

- Eliminates brain fog and boosts cognitive performance.
- Resets our immune system in as little as three days.
- Allows us to live longer.
- Protects us from obesity and other related diseases.
- Improves our overall fitness.
- Reduces inflammation.
- Decreases the risk of metabolic disease.
- Can help prevent cancer.

Spiritual Effects

The spiritual effects of fasting are married to the physical effects, with the added bonus that while our bodies quiet and our senses heighten, our depressed and anxious thoughts mute, and the whispers become louder.

Not consuming food for an allotted time initiates a sophisticated protocol in the body to ensure its survival. Instead of food, it begins consuming all the unnecessary cells in our body: Fat reserves, damaged cells, and cancer cells are all metabolized for energy, and there is a 2-fold benefit: we cleanse ourselves while our digestive organs get a break.

Metabolizing food is one of the largest ways our body exerts energy, using approximately 30% of our calories. With fasting, that machine is silenced, and that energy is freed to focus on regenerative work within the body, essentially healing itself. It is also redirected to our higher energy centers, allowing us to experience heightened states of consciousness that aren't available to us while we are in survival mode.

Our body has seven energy centers that start at our pelvic root and go up to the top of our head in a straight line through the center of our body, along our spine. Each energy center correlates to the body parts we use when in different states of need. For example, at the bottom is our root and sacral centers, which are located near our reproductive and digestive organs; they are activated when we must focus on our survival needs: Food, safety, and procreation. These are all wonderful things that we have been programmed to need to ensure that we not only survive as individuals but as a human species. However, those needs must be balanced with the soul's need for creativity, love, and evolution, which are activated when our energy is free to move up to our higher energy centers, located in the heart, throat, and center of our mind – where our pineal gland rests.

This balance becomes skewed when we get stuck in survival mode and our lower energy centers, we mistake our spiritual needs for our physical ones, and we might overeat sweets, not knowing our true hunger is for deep levels of love in our life. When I started this journey, the enormous feeling within me to write a book caused me so much anxiety that instead of exploring that spiritual need, I tried numbing it with junk food. When I felt disconnected from the Light inside of me, I always felt 'hungry' no matter how much I ate because food couldn't satisfy my emotional and spiritual needs. The thing I was trying to eat through was eating away at me, and mistaking my spiritual body for my physical one, I tried to prevent it from being consumed, so I ate and ate and ate. Incredibly, it was fasting that calmed my anxiety and made me feel spiritually full, igniting my ability to connect with the true source of nourishment and teaching me the truth that we do not live on bread alone.

When we fast and allow our lower energy centers to rest, our body automatically recalibrates and balances these competing needs, which is why many people are surprised to report that they no longer feel hunger after just a few hours of fasting. When the higher energy centers are activated, that is when we become connected to Source and receive divine inspiration and guidance, but most importantly, we are filled with love.

This connection doesn't require months of training; it can be felt on Day 1. The first thing I notice is the peace and calm descending within me, and then naturally wanting to close my eyes and feel into my heart; after a while of calm, quiet attention, I can feel it energize and expand, filling me with what I can only describe as a hug on the inside.

Unlearn to Learn

Li Ching-Yuen was a Chinese man who lived to be 250 years old; this number is so high scientists believe it is a myth. He died in 1933, leaving behind his 24th wife and 200 kids. Before he passed, he was asked what his secret was, and he said herb tinctures and fasting. It's not just that he grew old; his quality of life was superior to many 'young' people who suffer all of the health and psychological issues that come with aging and overconsuming.

As our society progressed scientifically, we stopped trusting our body, feelings, and intuition. Their results were not reproducible in a lab because, as individuals, our needs are individual; we cannot be reduced to a one-size-fits-all program. In an attempt to provide a general health guide, a food pyramid was created, and with it, an obesity epidemic.

Whether intentionally or not, we are severely uneducated about how much and what kinds of food our body actually needs, and most importantly, when to eat and when to give it a rest. The societal belief that we should be eating 3 - 6 meals a day has left me in a position where when I tell my family I only eat 1-2 meals per day, all they think is, 'Are you becoming anorexic?' even though I have tremendous amounts of energy, and still maintain beautiful fat deposits on my body. Instead of trusting our internal guidance, we gave our power away to external sources: Scientists, doctors, government, family, culture, and community became our guides, which is ok to a certain extent.

When my son was younger, he used to run full speed while looking behind him, and once he ran face-first into the corner of a wall and split his upper lip in half. We had to rush him to an emergency room, where the doctor gave him a numbing agent, and stitched him up with sterilized equipment. It was a Blessing. Health care is a blessing. Fasting could not solve this problem for us. So, I am not knocking the system or saying they are wrong about everything.

What I am saying is that we should believe that we are a part of their ranks and that some situations may require a hammer, whereas others require a scalpel. There is an intelligence inside of us that is the same one that created the entire universe, that knows what is best for us, and it should get at least as much respect as what's outside of us.

Once, when I was in college, I had the worst earache and no health insurance. I went home and told my mom, and she said, "Oh, when that happened to me as a kid, my mother would put olive oil in my ear, do you want to try it?"

Completely grossed out at the thought of putting olive oil in my ear, I made fun of her:

"Mom, I live in America, we use medicine, not superstition. I'm going to see a doctor."

Because I was in so much pain, they squeezed me into their schedule with an appointment the following day. I had to wait three hours until it was my turn because his earlier appointments were delayed, and it cost $100 for the visit, which I considered very expensive, but I was in so much pain I had no choice. It was finally my turn to see him, and he was a very kind older Indian man, aware of medicine from both the East and West. He asked me what was wrong, and I told him I had an earache.

He took a look, asked me a few questions, and then gave me his opinion:

"You definitely have an ear infection, and I could prescribe antibiotics to kill it, but I know that a few drops of olive oil poured directly into your ear works just as well and won't cause the side effects that antibiotics will."

My mom has a special way of making my jaw hit the ground.

I paid $100, sat in line for three hours to see the doctor for five minutes, only to be told the same thing my mother told me yesterday?! I went home, told her the story, and she pressed her lips and nodded her head, saying, 'I told you so,' without saying it. I followed her to the kitchen, where she got a metal spoon, poured a few drops of olive oil onto it, and warmed it for three seconds with a lighter. She tested it first to make sure it wasn't too warm and then gently poured it into my ear; I barely felt a thing. The next day, I woke up, and the pain was gone, like a joke.

I tell this story to illustrate that doctors don't always know more right answers than my mom, scientists are only right until new discoveries are made, and lobbyists have become a natural part of our government. If all of these institutions, with their money, tests, equipment, and brainpower, can get it wrong, then perhaps we have permission to trust how right we can get it when we listen to ourselves.

The Fastest, Easiest, Cheapest way, to listen to ourselves,
is by heightening our senses.

<u>Lost Wisdom Resurfaces</u>

There is a reason why Muhammad* heard the first recitation in a silent, fasted state alone on the mountain. Why Jesus* was alone In the forest fasting when he became ordained. Why Siddhartha became the Buddha* sitting alone under the Bodhi tree, fasting. These men all come from different places at different times, and yet the methods they used to heighten their senses and reach enlightenment, were TIMELESS and FREE.

Again, I am not suggesting that we should all fast for long periods of time or try to reach enlightenment. That's not necessarily the goal. The point is that these men all used fasting because it did something for them; it allowed them to become silent enough to hear the whisper. If my experience of fasting was anything like theirs, then I understand now that their intentions were much larger than mine, explaining why their fasting was so much more intense. I don't know

177

if they are correlated, but I know once I accepted this mission to write a book, hunger stopped being the main focus of my life. Fasting didn't feel like a choice; it felt like a side effect because the only thing I craved was hearing more guidance, and the easiest way to do that was through fasting, creating a loop within me that took over.

It's like when we get sick, both humans and animals naturally lose their desire to eat. We don't have to intentionally think that because we are sick, we should fast and allow our bodies to rest and fight invaders. Our appetite naturally suppresses, and our body knows how to manage its energy efficiently. It's the same when we fall in love; our need for food disappears when we are fed something much more filling.

When we used to be hunters, we would hunt when we were hungry, aware of every sound, eyes sharp, mind alert and clear, ready to move suddenly and quickly. In the new age, we hunt for new ideas, creativity, and love. Hunting, regardless of what for, requires heightened senses in order to be successful. Fasting eliminates the excess energy reserves within us, silencing the chaotic thoughts and making us naturally crave a meditative state where we can play with the depths of our imagination - The single greatest tool for creation in existence. Nothing has ever existed that did not come from someone's imagination. Some religions believe that all of existence is just a dream that is playing in God's mind.

When we close our eyes in a fasted state, our body naturally knows where to focus its attention; not a single meditation class is needed. It would be like going to class to learn how to make your heartbeat. Meditation is that natural to us, but we wouldn't know that because we haven't existed in our natural state or environment for many generations, so some of that wisdom was left behind.

It's in that natural meditative fasting state that our senses heighten, and we notice thoughts that are more subtle, inspired, and profound. They sound and feel different than the louder thoughts we have in our normally distracted state; just thinking them or feeling them feels good, feeding something inside of us, and right when we are happy and content just sitting in that feeling, a coherence occurs. The heart and mind align, and we connect to the part of us that knows what it's doing; it guides us, gives us creative ideas, and motivation. This alignment-connection-communion is our ultimate goal.

<u>Water fasting</u>

Fasting from food alone can accomplish much, but fasting from water amplifies it even further. It was recently discovered that water has a memory, and it also reacts to words spoken to it. The difference in water molecules under a microscope when words of love versus words of hate are spoken to it shows a stark difference in the symmetry and beauty of its shape. Taking that into consideration and realizing that the human body is made up of approximately 70% water, we deduce very quickly that we may have more stored within us than we realize.

During periods of dry fasting, the body still needs water to perform its normal functions; however, when water is not ingested, we must use our own stored reserves. Our body will pull water from our deepest, darkest recesses, and with it comes all the stored memories it holds. For many, pulling our memories to the surface is not a great experience, but when done in a heightened state, it becomes a gift. Like when the tide brings something that was lost at sea back to shore, unlike when it was thrown in, it reemerges as a long-lost treasure. Somehow transformed with the magic of space and time, we can look at those memories now and see that they have turned into pearls of wisdom.

Pulling old memories to the surface is one of the reasons why it is very normal to become angry or emotional in a fasted state, believing it is just because we are hungry, but not realizing all of the emotions that are being brought to the surface for the first time in a very long time. Releasing those emotions gives us a chance to exchange the old for the new, baptizing ourselves with every sip of water we take, which is why many religions pray over food and water before consuming it. They are charging it with blessings, knowing it will retain that memory and become a part of themselves.

Fasting isn't just the technical process of abstaining from food and water; it's a spiritual purification and the best tool I have found for heightening my senses. However, the physical benefits were enough of a reason to make this a consistent part of my everyday practice. It was in surrendering the excess food energy that didn't serve me and allowing my internal state to become silent that I was able to make my deepest and clearest natural connection to Source, allowing me to flow with life easily and confidently.

A Shaman once told me that in order to understand our own nature, we must observe the nature of the elements we are made of and how they behave in the world. He said:

"If you see water in a river or stream and it hits a rock, it doesn't fight the rock; it just flows around it and keeps going. We are made of water, and the river teaches us about the strength and intelligence in our fluid nature. In life, just like in the river, when we experience obstacles, we don't need to waste our energy fighting them. We only need to allow the flow of the current to carry us around them with ease."

In fasting, we learn how to access our flow state.

How I Failed at it

Food Addiction

There is no way to have a conversation about fasting without first talking about food addiction. Food is emotional. Whether thick or thin, anyone can have an unhealthy relationship with food, so this isn't just for those of us who have some pounds to lose. Food for me was like a security blanket I used under my skin to make me feel safe and protected from the feelings the outside world evoked in me.

I don't even remember a time in my life after becoming a teenager when I wasn't trying to lose weight. Right after I graduated from middle school and was finally free from my three-year prison sentence, my parents suddenly announced that we were all moving back to Jordan. I was stunned. I had never lived in Jordan before, and I didn't want to. It was nice when we visited, but I was American, I spoke English, my culture, friends, and future were here. I had already planted roots; this was home.

I knew they wanted us to learn the language and pick up the culture and manners more, but it felt like this was my dad's last-ditch effort to control me. I was getting older, and he couldn't lock me away or punish me the way he used to. I was also maturing and developing in ways that made him perceive me as a susceptible target for men in the near future. He didn't trust other men, and his greatest fear was that I would get pregnant. When I would ask him if I could go out with friends, he would say: "If I let you out of the house, the wolves might eat you," a fear as old as Jacob*. He was possessive and controlling, but I knew it was coming from a place of deep, convoluted love, and so he did what he thought he had to do to keep us safe and shipped us off.

That summer felt like I had entered an alternate reality; nothing was normal anymore, everything felt foreign. The smell of petrol and cigarettes polluted the air, drivers ignored lanes, the language, music, and expectations of girls were all so different. I was trying to process all that new information while also mourning the life I left behind: people who understood my sense of humor, music I understood, and the freedom to play basketball outside without a chaperone.

But it wasn't all bad; there was excitement as well. Going on trips to the Middle East was always fun; I had been there twice before, and our family was huge, I had 15 first cousins all around my age, and there was much more of a social lifestyle. People visit each other all the time and go out late at night to walk through the crowded streets and just socialize and enjoy life. It was completely different from the years of solitude I was used to. I felt more freedom there than I did back home, and I loved it, but by far, the experience that stole the show was the food. There were falafel street vendors a short walk from our house, so we would get fresh plates of hummus and fried falafel every evening for our late-night snack, and below our apartment was a sweets shop. The smell of out-of-the-oven honeyed kanafa, fresh pita bread, and sesame seed anise ka'ak wafted up to us all day. If food is love, I was swimming in it.

It's difficult trying to describe what it's like living in America my whole life and then tasting Middle Eastern food at an age where I could appreciate it. Without being disrespectful, It was like actually using my taste buds for the first time. There was a passionate intensity to it, and without exaggeration, it woke up my senses in a euphoric way. That coupled with the culture, which used generosity with food to express love, and my mental state of mourning my old life, I gained 30 pounds in one summer.

Everyone fed me all the time, sometimes literally with their own hands, believing there is a blessing in feeding others. At dinner, my aunt would make my favorite rice dish with chicken, fried carrots, caramelized onion, cinnamon, and cardamom, and the aroma alone made me salivate. If I only ate until I was full, she would force feed me by hand just a few more bites to make sure I was 'full-full.' You can't leave the table satisfied; you have to leave not being able to take one more bite, and they can sense the difference and take it on as their mission in life to right the injustice.

My grandpa would come to our house every day with fresh harissa because after I tried it once, I said it tasted 'good,' so going forward, this was defined as my new favorite food, and they would provide it every chance they got. I would always feel embarrassed not to eat it because of how happy they seemed to be when they fed me. They knew how hard this move was on us, and they wanted to make sure we were happy, and that we knew they loved us and welcomed us home. So I took on their emotional burden, too, and I ate.

In a way, it really did make me feel special. I never really thought about how loving it is to be fed by others. It was always so normal, but I realize now maybe others don't know what that feels like, not just getting gifts of food, but someone making sure you physically eat because you being in their life is important to them. There was a lot of love in the chaos, and the most prominent form of it in that culture was food. Eating also helped numb the anxious, tingly feeling in my stomach, hips, and thighs, which coincidentally is where I gained all my weight. When I ate, those places felt calmer, and like I was weighed back down to Earth, like a carrot might wish to do after being uprooted.

To all of our surprise, the saga abruptly ended. After only six weeks into the first semester at school, and failing to be able to learn algebra in Arabic, my parents realized how poor our language skills were, and it was never their intention to hurt us academically. So, they brought us back, just as swiftly as they had taken us. But the damage of the extended summer had been done, starting me on a 25-year battle with weight loss, insecurity, and food addiction.

I was quite thin, to begin with, so the 30 pounds sat beautifully on my body, and it didn't hinder me from looking good in clothing, although in the back of my mind, I knew it didn't belong, it also became comfortable over time. It became how I recognized myself while also fighting a battle to lose it. I was in a love/hate relationship with myself.

The weight gain encouraged me to keep doing my intense, physically punishing workouts – which I was also addicted to because of the endorphin release afterward. I was going beast mode on an elliptical once when an older Asian man walked past me and stopped; he saw how drenched and maniacal I was working out and said, "Wow, you work so hard, but you are still big, you must eat too much," I laughed. I know what having Eastern parents is like; they do it from a place of love. He was probably sad to see how much I was torturing myself and not having any results.

Also, he was right; I did eat a lot, and it's almost impossible to take weight off with exercise alone. I thought I was controlling the way I felt inside by numbing my feelings with food, only to learn that it was the opposite: the feelings inside were the ones controlling my eating habits, and I was just an innocent bystander watching the coup.

I Didn't Know How To Be Healthy

I had learned all of my dieting and food patterns from my dad, who was always on a diet rollercoaster. He would do the cabbage soup diet for three days, lose 10 pounds, and then reward himself with an ice cream sundae. He yo-yoed those 10 pounds back and forth for decades, and I did the exact same. I didn't know what a healthy balanced diet consisted of, how to make lifestyle changes, or how to translate my cravings to determine which nutrients my body was asking for. All I knew was that I was always hungry, carbs make you fat, but they are the most delicious thing on Earth, and life is almost meaningless without Margherita pizza and chocolate lava cake.

I was able to maintain some semblance of control via my yo-yo diets and exercise for most of my life until 2020 when the darkness descended on my world. By this point, I had lived what felt like five or six completely different lives. I had survived so much as a kid, overachieved as an adult, experienced a huge awakening, threw my entire materialistic life away to start over with a spirit-led life, and buried my nephew. Every time I thought I was getting my bearings and understanding the world, something happened to flip it upside down again, and I could never gain my footing. I was just being tossed around by the waves.

Mothers Always Have Room For Guilt

As if all of that wasn't enough, I poured guilt on the chaos sundae by repeating my own history with my children. After the divorce, a child psychologist instructed us that when we leave the family home with the children, we should never return to it. Apparently, it was more traumatic for them to see it again. So all of a sudden, one day, I uprooted them, we just left the house and never went back. They had no clue what hit them until it was too late; my oldest was four at the time and was obsessed with numbers, so he would often ask me:

"Mom, can we go back to 15018?"

"No baby, we don't live there anymore, someone else lives there."

"But I miss when we all lived together with Daddy."

I knew the hole forming within him and noticed his new habit of desperately biting his nails, chewing them down till they bled. Spiritually, our nails represent our power to defend ourselves, and by declawing himself, he was showing me that inside, he knew he had no power to restore the happiness in his life. I would've given anything to make it right, but my ex was bitter. I was the one who filed for divorce; he wanted to work on things, but I had nothing left in me. So, no matter how hard I tried to have a positive co-parenting relationship with him, he couldn't stand the sight of me, calling me a "stain" in his life.

Life was beating a dead horse. Food was literally all I had. It distracted me, entertained me, made me feel safe, and reminded me of what it felt like to be loved. I would mindlessly consume until I was so full I couldn't breathe.

Eventually, I would have moments of clarity where I would be fed up and say this must stop now, then, once I was done eating all the junk food in the house, I would start my healthy diet. I would really stick to it for a week or two, but inevitably, there would always be a birthday, holiday, or friends that wanted to go out, and the dam would burst open. All the willpower I used to shut my hunger up would reverse, and it was always the same thought:

'Well, now that we've broken it, we should just enjoy it… besides, we already made so much progress how much damage could a couple more good meals make… well start again on Monday.'

Admitting I had a Problem

The crazy thing is I didn't even know I had an addiction until I tried to fight it. When I told my sister I had a food addiction, she said I was "perfectly healthy and just bored, making up diseases to cure." I was inclined to believe her. We were both under the impression that food addiction meant being lazy and obese and needing to go visit Dr. Nowzaradan. I was none of those things; I was just an average-sized woman who couldn't say no to food, but I was learning how dangerous the world is when there are things we are powerless to say no to.

It never mattered that I couldn't say no before because I could exercise and balance the effects of my eating. But with all my energy gone now, things started to spiral quickly. I started gaining weight, making me feel even more tired, and without the dopamine and endorphins that normally unlocked the good thoughts within me, my internal chatter became really dark. Even in my darkest days as a kid, when I thought I was alone, I still had the connection to the thoughts in my heart that balanced and saved me, but now even that was gone. I had no tools left to pierce the darkness and hear the love. It had descended on me so gradually that I didn't even notice it at first.

After a few months, my thoughts went from compassionate sadness and encouraging:

'You deserve a break,' 'Treat yourself!'

To vicious anger:

'You are so weak,' 'You have no control,' 'I hate myself!'

I couldn't even discern which were the good voices and which ones were bad. Initially, I thought the kind, compassionate voices were my friends, wanting me to feel comforted and cared for, but then, when I saw where they led me, I felt betrayed.

I was always taught that anger was bad, but I noticed those thoughts energized me and caused me to move. They didn't want me to stay in my current state; they may have judged me, but only because they knew I could do better.

I was like a seed that had been buried deep in the dark soil, and it was the viciousness of these voices that were cracking my shell, telling me it was time to make some big changes. They made my internal state so intolerable I had no choice but to do something.

My mind would go back and forth all day, and I just watched as the war waged within for control over me.

'Tea and biscuits for breakfast is fine, I need the energy to get me going,'

'ugh, you're so worthless, you said you weren't going to eat sugar for breakfast anymore,'

'these extra curves aren't so bad if I just dressed up more, I would feel sexy again,'

'You can't even walk a mile without your knees and feet hurting from the extra weight, stop tricking yourself into thinking this weight is good for you, you're delusional.'

It was one of the scariest things I have ever experienced. Not being able to control my thoughts, nor align my actions to my will. I was a slave. I didn't know if I had freely given away my free will, or it was taken, but what I did know is that I no longer had the *power to decide* to stop eating. The mechanism that drove me into the darkness was so subtle and alluring, and I was so tired and restless that I succumbed to the pull of my desires, thinking they would save me. Only to find the opposite, the darkness drowned me even more and then blamed me for being weak. Not knowing how I got there or how to get out, I had to take the first step that everyone overcoming addiction has to take. I had to admit that I had a problem, and that I couldn't fight this battle on my own. I needed help from a higher power to get me out of the dark.

Rock-bottom humility is where I consistently found the door to the divine. His voice had been there all along, but I ignored it, drowning it out and, in turn, drowning myself. It was at this point where I prayed, and God threw me a lifesaver. He amplified my intention to write a book and reminded me that the feeling I was running away from was the same that I would now be fighting for. But even with the brilliant shine of my intention within, I could only get fleeting glimpses of it. My brain fog was too intense, and my senses had dulled after years of overstimulation. I needed a reset to clear the chaotic thoughts inside me so that I could hear my inner guidance and refocus my priorities. Because when I fasted for spiritual (internal) reasons rather than physical (external) enhancement, I actually stuck to it and got both of the benefits anyway.

What I Learned

Fasting Is Not Starvation

I had fasted most of my life, being raised in a Muslim household, but when I embarked on this journey, it was really demoralizing. It took months of slow momentum to build the endurance necessary just to start fasting again. Before, when I had tons of energy, fasting was normal, nothing to complain about or get excited about. I would get hungry during the day, but I had the willpower to contain it, knowing I would make up for it when I got to eat at night. My body was so comfortable in a fasted state, that I planned my workouts for right before eating time so that I could drink water as soon as my workout was done, knowing I could handle it.

Seeing how far I had fallen added to my mental anguish. My only saving grace was that years of fasting eliminated my fear of it. For many people, it's not just their fear of hunger but also their inexperience with what fasting does to the body, that adds an element of the unknown to their anxiety in trying it for the first time.

Yet even with years of experience and knowing how it worked, how it affected my body, and all the benefits of it, I still failed at it. I tried inserting fasting into my yo-yo diet program, where one day, I would muster up all the energy in my body to not eat anything, but then the next, I would binge. I wasn't intentionally trying to whiplash myself; it was just the only diet I knew, so naturally, I gave it my first shot, but from it, I learned how extreme I was; people have made that observation about me my entire life, 'You are too intense.'

My sisters, friends, men, and even life coaches have told me this, but it wasn't my fault. I was born with a lot of energy, and I didn't know how to use it properly and where to direct it, so it just existed as this intense passion that I injected into everything I did. When no one around me understood my commitment to fasting, I compared myself to Olympic athletes, but instead of training for a sport, I was training to hear God. Later on in my journey, when I would fast for very long periods of time, my mom would say: "That's not in the traditions. Our tradition is one of moderation." In my mind, I translated moderation as something ordinary people do that never achieve great things, so I ignored her… sigh.

I would juice or water fast for anywhere between three days to two weeks, and although I would achieve some amazing feats in my clairvoyant abilities, very quickly, my body started running out of reserves. Not that I ever became emaciated because I always had my binge days to make up for the fasting days, but I realized at the end of it just how much damage I was doing to my body by constantly putting it in feast or famine mode. My energy was shot, and my body was either starving or about to burst. It wasn't a way to live. I was chasing short-term rewards and not thinking about success in the long term – I was back to impatiently running towards a goal and not living in the moment.

I say I was fasting, but what I was really doing was starving myself to achieve heightened states of consciousness, and when I could go no longer, I'd crash back down into a dulled binge state. No true gains were made, but it was in that extreme yo-yo state that I learned the mechanics of the 3rd Law of Motion, alive and well, inside of me. Newton says that for every force, there is an equal and opposite force; our bodies being energetic, we are also subject to the laws that apply to the universe, and after a lifetime of experience on the rollercoaster of bingeing and starving, I asked the same stoic question as Chastity from the movie *Ten Things I Hate About You*: "I know you can be underwhelmed, and you can be overwhelmed, but can you ever just be whelmed"?

The initial failed attempt at fasting, through extreme starvation/bingeing behavior, taught me what fasting wasn't, which was incredibly important because although I hadn't made any real progress yet, it showed me how to move forward. I painfully learned over and over in every area of my life that if I wanted to experience real change, it would have to be the result of slow, consistent, balanced habits. Also, with extreme fasting, by reaching those heightened states of sense perception so quickly, I learned that the state of connection I was yearning for was possible, which motivated me to do the patient work of slowly changing my lifestyle. The word slow made my skin crawl; I was always impatient and wanted results fast. It's even called fasting, not slowing, but I knew after a lifetime of racing to the finish line in the pursuit of happiness that it wouldn't be there; I was missing it somewhere along the way.

Patience Brings Power To The Present Moment

I was amazed that I could feel such a powerful connection to God through fasting. It reassured me that I could naturally induce such an intensely heightened state without assistance from psychedelics, but it also frustrated me because I was impatient and didn't want to spend time cultivating this skill; I wanted the connection immediately.

> Just to clarify, the connection is always there; we can NEVER be disconnected from it. We only feel disconnected when we can't hear it, but that is just because of the noise. Once the noise is cleared, we realize God was there all along, but it's hard to believe that when all we know is the noise.

Nonetheless, it was through my impatience that I was taught how to relinquish control. As I realized that I was using starvation to cut through the noise to access my intuition on demand, rather than allow my body to teach me its natural ability to flow around the noise to hear my intuition, I was going against my nature by trying to fight the obstacles instead of flowing around them, and I learned that although letting go of control can hurt, starvation hurts more. It was when I finally accepted that I couldn't jump straight to the finish line that I surrendered the obstacles within myself, in the form of all my old beliefs about diet and health, so that I could move forward.

I had to stop thinking of dieting in terms of 'starting tomorrow' or what I would ultimately achieve. In order to flow with the connection now, I had to collapse time and make all days - Day 1. By making this mindset shift, I could no longer rush or procrastinate success; there were no other days. Each day was the day that I had to choose whether to eat food that would allow me to hear my inner connection or not. In collapsing mental time to no longer think in terms of the future and to be hyper-conscious of how I feel today – moment to moment, I felt the seriousness and intensity of my current state.

Although there was pressure to make good choices in real time, I found it was easier when I only needed to prioritize having a great day rather than expecting myself to be perfect for a week. The lack of future planning was foreign to me, but with my energy pulled back to the present moment and no longer feeling the need to sprint, I started having the power to make better decisions on a daily basis, and the momentum of that accumulated over time.

This collapsing of time allowed me to slowly pay attention to my day in detail, and for the first time, I studied myself and noticed a natural rhythm at work inside of me. I was always most hungry in the morning and afternoon but didn't care to eat in the evenings. Also, there were some activities that triggered eating specific foods out of habit. Like if I had a cup of coffee or tea, I needed a cookie or biscuit to dip into it, but if I didn't drink them, I didn't crave the accompaniments at all. It was the same when I watched TV at night; I always wanted snacks to go with the movie because they just went together.

In becoming mindful of my habits, I found that rather than using force to fight craving, I could trade them for better ones effortlessly when I was working with my body's natural inclinations, for example:

Because I noticed that I didn't care to eat dinner, instead of starting with long fasts, I tried an intermittent fast and skipped dinner with no resistance at all. I didn't even feel the urge to eat extra the next morning after eliminating a meal because my body didn't notice that I was giving something up. However, if I skipped a morning meal, I would be hungry for the rest of the day no matter how much I ate, so I always made sure to eat a whole healthy meal to start the day.

Another trade I made was replacing my nighttime TV habit because even though I wasn't hungry, it would trigger an oral fixation for snacking. So, instead, I picked up a better habit and read before bed, which had a twofold benefit. The nighttime snacking not only caused me to gain weight, but the excess calories would cause me to toss and turn all night from the extra energy. Without that caloric stimulation at night, I not only lost weight but slept more peacefully and felt happier and more energetic in the morning rather than lethargic like I was used to. Also, because I was filling my head with such great content, when I woke up in the morning I felt like jumping out of bed so that I could get my ideas down.

Eliminating caffeine was a domino effect of that change because I was never a big fan of it, but I drank it out of habit as a cheap energy source because of how tired I was all the time. When I stopped eating excess calories before bed and started waking up feeling focused and energetic, I noticed I didn't need the caffeine anymore, so when I gave it up, it felt easy and again was a double blessing. The caffeine was so loud within my body that it frazzled my nervous system and fueled my negative thoughts. When I stopped drinking it, not only did I feel calmer, but I also stopped craving the cookies that had to go with it, and by reducing my sugar intake, I noticed a subtle anxiety within me disappear. Everything was connected, and without my caffeine and junk food high, I felt my body's natural energy start to return after being manipulated for so long, illuminating my direct connection to Source energy.

Bit by bit, I made tiny changes that had huge impacts on my energy levels, and although for a long time I didn't change my diet during my eating periods at all, I still felt really great and accomplished each day. Eventually, the momentum of these tiny successes built up so much that it became a self-fulfilling cycle, which empowered my new addiction to feel successful in each moment, and so I no longer dreamt of a better tomorrow because today felt so good.

Momentum Of Moderation

I used to think moderation was something boring and uninspiring, not realizing I was addicted to the dramatic highs and lows of life, but with time and consistency, I found that moderation is actually the forward momentum of life that saves us from being whipped from side to side on the energetic pendulum. When I patiently established the habits necessary to firmly flow with this positive river of energy inside of me, I found that similar to my addictions,

IT moved ME, with a few notable differences, the main one being that this time, I was being carried in the right direction.

Another difference with practicing moderation was if I occasionally broke it the way I used to break my starvation diet before, by going to dinner with friends at night or eating some of my kids *M&M's* during a movie, it would only destabilize me for a short while before I was naturally back on my forward momentum again. There was no longer the urge to binge out of fear that I couldn't enjoy life anymore because I always allowed myself to eat whatever I wanted, but all I wanted now was to feel that connection. I also noticed how quickly junk food could break my good habits and cause me to crave more of it when I indulged, so over time, these breaks would happen less frequently because not only was nothing worth losing my connection, but I also hated the feeling of something having control over me.

For example, After taking a break from eating candy for a while, I noticed that when I would indulge in it one day, the next day at a similar time, I would crave it again for no reason. This happens because sugar is extremely addictive as it is an easy-to-grab energy source, and our bodies come to expect it more quickly than anything else we eat. Because I had taken the time to reduce it from my system, I could distinctly feel its unconscious pull on me, and I hated that feeling of being controlled. Over time, I armed myself with the tool of moderation, which told me that I could have sugar anytime I wanted it, but I needed to decide how I wanted to feel at that moment. I knew that if I indulged again, it would firmly establish that addiction habit and that the aftereffects of eating it would be a loud and hyper nervous system, which would distort my ability to hear my internal guidance with clarity and because hearing that internal guidance was my highest priority in life, it gave me the power to say no to sugar with ease more often.

Eventually, I got to the point where I would take a bite of a candy bar and feel it already frazzling me and break my successful momentum towards more clarity and connection. I hated that feeling so much now that it would immediately cancel out the high of eating something I craved, causing me to not only lose the desire for what I was eating mid-chew but also to have the willpower to say no to my cravings even while in the act of indulging in them. I cannot convey enough what this feels like; it is nothing short of discovering a superpower.

Experiencing this level of internal trust and willpower elevated how I felt about myself. Before, even when I was 'good' and lost weight on my yo-yo diets, I never felt any different inside. I still had all the fear, hunger, and self-doubt, knowing it was just a matter of time before I relapsed and gained the weight back, so I always felt like a skinny imposter. But when I fasted with moderation and according to my natural rhythm, I felt confident, radiant, and incredibly – not hungry.

Before, I thought surrendering my control to the higher power within me would make me feel defeated, but it did the opposite. It took me from a state of need and weakness to finally having true confidence in myself and my willpower. My thoughts and actions were finally aligned, which made me feel whole and complete in a way I never had before, and ultimately, it allowed me to give my intention of writing a book the honor it deserved.

This transformation through moderation happened over such a long period of time that I barely noticed when, one day, I felt confident in my connection. I had tuned to it so subtly that I didn't recognize it at first because it wasn't the big slap-in-the-face communication that I would get when I would do my extreme intense fasting. It was calmer and just always there, gently guiding me and becoming stronger the more I followed its suggestions to pursue the better feeling option. I don't know how to describe what it feels like to know that every step you take is being guided. It's not just that you aren't alone, but you know it and can feel it. I had always known that God was out there watching out for me, but that was just based on my faith alone; this experience, however, was a tangible reality. I could feel His ever-watchful eye alive inside of me, diligently making sure I was experiencing my highest potential, but He always made it clear that it was my choice; I had the free will to follow His guidance or not.

Although, at this point in the connection, I was so compelled by the Light inside of me that it no longer felt like a choice, one of the greatest benefits was that even when I experienced a detour or slip up, because I was so connected I would understand what that obstacle was teaching me real-time (mainly patience), and so I was no longer constantly drowning in confusion and guilt, just the wisdom that was truly hidden in an empty stomach.

Trees Grow Tall With Deeply Grounded Roots

As time went on, my feeling of inner wealth grew as I consistently went to bed each night content with my gentle productivity. I discovered the magic hidden in the daily mundane acts of slow, consistent habits and their holistic effects on the body when used to benefit the entire system. I learned that moderation meant slow progress but with no limit. There is an African proverb: "If you want to go fast, go alone, but if you want to go far, go together." Before, my mind would outpace the rest of me, using sheer willpower to force me to go as fast as possible, but my body would hit a limit and stop. When I aligned the goals of my mind with the ability of my body and the guidance of my heart, we went slow but further than we had ever gone before.

During my year of Day 1 Mondays, while I diligently made those tiny, effortless adjustments to my lifestyle, such as adding something green to each meal, or reducing foods that made me feel awful after eating them (like dairy and sour gelatin candies). My biggest effort was spent in maintaining my slowness with grace because I kept wanting to run, but by consistently ingraining those new habits every day, I was firmly embedding their roots so that the tree that grew from them would be strong enough to withstand the heavy winds of life. I don't know if this is true, but my mother told me that Noah* lived for hundreds of years, and when he was commanded to build an Ark, he first had to plant the trees and wait for them to grow before he could cut them down and use the wood to make his boat. If this is true, then the amount of patience, determination, and faith he exhibited is something I aspire to.

It was difficult for me to fight my internal desire to revert back to my extreme ways when I would see a little bit of progress and want to kick it up 10 notches, so I was very careful at the beginning, always making sure that I was maintaining balance with each step I took. Occasionally, I would force myself to take a bite of a *Snickers* or *Twix* to remind myself that I could always have them, but over time, this tactic would unintentionally end up revealing the opposite to me - that the craving was truly gone and even when I tried to revert back to my old ways, those habits were uprooted and replaced.

I thought I was forever going to be like an alcoholic who couldn't go near a bar, but now I was sipping my old favorites and felt nothing. Although this brought me a tremendous amount of relief, I also knew how easily those old habits could come back, so I never relinquished my watchful diligence. But I couldn't deny that the differences were palpable. I thought certainly, during my monthly cycle when my hormones would fluctuate and cause cravings, that it would open a door for addiction to sneak back in, but even those had changed. They were less urgent and were satisfied easily with healthier options. Before, I needed nachos bel grande and a pint of peanut butter chocolate swirl ice cream. Now, a couple of pieces of dark chocolate did the trick.

Because I was going so slow, I didn't notice the changes initially, then something magical happened around the 9th month when everything seemed to click into place, and my internal progress started to have physical effects, and even though changing my external appearance was never the point, it still felt amazing to get the added bonus. Beyond the willpower, change in food preferences, better sleep, inner peace, and increased clarity, the weight started falling off of me. I saw numbers I hadn't seen since high school. Also the acne on my skin cleared, my thin hair thickened and grew longer, and my flimsy nails became stronger. Beyond feeling confident in my connection within, I was also feeling confident in my external appearance and could finally see the fruit growing from my deeply rooted tree of good habits. It was another moment where when I focused on the Kingdom within, everything else was added to it.

Eventually, as I grew stronger, I got to a point where I could responsibly push myself to fast during "hungry" periods of my day, and the small pang of hunger was no longer a surge but a far-away echo. That's when I started implementing the tradition of Muhammad* and fasted the first three days of the month, and every Monday and Thursday, and incredibly, it gave me better benefits than the longer fasts I used to do. For one, it felt too easy! Compared to the weeklong starvation sessions I used to endure, this amount of fasting felt like nothing, and it was more effective. On days that I fasted, I got the light, energetic, connected feeling I was wanting, then the next day, my appetite would still be suppressed, so it made it very easy to pick healthier options without feeling like I was missing out. It perfectly balanced my week so that right when my hunger would try to take control, another fasting day would pop up to silence it and take its power over me away.

Another more unusual benefit was that before, when I would tell my mom I was fasting, she would lecture me and say I was doing too much. Now, when she would ask me if I wanted something to eat, all I would have to say is, "It's Monday," and she immediately understood I was following the Prophet's* tradition and let me be. I cannot stress enough what it feels like when your Arab mother lets you be without a fight. So much of diet and fasting is sabotaged by family and friends who cannot socialize without food, so when that social pressure is not only released but now your efforts are being supported, it feels like a boost and relief.

I am always thrilled when I read about the Prophet's* life and traditions and find his response to people like me who lived among him. There was a man at his time who was strong and would fast for long periods of time, and so the Prophet* had a conversation with him:

"I have been informed that you pray all the nights and observe fast all the days; is this true?"

"Yes."

"If you do so, your eyes will be weak, and you will get bored. So fast three days a month, for this will be equal to the fasting of a whole year."

"I find myself able to fast more."

"Then fast like David*, who had the most beloved fast to Allah. He used to fast on alternate days and would not flee on facing the enemy."[5]

Perhaps one day I will fast like David*, but for now, I have found that with moderate intermittent fasting, my body always feels light and grounded simultaneously. Before, with my intense fasting, I would feel like I was having an out-of-body experience and was going to float away, until I ate a big me and crashed back down to earth and felt horrible. But now, with moderation, I have learned that my soul's ability to safely reach higher levels of consciousness through fasting had to be balanced with my body's stability, which was obtained through my consistent slow commitment to deeply embed dependable healthy habits, like the branches of a tree that can only reach up to the heavens when its roots are firmly grounded.

"You must not get overdrunk with ecstasy. Much work yet remains for you in the world. Come, let us sweep the balcony floor, then we shall walk by the Ganges."

"Master, I knew, was teaching me the secret of balanced living. The soul must stretch over the cosmogonic abysses while the body performs its daily duties."[6]

<u>Forgiveness and Love</u>

I grew up in a world of 'No pain, No gain' and 'You can't have your cake and eat it too,' and I believed it. But after going on this journey, I learned the difference between pain and effort, that effort could be done with ease, and that I could have my cake, but I had to savor it slowly, piece by piece, and not swallow it whole in one sitting.

After going so long with warped ideas about diet, health, and fasting, it was a relief to learn how to go inside to reclaim my power from the pharaoh of the food pyramid. Finally, finding my perfect personal eating rhythm felt like an intimate gift I gave myself, and all I had to do was pay attention. Sadly, I spent years treating my body like an enemy or a prison, trying to escape it, beat it into submission, and force it to do things that didn't come naturally to it, but it could not ignore the wisdom that was programmed into it. I treated it with so much disrespect, arrogantly thinking I knew better than it, and yet it never delayed its forgiveness and in sharing its wisdom with me.

So many times, it sent me warnings through my health and crashed energy levels, but I didn't know how to listen. Once I finally took the time to Know Myself, figure out how my body communicates with me and then listen to its guidance, it went straight back to homeostasis. No judgment, no hard feelings, just a good mood as a reward for coming back. My body showed me more compassion than I had ever shown it, always judging and criticizing it. I was literally made out of nonjudgmental unconditional love and complained that I wasn't good enough.

Before it irritated my soul to be bound to Earth, I couldn't understand the benefit of being stuck in this heavy, dull creature. But now I understand that the only way the soul can truly know itself and the love it is capable of is through the holy temple of the body, when it comes to the humbling realization that all along it has been carried and not caged.

<u>What Success Looked Like</u>

<u>Inner Peace</u>

After a year of experimenting and finding the fasting that was right for me, the benefits of embedding this habit were innumerable. Most notable was how aligned my mind, body, and spirit became, causing me to have so much inner peace. Fasting had cannibalized the old cells in my body and replaced them with new healthy ones, which made my sense receptors feel renewed, and coupled with the focused silence it created within me, I could easily hear my intuition in a clear tone – Which was my ultimate goal.

To add to that, I gained a newfound trust in my body, and trust being the key that unlocks all doors, I fell deeper into my connection with God. I found that inner peace was the ultimate ark that would continue to guide and protect me through the crashing waves of life and carry me to safety. This is why we wish peace on the light bringers of the past when we mention their names. Even though it may seem tedious or strange, anytime we wish peace on someone else, we are filled with that peace first. By sending them blessings, we bless ourselves first.

<u>Perspective</u>

With the protection of my ark of inner peace, I was able to travel through time and traverse the emotional waves of being uprooted as a child so that I could safely understand that experience with a heightened perspective. What I saw was that God was teaching me many lessons at a young age, which He knew would ripple out to positively affect me later in life, but the most important lesson was:

Don't get too attached to the external, it is temporary,
you are just a visitor, home is inside.

Because of the external world's temporary nature, it could change in an instant, and by being suddenly uprooted, I was receiving a sharp lesson in understanding the reality of the world I was living in. Because it happened at such a young age, I never got the chance to put down deep roots and really attach myself to the world, which served me later on in life when I truly grasped how much of an illusion it is, making it easier for me to surrender my attachment to it, and gave my soul the ability to fly freely to different states of consciousness and see the true higher reality.

If I hadn't been uprooted and been allowed to believe that my external reality was solid, when it came time to gain enlightenment, I would've had to break a firmly grounded belief, which is so much more difficult in comparison to having it broken already and only needing to learn how to ground within myself later on in life. This insight infused me with confidence in God's plan and showed me that what happened to me as a child was the more merciful option, especially considering my goal to commune with God in this lifetime, which would require mind-bending amounts of surrender.

Even though it didn't feel merciful to be uprooted at the time, looking back with 20+ years of hindsight, I was safe, happy, and gained some incredible experiences. I got to know my family abroad, learned a bit of Arabic, and gained a deep appreciation for our culture and especially our food. The few months I spent there changed me so significantly that by the time I got back to America and started high school, I was no longer the fit girl in a cool clique; I was now a chubby, fobish girl. I didn't fit in at school the way I used to, and in a way that might have protected me. Perhaps if I hadn't experienced everything that I had up until that point, I might've become a popular target at school, and my dad's fear that I might come home pregnant one day would've come true. I had very low self-esteem, and that could've made me desperate enough to succumb to peer pressure to fit in, but now that I was such an odd person out, no one really cared to pursue me.

There is no telling what could've happened, but what I do know is that by having my persona altered at one of the most formative points in my life, I was gifted with the awesome lesson that it's not only the world around us that is susceptible to change, but that I should not even become attached to my own body and personality because they were temporary and could quickly change too. I was not only different from how others perceived me, but from how I perceived myself, and although at the time I felt like I was having a foreign experience of life, now I know that I was being prepared for the huge ability to internally adapt that I would need as an adult, in order to have the limitless courage required to achieve my purpose in life.

One of the things that really confused me as a child about the external world was the clash between how chaotic and cursory it felt versus all the stability I could easily access in my innermost world. For so long, I tried controlling my external environment by imposing my stability on it by collecting assets, money, and food for tomorrow's rainy day. But when changing the world didn't bring me happiness, I was truly baffled at what the point of experiencing this contrast was.

When I peacefully looked back at my memories, I found another truth revealed. So much of our education in this world is derived from experiencing duality. In Heaven, where only calm, peaceful love exists, we cannot distinguish ourselves from the world around us and are in a constant state of oneness. By coming to Earth and experiencing separation and opposition, we come to Know Thyself by experiencing what we are not.

In learning the lessons and truths hidden in my uprooting, I found deep peace for what God had taught me at a young age, which also healed my guilt for doing the same to my son, knowing now that he is being prepared to fly with me one day.

The Greatest Tool of All Time

Fasting was single-handedly the most powerful tool in heightening my senses, while also silencing and renewing me. The ability to constantly commune with my inner guidance built so much trust within me that even when I felt at odds with the whole world, I still walked in my truth with absolute confidence in its wisdom. That confidence, contentment, love, trust, and self-respect spilled into every area of my life.

I loved the way I looked and felt, but it wasn't just the weight loss; I felt more attractive energetically. This wasn't the type of attractiveness that needed to dress up to get attention; it was a magnetism that even in an oversized tee and leggings, people would comment on my glow or pull me aside to tell me how inspired they were by me in class. By being constantly in touch with my inner self-love, it turned into understanding that what I was actually feeling was God's love for me, and in feeling that way internally by law, it had to be reflected back to me externally. I was drowning in love.

I also had more energy to play with my kids, and because I was no longer projecting my baggage and guilt onto them, I relaxed into allowing life to shape them the same way it had shaped me, the organic way. Knowing I didn't need to protect them because they were growing character and strength of their own, it allowed me to enjoy the precious time we have together because, My God, they grow so fast!

Not only was I benefitting physically and mentally, but spiritually, my writing felt inspired, deeper, and more powerful. I was able to explore my depths without any resistance, and words started to flow out of me effortlessly. They were no longer obstructed by my self-criticism or drowned out by the noise.

To this day, my world is no less chaotic, but now I know how to flow with it and appreciate it while being anchored in my own internal stability, which the world can never take away from me because it isn't just mine, it's me.

A Summary of Key Tips for Fasting

Disclaimer

This is a summary of fasting techniques that I discovered on my journey that worked for me. I am not a doctor or nutritionist and suggest that if you would like to try fasting, you heavily rely on your own *intuition* and do what feels right for you.

Intention: Please note that I used fasting for the purpose of spiritually aligning and heightening my senses so that I could consistently hear God. Over time, one of the many side benefits of that was weight loss, but in the beginning, I probably gained a few pounds before I started losing any. So, setting your intention before you embark on this journey is critical, and please don't let the initial hurdles and setbacks stop you from claiming your ultimate prize at the end.

Tip #1: DO NOT - I repeat, DO NOT begin fasting - until you have ADDED love to your life first. A hobby, art, adventure… that you do CONSISTENTLY.

Here is a short list of fun things I added to my life Before I incorporated fasting:

- A daily writing practice
- Writing classes
- Mixed Martial Art classes
- Spiritual healing classes
- Walking
- Reading for fun

<u>Here is a list of foods I added to my diet Before I started fasting:</u>

- Protein and fat with each meal
- More fruits and vegetables

As I mentioned before, this path requires baby steps, and for a long time, you will feel like you are going backward before you start going forwards, just like you have to dig underground to lay the foundation before you start building the house on top of it. It is the exact same methodology when we make changes within ourselves; we have to lay the roots of love down first so the tree can grow good fruit.

For example, one of the first standing changes that I incorporated was each morning, I would go for a walk, take a shower, and then have a whole meal afterwards, exactly in that order. I found that I felt so fresh and accomplished by the time I sat down to eat that, over time, I ate less because I was so spiritually satisfied.

Also, my meals always had to include a protein, fat, and carb element, and then anything else I wanted, because at no point was I allowed to deny or starve myself - It was the opposite; I needed to feel spiritually full and abundant. So, if I normally wanted pancakes (carb) for breakfast, now I had to have eggs (protein) and avocado (fat) with it, and if I was still hungry after, I was allowed to have that leftover piece of cake from the night before.

This same methodology was applied to all snacking as well. If I reached for a candy bar (carb), I had to also grab some chicken (protein) and nuts (fat) to go with it, and I had to eat the protein and fat first.

I'm certain just by reading this, you can ascertain that over time, I was so full from my bigger and healthier meals and snacks that I didn't even crave the junk I used to go for before. They were cheap and easy to reach for, and in the beginning, I had to learn how to honor my body and feed it food that would replenish it without ever denying it.

After years of being on Atkins-type diets that had taught me to shun carbs, I had an aversion to them, but after learning that those crash diets never really served me and only caused me to quickly yo-yo, I understood the value of slow benefits through moderation and balance. Also, bringing healthy carbs back into my life gave me more internal stability and caused me to crave junk food less, which increased my willpower over time to easily resist them.

Tip #2: **Once you have incorporated all the fun and health you can squeeze into your heart and body, your spirit should start feeling very full. That is when you can start to reduce your food intake, but don't start with elimination, only reduction at first.**

Intuitively, I knew my body was ready for reduction when I was leaving more food on my plate, and I stopped craving snacks as often. The initial period of 'addition only' lasted about three months for me, and during it, I was paying attention to how I felt at different times of the day and after specific meals. I even noted on my calendar what I roughly ate each day so that if I wanted to remember why I felt so good a few days ago, I could refer back to what I ate and incorporate more of that.

Again, I *intuitively* knew where I could easily make some small changes because of how diligent I was in paying attention to how I felt after doing things consistently over time. Just like a scientist in a lab, there has to be a constant so that experimental changes can be measured against it. When we exercise and eat well consistently, we learn how changes from our normal routine affect us.

For example: By habit, I was eating three square meals a day, but I didn't know why I was eating dinner because I didn't crave it at all. I think it was established as a habit because of how social dinner is. Whether I was at my mom's house, at a dinner party, or out to dinner with my friends, I never cared to eat but unconsciously did because everyone around me was. But when I was on my own at home with no one around, I was happy with 'Girl dinner': A snack plate of apples, guacamole, nuts, and some popcorn.

It was really eye-opening for me to realize that I didn't care for dinner and that, as an adult, I could cut it. As a child, I was forced to sit at our dinner table to eat, but now I could make my own decisions, and it felt like I was breaking some unspoken law until I learned more about the Prophets* and how little they used to eat.

Eliminating dinner was a slow process, even with the fact that I didn't like it. Initially, I reduced it to a healthy high-vibrational snack (fruits/veggies/nuts) and then waited to see how my body reacted to that. When I saw that there was no difference emotionally, and I wasn't eating more at other meals to make up for it, I replaced it completely with a cup of hot herbal tea.

This isn't to say that I never ate dinner again; I still do, especially and almost exclusively socially because I don't crave it alone, and I don't want to completely disconnect from society. One of the toughest hurdles I found when I started the path of fasting was all the peer pressure from family and friends to eat – Especially from my mom, and I'm almost 40! With experience, I found that instead of fighting it, it was much easier to initially isolate myself while making some of my bigger changes and then to find fun solutions so that I could still enjoy company while being true to myself.

Now, when I go out to eat with a friend, or have dinner at my mom's house, I'll have a plate and take a few bites while we are all sitting around chatting and enjoying each other's loving company over a beautiful meal, then I box up most of it and eat it the next day for lunch when I know I will be hungry.

Eventually, after months of consistency, once the momentum of fasting took over, I could start to push myself without the repercussions of bingeing later. I started with a juice fast one day a week and then transitioned to a water fast two days per week, which led me to fast according to Muhammad's* tradition with a slight modification. He used to do a dry fast, meaning no food or water from sun up to sun down, whereas I would include water but fast for an entire 24-hour period every Monday, Thursday, and the first three days of each month. On those three consecutive days of fasting, I would have one meal during the day rather than at night.

<u>Tip #3</u>: Troubleshooting: What to do if you don't feel spiritually full and are still hungry?

If you have tried to reduce or eliminate a meal and find that you are making up for it by eating more at other meals, then immediately add that meal back. DO NOT EVER mentally go into starvation mode at any point. If your mind is still hungry, it can mean a couple of things:

1. You have not added enough of what you spiritually love yet, consistently enough, and you need to relinquish fasting completely until you have found something that truly feeds you spiritually.

First, Ask God for help. Tell Him to send you an idea or dream of what would authentically fill you. Perhaps you tried taking up belly dancing classes because you always wanted to learn, but through divine inspiration, you find that what your heart really yearns for is to start a big brother/sister program and mentor youths who need strong and healthy role models. So even though your first attempt to fill yourself with love was an excellent one, it wasn't big enough for your life's journey. Or, who knows, maybe you will meet someone in that dance class who has the same dream and will become your business partner one day. God works in mysterious ways, but just remember that this process isn't just about diet, weight loss, and willpower. It's about bringing our purpose for existence to life, by exploring the desires buried in the depths of our soul so we can bring to light our truest highest expression. So solemnly prepare yourself before you begin this earnest work, and only proceed when you are really ready to transform.

2. There is something you are unaware of that is spiritually eating away at you, and you need to heal that first.

Since fasting naturally happens when we are spiritually full, if you know you are following your true purpose and are still not feeling full, then there are some deeper roots that are asking for your attention.

It is possible there is a memory or trauma stored deep inside that is eating away at you and draining your happiness and health. In order to address these past traumas that live in some deep, dark place in our psyche, we have many options, but ultimately, this is where our self-responsibility kicks in.

Remember, the first step is always admitting that we have a problem and we need help.

We should pray for God's help and guidance and then immediately take the steps to seek out grief counselors, life coaches, therapists, spiritual healers, etc., to help us navigate these areas of our lives. I cannot tell you how much I have spent on these invaluable services and how much they sped up my healing process.

So please allow these people to express their gifts to assist you on this path because nothing would give them greater pleasure than to see others impacted by their help. It's a win-win situation when we are all lifting each other up and helping each other find the way home. However, please note that the first person you find to help might not be a perfect fit, so don't despair; just move on until you find someone you love working with. If this is the case, know that this is truly a part of the journey, and you aren't behind or ahead; you are exactly where you should be. By taking steps to know yourself more deeply, you fulfil the only thing God asks of us – to Know Thyself.

Tip #4: How to get quick and clear guidance when you need it immediately.

Sometimes, when I need to kickstart my healthy habits or get quick and clear guidance when urgently needed, I will do a temporary juice fast for three days, where I only drink green juice for every meal. I used to do this about once a year, but because fasting is such a normal part of my life now, it doesn't serve me as much as it used to. However, it really helped to reset my system annually. After about two days into the fast, I would start to feel my senses significantly heighten and be able to deeply access my intuition.

There is an entire documentary about this fasting technique called *Fat, Sick and Nearly Dead,* where an obese man (monitored by his doctor) drinks only green juice for 60 days to reset his health. If you are interested in learning more, here is the recipe:

<u>**Green Juice Recipe**</u>

- Green apple (1 per cup of juice)
- Lime (1/2 per cup of juice)
- Celery (make sure to take the leaves off, otherwise it will be horribly bitter)
- Spinach
- Cucumber
- Ginger (1/2 inch, optional)

<u>**Quick Reference Fasting Tips List:**</u>

1. Set your intention
2. Add love
3. Spend lots of time paying attention to your preferences
4. Reduce the low-hanging fruit first
5. Ask God for help
6. Allow the people he sends to help
7. Keep going

Fasting Flow

Be empty
Be famished
Be ache.
Let the fire in your stomach burn.
Bake the clay, create.

When your mind Needs anything,
It goes deeper to find it.
Necessity Is the Mother of Invention.

Allow the hunger, to create.
Creating Space.
For new things to desire.
Desire a premonition of things to come.
Hungrily dreaming our future,
into reality.

At night, we fast, we dream.
One month we fast.
We dream all day and night.
Doubling the power of things to come.

Needs magnify the blessings we dream of,
Beyond hunger and thirst,
Need of sleep, warmth,
And deep concentration.
We focus on one.
One need above all.
You.

We focus on you.
I.
Eye.

You fill us with the cold, burning light.
Cleansing us.
Making us new.

A new chance.
An empty slate.
Armed with the wisdom, Free of the weight.

To Walk on Earth as in Heaven.
Feast on the Nothing
On your plate.

When I was 13 years old, my father handed me a $20 bill and said:

"This is your monthly allowance, now you will be my slave."

He didn't say those exact words, but the sentiment was clear.

He paid me – I owed him.

Money was yet another way to feed his hunger for control, and it was universally known that whoever has the money, has the power.

By accepting that $20, I sold my soul.

A few years later, when I was 15 and old enough to do something about my frustrations regarding his obnoxious demands on my life, I threw it back at him and said:

"I don't need your money. I'll go get my own!"

I felt like I had taken my power back and that I was finally free.Not knowing how badly it would mess up my beliefs about money and men for decades to come.

Chapter 4: Charity

"Those who spend their wealth in God's cause are like grains of
corn that produce seven ears, each bearing a hundred grains.
God gives multiple increase to whoever He wishes:
He is limitless and all knowing"
- Quran 2:261

Money is survival, luxury, and power all in one. It's the bread,
cheddar, and cake of life.

For so long, every decision I ever made revolved around money.
When I chose my major in college, it was because it made good
money, and despite globalization and outsourcing, businesses would
always need accountants, ensuring my safety and stability.

When I chose my husband, I assumed I hit the jackpot. My
attraction to him wasn't just because he was handsome; he was also
highly educated, and I thought that meant he would be a good
provider – further securing my survival.

Even small decisions like going out to dinner with friends, buying
clothes, or spoiling myself were always measured against an
opportunity cost. Would I rather have fun now or have money saved
for when I need it later? I almost always chose the latter. I thought
paying $5 for a cup of coffee was a sign of the end times, and even
when I had money, I refused to throw it away.

Money was attached to everything: My safety, love, attraction,
prestige, survival, dreams. I thought money was the only true way
to show love because there wasn't anything else of real value. Time
and money were one and the same to me, and if I wasn't giving one,

I was giving the other, and strangely enough, I never gave either to myself.

I gave generously to everyone around me with the intention of sharing my stability with them because they always seemed so unstable, but what I was inadvertently doing was trying to control my environment, and painfully, I learned that the road to hell is paved with good intentions. Sadly, I thought charity and giving were the same thing, and I had only ever known giving as a form of control, a transaction. I scratch your back, you scratch mine. So, when I helped those around me, it was with the expectation that they would conform to my needs as a way to show their appreciation and repay me.

In my heart, I thought I was a good, helpful, charitable person, and I didn't understand how everyone could use me so injudiciously. After giving for so long and never getting what I needed back, I was drained. I had only ever been a cog in the never-ending 'pursuit of happiness' wheel, so even though I was 33 years old, I didn't know how to fill my own tank. It was in this state of complete emptiness that I realized I couldn't live on bread alone, forcing me to hunt for my true source of nourishment.

"When the last tree has been cut down,
the last fish caught, the last river poisoned,
only then will we realize that we cannot eat money."
– Native American prophecy

What Is Charity?

Charity is renewal and purification.

Charity is a law of nature that automatically recycles by taking the old and making it new, and so it's no surprise that once again, observing water in nature illustrates this process for us. In order for it to rain, water must enter the cycle of evaporation and condensation. First, heat breaks the water's bond, allowing it to release heavy impurities and become a vapor, light enough to rise and accumulate in the heavens before falling back down to Earth, pure and new.

I don't know anything more prayed for in the olden days than rain, even more than food or money. There were songs, dances, prayers, and sacrifices made for it. Without clean water for just a short while, crops, animals, and people died. Nowadays, most of us have never known this dependency because irrigation has solved this problem, but before that, rain was holy.

Rain teaches us the art of charity through the cycle of giving and receiving. We have to know how to do both equally because charity doesn't work if we are doing too much of one or the other. We would go back to the extreme ends of the pendulum again, where we are either too empty or too full. Neither allowing us to move forward and up the steps of surrender and evolution.

Because giving is so engraved in the nature of our being, even the most miserly person gives, whether intentionally or not. Those with a generous nature can give even when there is nothing left in them; just ask a newborn's mother. But giving also includes releasing, and that is where things become difficult; just ask a stillborn's mother. Releasing grief, anger, pain, hopes, and dreams is the charity we give ourselves. When we don't let go, we become too rich and full of these heavy emotions, and it blocks the cycle, simultaneously making us feel so empty of goodness and so full of rage.

"It is easier for a camel to walk through the eye of a needle than a rich man to enter paradise."
- Matt. 19:24, and echoed in Quran 7:40

This quote is often understood to mean financial riches, but what it truly means is that:

The process of becoming light enough to enter heaven begins just like that of rain.

We first have to break our emotional bonds to the world, in order to release the riches held within, which are our heavy emotions that weigh us down.

This is very difficult when our hearts are deeply attached to the physical world, but the only way water can become vapor is to accept its transient nature. So we must detach from what is temporary, in order to become light enough to rise.

To be clear, there is nothing wrong with enjoying the material world, money included; many holy people have received God's favor, the difference is that they never attached their hearts to it. Evidenced by Buddha* who left his crown behind. Jesus, who rejected the devil's temptation to rule the world, and Solomon*, who had all the riches at his fingertips but only remarked that they were "meaningless. meaningless."[1]

Having money is what supports our survival while on Earth, and since we are programmed to survive, it makes it very difficult to override that command. But there is a point on the journey where we must be willing to detach from our strongest instincts in order to transcend what is temporary in exchange for what is eternal. This doesn't mean that we stop enjoying life; it means we stop craving survival. In order to achieve that state, we must love death (or detachment) as much as we love life. Love your enemy.

Nature Abhors A Vacuum - Aristotle

Once we reach an internal state of acceptance, both parts of the giving/receiving cycle work in perfect harmony with each other, and by allowing ourselves to release the attachments that sit heavy in our hearts, our body becomes ready to receive, as it is always seeking homeostasis.

In my experience, it worked in either direction as well; for example, when I focused on building good habits first, I not only received the feeling of success within, but it then became even easier to release the old addiction habits that no longer served me. However, regardless of how we start, eventually, in order to accept more, we must make space.

That space acts like a vacuum, calling back to us what we need in order to balance the energy given. This is why it is universally acknowledged that the more we give, the more we get. Even Feng Shui understands the benefit of leaving a drawer empty to attract good luck.

Giving and receiving can be scary when we don't understand this law. It can feel like a risk to give so much away without knowing whether it will return. This is where knowing the law and how to receive becomes critical.

We must understand that:
- All concepts of giving/receiving refer to an energetic transaction.

- Emotions are energy, and
- Energy cannot be created or destroyed, but it can change form.

Which is why it is critical to understand that because energy works the same way within us as it does the entire universe, when we give and a vacuum is created, we KNOW that by law that space MUST be filled, as long as we know how to receive. However, what we receive will not necessarily take on the identical form of what we have given or what we EXPECT to receive. In receiving, we must let go of all expectations.

Do not give $100 and expect to get $7,000 back the next day. Not to say that this couldn't happen, but instead, give the $100, knowing with certainty that one day you will receive $7,000 worth of value returned to you. It will happen when you LEAST EXPECT it because when charity is given without expectation, it includes a guaranteed return. It also works most effectively when we do it to appreciate the subtle feeling of not sticking to anything.

Long ago, Buddha* mastered the superpower of detachment, where he learned to release his attachments to the world to free himself from the constant suffering of life. I admit that before going on this journey, the idea of detachment was intimidating to me; I was afraid that if I let go of my emotional attachment to the world, I would become stoic and dull. But it was exactly the opposite; I was able to feel more for the things I loved because detaching didn't mean letting go of the love; it meant letting go of the fear of losing it. Where before, there was always this underlying current of anxiety and depression lurking in the background of my emotions, fearing things that could go wrong in the future or mourning things lost in the past. When I released the fear of losing things, knowing everything meant for me would always be returned, the energetic drain from the anxiety was returned to me, and I could appreciate what I had so much more.

Detachment didn't mean not feeling anything; it meant focusing on the better feelings of joy, appreciation, and gratitude so that the heavier emotions of fear, guilt, and loss could fade away naturally. It was the only way to really live. Otherwise, every day would feel like a funeral. I still lost many things, and I would've lost them anyway, but now the way I felt about those losses changed. I knew that love was an energy that could not be created or destroyed, and that it would always be returned to me, just in a changed form.

The First. The Last. The Self-Sustaining.

Mysticism of Charity

There was a year between my divorce and getting my own house, where I moved in with my mom. I was 33 and had two kids under the age of four, so she wasn't thrilled, but she didn't say no to us either.

I paid her house off when I was 20 years old. It was $48,000 when they bought it in the 80's, and 20 years later, because of the crazy interest rate on the mortgage, she still had around $30,000 left to pay off. I had been working for five years at that point, and saving money was my superpower. I decided that instead of using the money to travel or wasting it on cheap thrills, it would be better spent on making my mom feel secure.

To this day, I have never met anyone who stresses about money more than her, and since we lived together, when she was emotionally stable, our home felt stable. She would show how grateful she was for me and the way I took care of her by always praying to God to bless me, and since I didn't know how to connect to God myself, giving to her was the way I prayed.

Despite our strong bond, five years later, when I got married, our relationship deteriorated when I moved out for the first time to go live with my husband. I was 25 years old and had been taking care of her since I was 16 when my dad left. She was 45 years old now, so I thought she was more confident and could handle being alone with my youngest sister while I started my new life. I always knew that when she was ready to retire, I would also be ready to take primary responsibility of her again – as is expected in Middle Eastern traditions.

But to my complete shock, when I left, it completely destabilized her. Instead of being happy for me, she acted betrayed, and her behavior became bizarre. She became desperate to find a husband, causing her to do things I never dreamed she would do. When I challenged her about it, asking how she could act that way while still being a role model to my youngest sister, she said: "You and your sisters are allowed to go out and do whatever you want. For once in my life, I should be able to do the same." Shortly after, she met a man online, and two weeks later, she married him.

Without exaggeration, her behavior almost killed me. I thought I was going to have a heart attack from the amount of pain and disappointment crammed into that year of my life. My father had died at the start of that year, which was a few months after I graduated college and started my first public accounting job. Two months after his death was my wedding, which was an absolute disaster, and then the first year of marriage, which included the typical friction of combining different habits and behaviors under one roof and seeing what people are like behind closed doors, which was a gut-wrenching disappointment and made me even more homesick.

On top of all that, the guilt of leaving my baby sister behind never subsided. I had three sisters, one older and two younger, and my older and younger sister left for college out of the city as soon as they could, leaving me behind to care for my mom and baby sister alone. She was 11 years younger than me, and I had always tried to protect her and make up for my parent's emotional and financial shortcomings. She was only five years old when my dad left, so I stepped into his role and chaperoned her field trips, ate lunch with her at school, signed her up for the soccer team, bought her uniform and gear, and took her to her practices/games. So when I moved out to live with my husband, even though she was much older and I left her with our mom, it still felt like I had left my own child behind.

By taking care of my mom's biggest needs before I left, I hoped she would feel supported, and that would make her emotionally stable enough to responsibly care for my sister alone for a while. I also intentionally bought a house in the neighborhood across the street from my mom to reassure her that I would never go too far away. I assumed that after all of that, she would feel grateful for my years of unrelenting support and that she would put her feelings aside and be happy for me, but instead, she relapsed into a state of fear that was even worse than when my father left her.

I didn't know it back then, but in my helpful innocence, I had unintentionally created in her a crippling dependency on me. By not allowing her to suffer when she was younger, I stripped her of her confidence to take care of herself, and like puzzle pieces, our most toxic traits fit perfectly together. She was forever in need, and I was a savior.

Since I didn't understand codependency at that time, I also felt betrayed by her. After spending years creating stability for her and my younger sisters, she immediately invited chaos as soon as I left?! It was one thing for her to put herself at risk by marrying a random stranger she found on the internet, but how could she dream of allowing him to live with her when she still had my 15-year-old sister in the house? My mind exploded in rage at how ungrateful and irresponsible she was behaving. When I told her he wasn't allowed to live in the same house as my baby sister, my mom asked my sister, "Where are you going to live then? " implying that her husband was moving in, so my sister had to find somewhere to go – choosing a stranger over her own child.

To this day, out of everything I have ever experienced in my entire life, the scariest demon I have ever encountered is unchecked survival mode. Our survival instincts have their uses, but when allowed to take complete control, we become like reptiles that can justify eating their own young.

I put my foot down and told her that there was no way he was moving into that house, exerting the power I had paid into it years ago. Having to play this card devastated me. Paying off the house for her was a defining moment in my life. I thought it would finally make our chaotic house into a calm and stable home, and it was tied to my first really big feeling of giving charity. That feeling was spoiled now by having to use it as a power play to kick her and her husband out to protect my baby sister. It wasn't just that I felt she was ungrateful; it felt like she had thrown poison on the greatest gift I had ever given her and robbed me of my blessings by forcing me to remind her that I had taken care of her. When I had given her the money years ago, I felt like the best daughter ever and so selfless. Now I felt dirty.

They ended up getting their own apartment, and my other younger sister, who had just graduated college, moved back in to take on the role of mom and take care of our baby sister. The pain of this experience was so convoluted, but mostly it was anger. I had never given my mom the opportunity to show how she would act if she was the one in charge; now that I had seen how fragile she was, it made me understand why, at such a young age, I instinctively knew I had to take on the role of man of the house when my dad left. Perhaps I had seen this side of her before and never wanted to see it again, so I suppressed it by sacrificing my years of playful youth in exchange for providing our family with responsibility and stability.

We didn't speak to each other for almost a year, but it couldn't last forever. She was my mom, and in my own personal religion, parents -no matter what- are holy teachers. I couldn't write off years of her own sacrifices and caring for us as small children because she snapped during a midlife crisis. We eventually reconciled, and although our relationship wasn't as warm as it used to be, I still had the desire to take care of her no matter what; I knew that urge would never go away.

As I got to know her husband, it turned out that by some miracle, he was a living angel. We were so similar that I felt closer to him than I did my own biological father; we had identical mentalities - selfless martyrs. After a few years, when my youngest sister moved out for college, he and my mom moved back into the house, and we got into another big fight. He was smoking in the house, and I felt that was so disrespectful, but again, he showed me his good nature by offering to pay me the money I paid into the house long ago. By buying me out, it was their house now, and they could do whatever they wanted. It simultaneously elated and deflated me.

He grew in measure in my mind, I never had a parent who made things right so quickly and generously before. While our relationship became stronger because of that respect, it also changed the dynamic between my mom and me again. Our relationship was based on me providing for her and her loving me for it, but now that I was no longer her provider, I felt a subtle shift in her attitude towards me, like she didn't need me, and so she loved me less.

It wasn't something she ever said out loud, but I noticed over the years that whenever my other sisters needed a place to stay, she would happily open her home for them. She was so excited to have them back, and she never asked them to help her with money or let them feel as if they had worn out their welcome. She wears her heart on her sleeve, so I could easily tell by her half-smiles when I asked if I could move back in for a while that she didn't really want me there.

We had never been in this position where I was the dependent, and she was the provider, so it was uncomfortable and awkward for both of us. But I had always assumed we were partners. That we would lift each other up over the course of our lives, and that because I stood by her side so diligently and for so long when she was younger and had my two little sisters to take care of, she would jump at the chance to return the favor when I was finally in a similar position to need her.

Her unenthusiastic reaction to me coming back to live with her made me feel such a deep sadness; I was at the lowest point of my life, and the person I helped the most made me feel like a burden. Even deeper than that, I thought the relationship with your mom is different than the one with your dad. I had already learned the lesson long ago that the people you are there for aren't necessarily the ones who will be there for you, but I thought moms were the exception to this rule. I was wrong again. But incredibly, this feeling was alleviated by her husband, who was thrilled to have me move in with them. He would check on me often to see if I needed anything, knowing how hard the divorce and move were on me. He made sure I was happy and comfortable and always played with the kids after work, even when he was exhausted. I don't know if he was sent as an angel for her or for myself, but it made me realize how critical a stepparent can be in a child's life, no matter what age.

To make the move more palatable for my mom, I did what I always do: I offered her money. I knew her expenses would go up with me and the kids in the house, so I gave her money for rent and food while I was there. It stung a little because it poked at the pain of having to pay rent on a house I remembered paying off long ago, but nonetheless, it was how I showed my love and appreciation for letting me come back.

As a move-in gift, I also told her I would clean out her garage. After my dad died of a stroke, combined with his history of heart disease and diabetes, we moved all of his medical equipment into the garage. Before he died, he told us not to throw them out because they were worth money. There was his old electric wheelchair, his hospital bed, and walking canes, in addition to all the stuff he collected/hoarded over the years. She always complained about not being able to walk through the garage, but we never got around to clearing it out until now. I called a junk company, and they quoted me $1,000 to pick it all up, and I agreed.

While I waited for them to come, I went outside to get started so that I could save myself a couple of bucks before they got there. As I lifted the garage door up, I said a silent prayer, 'God, please send someone to come help me,' and before the door even got all the way to the top, I felt a vehicle rolling up the driveway behind me. I turned around, and an older Hispanic couple got out of their small, beige beaten-up truck; they smiled and kindly asked me what I was planning on doing with all that stuff.

"I was about to throw it away," I told them.

Their faces lit up as if they had just won the lottery. They asked if they could have it, and with surprised confusion, I said, "Of course."

'Why would anyone want this stuff?' I thought to myself. Then I watched them go into the garage and take every single thing that was not nailed down and pile it like a small hill onto their truck bed. I asked if I could help them, and they refused, saying:

"No, ma'am, just relax, we will take care of it."

Afterwards, the man asked me for a broom, and I watched him sweep the entire garage floor clean. Once he was done, he didn't make any small talk; he just handed the broom back to me, said thank you, and left.

My mom had come out to see what was happening, and we both stood there together, our jaws stuck open in shock. We didn't even speak together; we just watched them take everything and leave. I found out later that they work for a nearby flea market that scours neighborhoods for things discarded in order to refurbish and resell them. I don't know if I gave them charity or they gave me charity, but either way, it was remarkable. I took it as a sign from God that now that I was following his directions, he would send people to help, even if they weren't the people I expected.

A few months after I moved in and started diving deep into my spiritual practices, I went to Ecuador to have my Ayahuasca experience. It was during one of my ecstatic journeys that I was gifted with the experience of being 'in divine presence,' and the only way I could describe the feeling was like going home. Not a home I had ever experienced on Earth, but the type of home I had always been trying to subconsciously recreate. The home where everyone is calm and stable, and we take care of each other selflessly without expectation, with the promise that no matter what happens, as long as we have each other, everything will be okay. The closest word that encapsulates the energy of how that experience felt, is charity.

That spiritual journey pierced the darkness of my memory to remind me that our real eternal home is in charity and made everything I had experienced up until then make complete sense. Why somehow charity, in terms of giving selflessly, and home was always linked in my life experience. Charity was never something I deeply felt when I gave a few dollars to strangers, I felt it most when I gave selflessly and ceaselessly to the people I loved the most at home. It also explained why every time I tried to recreate the experience of 'Home in Charity' on Earth, it failed. The first lesson of life was always reappearing:

Do not get attached to home on Earth, it is temporary.

God knew that I believed my home was wherever my parents were and that it was my internal default to worship my parents. In order to protect me from false idols, he sent me parents so weak and broken I couldn't worship them, no matter how hard I tried. What seemed for so long to be an unmerciful injustice, I realized now, was my salvation. No god, but God.

I finally understood why every religion on the planet instructs us to experience charity so often. It also may explain why Mr. Beast is such an international phenomenon; his videos hit the core of us, by watching him give so freely and abundantly, for a few moments, he takes us all home.

How I Failed

Early in my marriage, I had fertility issues and decided if we couldn't have kids, we should chase our dreams. Why work so hard to build something no one would inherit? So, I quit my exhausting public accounting job and got an easier position in the oil and gas industry – my idea of a dream job at the time, and I encouraged my ex-husband to get his PhD, which he had always regretted not getting before. The month after he was accepted to Rice University with a full scholarship and paid stipend, I found out I was pregnant.

My life was drowned in joy. Probably the most I've ever experienced in my life.

After years of being crippled with infertility, and riding the rollercoaster of hope and disappointment each month, one day, I finally got the two lines. I sobbed as the relief flooded me because, for the first time, I felt like my life meant something and that I had a purpose. My son was extra special because he was the first boy in the family. My father had four girls, and he always blamed my mom for not producing an heir for him. My mother and I internalized that failure, believing that if she had given him a boy, he might've loved her, and if I had been a boy, he might've loved me. When my mom came to the hospital after his birth, she held him in her arms and said: "I waited 30 years to have my boy," with his birth, he healed us both.

For a few weeks after, I was in 7th heaven. Despite all the physical pain and lack of sleep, I got to stay home and not go to work for the longest time since I was 15 years old. Also, since my husband was in school and didn't work, he naturally helped around the house more. My dad never did such things like putting the laundry in the washer or the dishes in the dishwasher or vacuuming or changing diapers, so I was grateful that he was so progressive. Our life was smooth sailing up until I had to go back to work.

That's when I learned how expensive kids are and how exhausting being a working mom is. In order to go to work, I had to put him in daycare, which was SO expensive, and then being around other kids made him sick all the time, so he couldn't sleep through the night, and we probably spent the entire first year at the Doctor's office. I was sleep-deprived and stressed, and even as a super-conservative CPA, I was barely breaking even with all the new expenses. I had already paid the house off, so daycare became my new mortgage payment, and to this day, I don't know how single providers can pay rent and daycare.

But it wasn't just the physical and financial exhaustion; mentally and emotionally, I was drained. I had to go back to work when he was 12 weeks old, and I would be completely braindead after spending all night taking care of him, whether it was because he was sick or breastfeeding. Then, during the day, I didn't have to just deal with work, but pumping, which may have been done in a bathroom more than once while crying because my hormones were all over the place. Then there was the added pain of being separated from him all day when every instinct in me wanted to keep him as close to me as possible. Fighting that need left me feeling spiritually bruised and battered by the end of the day.

I was exhausted at every level of my existence, and that turned into frustration and, eventually, injustice and rage. My thoughts became angry and accusatory. How was it fair that I had to work during the day to pay all the bills, while his father got to stay home and study for a few hours? How come I had to take care of the baby at night, while his dad slept in the guest room upstairs? When I asked him to get a part-time job to help with bills so that I could get a break, he said his creativity required a very delicate routine, as inspiration only came to him when he was relaxed and inspired.

It never occurred to me when I told him that I supported him going back to school that he would stop working completely. I never stopped working throughout high school and college, so I didn't even understand the concept of going to school and not having a job. But he came from a more affluent world than me, where it was expected that you wouldn't work while in school. In the beginning, when I would ask for help, he would say:

"If I get a job, it will impair my quality of life."

When I got desperate for help and told him that was an unacceptable response, he changed it to: "Getting a job will delay my thesis, and I am so close to finishing. The faster I graduate, the quicker you can quit working, and I can take care of you the way you took care of me."

But I couldn't wait years, let alone minutes longer. I needed help immediately; I was drowning.

I thought he would naturally feel some sort of responsibility as a husband and father, but instead, he was in his own world reliving his 20s, even considering trying out for the university's football team. He was 40 years old at the time.

He had never been great with money, but it didn't matter when he had it coming in or there wasn't a shared person to take care of. But now, with my hands over full, he became another burden, and I was desperately seeking help from him. Although I had considered getting a divorce at the time, I didn't because I knew I would be making the decision from a negative state of mind, and so instead, I put my head down and got through that first year. Eventually, things got easier as the baby started sleeping through the night, and my energy started coming back, and my hormones started balancing. We fell into a better routine when I was no longer breastfeeding, and the ratio was two adults for one child. It was the following year, after my second son was born that I experienced the final straw that broke the camel's back.

It was tax season, and after calculating our taxes with two kids now, we got a huge refund. It was the first time, and in the spirit of excitement, instead of saving it or using it to pay bills, I decided we had been through enough; we should enjoy ourselves with this 'extra' money. He had his eye on a new camera, an expensive hobby he developed after our first son was born. We wanted to document every step of his life, so I bought a camera for him, but eventually, it blew up into an addiction. We split the cash in half, and he bought his camera, and I bought myself some jewelry. Then, to my surprise, he came to me a few weeks later, saying he had miscalculated how much the camera would cost and needed me to cover the difference charged to his credit card. We had separate bank accounts, so I never really knew what was going on with him financially. I had learned too many hard lessons as a child about giving someone else control over my money, so I gave him his privacy, and he gave me mine.

He was never responsible with money, but he had never been this far off either, so I offered to help him figure out the difference, assuming he might've been incorrectly charged. He opened up his banking app on his phone, but he was uneasy. It didn't really register to me why until I saw his statement. He had SO many charges: $200 for a two-hour massage, going out to eat constantly, camera equipment, and these huge amounts that he was being charged monthly. I couldn't tell what they were based on the description, so I asked him, and he lost it:

"See, this is what you do every time I ask for help! It's your fault I have to lie! I can never tell you anything because you're so judgmental."

In my mind, I thought I had entered an alternate universe.

He quickly became so irrational and unhinged about such a simple inquiry as if he was prepared for this fight. I didn't know how to react. I just stood there stunned for a moment while he kept berating me, his eyes getting wider and wilder. Beyond the shock, something in his attack mesmerized me until I recognized something that I hadn't seen in decades. It was that same rage that takes men to the unmerciful darkness.

I knew that I had asked him for help financially before and that it would always result in a huge fight because he either 'didn't have the money' or refused to go get a job. But I didn't think what I was asking for was unreasonable or unjust. I didn't even think it was right for me to have to ask, as I had expected him to take the lead financially, and when he didn't, I was often disappointed in him, and I knew he sensed that. But now was the first time I saw that he did have money; he just didn't prioritize spending it on me and the kids.

There was no self-awareness whatsoever, no 'wow, I feel really humiliated for lying to you and splurging while you work so hard and pay all the bills,' or 'I'm so sorry, I need help with spending, I have a problem.' Instead, he retorted that I never acknowledged that he does help with the bills by pointing out that "I pay the lawn guy $60 each month to mow the lawn."

His guilty conscience perceived my simple inquiry as a threat, and after years of having the same fight over and over, he used offense as a form of defense and attacked. I had seen glimpses of this incoherent, vicious side of him sporadically throughout the marriage when I would question him about curbing his money-spending addiction, but I would let it go for so many reasons. For the most part, I thought his spending was annoying but harmless and not worth the fight. But at an even deeper level, it was because I loved him and believed he was too good for me, so I didn't feel that I deserved his love but rather that I had to earn it. This was confirmed later on, right before we finalized the divorce when I asked him why he had married me, and he said: "Because I knew you would be a hard worker."

It was because of my own lack of worth that I stayed and allowed him to use me. Before, I was strong enough to overlook it and take care of both of us. But now that the years, children, responsibility, and exhaustion had worn me down, the illusion of love became too heavy for me to carry alone anymore. I had to face the fact that I married my father.

I went straight to our room and locked the door; I cocooned myself in there, simultaneously numb and hysterical. I felt so detached from reality, like I was having an out-of-body experience. In the distance, I could hear him pounding on the door, the kids crying and distressed, the phone ringing – my mother's faint voice of concern and him asking her to come immediately. My childhood instincts ignited, and even though I hadn't been there in so long, with all the chaos going on outside, I closed my eyes and fell inside.

'What's going on? Why is this happening to me? Help me?'

I was losing my mind. The entire world didn't make sense. I didn't understand how you could be so responsible, loving, and selfless, and the world never gave you a break. It never relented or sent someone to come take care of me for a change. How was it fair that I worked so hard and did so much, and he did nothing in comparison, but he got to stay home and relax for years and could somehow only see our problems as my fault? Was he insane, or was I? How could I be so blind to marry someone who was so irrational when I thought he was the smartest person in the world, much smarter than me? My inspired thoughts came in succession:

'The way I see the world must be wrong.' 'I'm wrong.' 'I'm not perfect'.

It was the first time ever in my adult life that I questioned that there was something missing in my ability to properly perceive the world around me. I didn't think I was the smartest person; I just thought I could understand and learn anything. But now I realized that there is no way I would've allowed things to get this bad or go this far if I had been able to see the signs or patterns leading to it, but I missed them all completely. I had always considered myself an excellent judge of character, and because I followed all the rules, never stepped out of line, and always did the responsible thing, I assumed I was perfect and, therefore, my life should be perfect. In that perfection, I assumed that when people around me made mistakes or struggled, it was because they were not using good judgment and that their lives were their fault.

By using that logic against myself, that must mean that because I am struggling now, somewhere, I made a mistake and didn't know it. My judgment was not as sound as I believed it to be, and this experience was turning all of my previous assumptions over on their head. I had done everything perfectly, but things were not perfect. Therefore, I must've done something wrong - I am not perfect. I know for some, this may seem like a trivial or obvious observation, but for me, it was Earth-shattering. I wasn't the hero… I was the villain.

I thought by helping everyone around me, I was saving them, but now I realized I was actually elevating myself. I had been stroking my own ego all along, believing that because they needed help and support, they were lesser than me, and in that realization, the selfless martyr revealed herself to be a petty dictator. I didn't know I had a superiority complex. After walking blind through life, feeling like a doormat for so long, I finally saw myself for what I really was, and it stopped me in my tracks. I was not the victim; I was the perpetrator, and I had NO clue. He was right. Inside, I was judgmental. I thought I was perfect and could do no wrong. I was not compassionate, or understanding, or merciful. I was black and white, with no grey in between.

My mom arrived while I was in this state of humbling realization and assured me (based on her experience) that all men lie and get really angry and that it was my job to be patient and forgive him, and that is how love grows in a marriage, by going through hard times together. She tried making me feel better by saying that my overreaction and pain was understandable but that all marriages have problems, and they work through it.

I thought he was my soulmate, and I wanted to keep my family and marriage alive, so I allowed what she said to calm me while also realizing that I was part of the problem too. After years of blaming him for everything, I couldn't blame him for blowing up at me; he must be hurting as much as I was right now. We spent years going to couples therapy, and he tried so hard to explain his point of view to me, but I always disregarded it, believing mine to be the only right one. No wonder he stopped trying. But I couldn't give up on us, not while I realized I had so much to learn.

I came to him in utter humility. Apologizing for putting him in a position to lie to me for all those years and for never really letting his words and frustrations enter my heart and instead dismissing them. I don't think I ever listened to him even once. All of our fights were me trying to prove my point without hearing him out or talking over him and not respecting his time to speak. I had dominated every aspect of our relationship and existence, and in his mercy, he allowed that, but he also had to find outlets for his own frustrations, so he spent money on himself. I promised him that I was going to change and not blame him for everything anymore and that I was going to take responsibility for my actions and the way I behaved towards him.

He saw how completely different my reaction to this fight had been from any other fight we had before, and I saw a glimpse of light in his eyes that I had never seen, perhaps hope. My mom was right; getting past this first hurdle brought us closer together than we had ever been before.

That night, while putting the kids to bed, I felt something awaken in me. The jolt of pain from the fight and realization that followed were so jarring that they reopened something I had shut down years ago - my feelings.

I had muted my senses so severely that I remember one time when I was done cooking, I handed my husband the pan to serve the food hot off the stove. Seeing that I was holding it with my bare hands, he assumed it was cool enough to hold it the same way, so he took the handle without question. A second later, I heard the cling of the pan hit the tile and him yelling: "What the hell is wrong with you? Are your hands made of asbestos?" I quickly turned to look, and his hand was bright red, almost burnt, whereas I only registered a little warmth. Feelings weren't necessary while I was in survival mode; my only concern was waking up and making money, so I not only suppressed the way I felt about things emotionally but physically as well. But now, my survival tactics couldn't help the situation I was in; the only way I could navigate myself out of this mess was with my heart.

As if I were a sleeper cell that had suddenly awakened, I felt every cell in my body light up at once. It felt like I had been thrown into a cold, burning fire. That night, I lay wide awake in bed, hoping I would not wake the kids with the sound of my teeth rattling as my entire body shivered. When I emerged the next morning, I noticed there was something subtly new about me. Or rather, there was something old that had come back to life, a receptor or filter that changed the way I sensed things. My eyes perceived everything softer; even the sunlight coming through the window looked kinder. When my husband and I spoke that morning, I was softer in the way I spoke, and he seemed to return that same tone to me. During the day at work, I felt things I hadn't felt before, mainly people's emotions – rather than trying to decipher what they were feeling based on the look on their face, I could instead feel their emotions and know when their face was hiding the truth. It was exhilarating; the information about the world that I had been missing my entire life had appeared; I had become empathic overnight. Demonstrating for me how limitless God's power is, in that even though my senses had been buried for 25 years, He could still raise them from the dead.

As soon as I broke the false idea that I was perfect and that I was always doing the right thing while everyone around me was always using me. My bond to a victimhood mentality burst open, allowing my heavy emotions of rage, injustice, and blame to spill out. By the law of charity, when a release is offered back into the world, a space is created within us, and it acts like a vacuum, pulling in the purified emotions of compassion and love. This renewal of emotions showed me the stark difference in how severely my perception of life could be altered based on how I feel, and after seeing with the light of truth, I could finally differentiate between the world I created, versus the truth of reality.

What I Learned

Breaking Mental Idols

As a kid, giving to those around me was more natural than anything else I can remember. My first instinct when seeing people stressed or in trouble was to jump in and save the day. I always felt like it was double rewarding because they would become so happy and grateful, and I would feel strong and good. It informed me of my identity and who I believed I was as a person: I was the leader, dependable, and independent. This default egoic perception of myself was amplified by being born into a family that seemed to have endless needs. Since the tables never turned, I never got the opportunity to give to myself, and buying things for myself never felt as good as the look in their eyes when I saved them.

This bias was confirmed when I was around my wealthier friends as a child. As a way to elevate my ego and not allow myself to feel lesser, I judged them. Although I saw that it was nice that they had expensive clothes and cars and could have so much fun all the time, they always seemed so spoiled and ungrateful, not in a mean way but in a naïve way. They had the expectation of things given and not the appreciation of something earned. So, I never admired them. Instead, I pitied them. I noticed that even when they turned 18 and became adults, rather than be thankful for everything their parents had done, they would resent that they hadn't given them more. I thought there was something lacking in them that no amount of money in the world could buy – True, deep gratitude.

On top of all that, as a girl, I was taught to be patient and to allow myself to be sacrificed for the good of others. This was ingrained into me as the definition of not only being a woman but also of being good and holy and the way to enter heaven. Which I believed because when I looked at the examples my mother and Jesus* set, selflessly sacrificing themselves, it all added up. In my mind, God only loved and admitted people to heaven who gave everything of themself to others, and Earth was just a test to see how selflessly charitable you could be. This was my truth.

It was in this deep web of experiences, prejudices, and beliefs that I lived most of my life, so my first step in learning about charity was an act of destruction. I had to acknowledge that the depths of who I believed I was as a person were false, and I had to crush the mental idol I had created of myself. It's easier to crush a mental idol that I thought was bad, but it never occurred to me that the good ones were worse. They were deceptive in their helpfulness and made me believe that the goodness came from me instead of through me and that because I was good, I was superior.

Once I realized that I was not perfect, nor better than anyone else and that God had never demanded perfection from anyone, I lost myself. Everything I knew to be true in the world fell, and 'I' fell with it. It was in this state of knowing nothing that the questions arose:

'If my job wasn't to be a sacrificial hero, what was I supposed to do with my time on Earth? What was the real way to get to heaven?

What was this transformation I experienced, and how do I get more of it?

What was my responsibility to those in need?

What was my responsibility to myself?

Who am I?'

Know Thyself

In an attempt to save my marriage and understand the transformation that occurred within me overnight, I became ravenous for information. My journey began with a simple Google search: 'What is compassion and unconditional love?' and from that, my spiritual journey grew wings and flew. I read everything at the pace of someone starved and finally finding an oasis. Within a few months, I read the Bhagavad Gita about Kriya yoga and Buddha's greater and lesser vehicles. I inhaled the New Testament, especially the book of John, and although I had trouble understanding the Old Testament, Neville Goddard and Joseph Campbell's explanations revealed their wisdom to me. I had already read the Quran many times before, but I reread it with fresh eyes. I don't know if it is because I read them all in succession or because I read them looking for something specific, but it was then that I realized they were all the same. Not a single one of them deviated from the core message of unity, compassion, and one love. They may have been from different places and times, but they were all pointing in the same direction.

"People, We have created you all male and female,
and have made you nations and tribes,
so that you would **recognize** each other.
The most honorable among you in the sight of God
is the most pious of you.
God is All-knowing and All-aware."
- Quran 49:13

Once I finished with the traditional religions and philosophies, I moved to nature-based beliefs and practices. I learned about spirituality, astrology, shamanism, and plant medicines. No matter what I learned, or how I read it, or the direction the author drew the picture from, it was all the same. Everyone was trying to explain the Great Spirit, and not as an external other, but as the fabric of everything. It was a beautiful kaleidoscope of voices, images, and teachings over thousands of years that had culminated in my mind and allowed me to reach my final conclusion.

My job wasn't to sacrifice myself, it was to Know Myself.

In knowing my true self, my purpose in life would reveal itself. Without gaining this critical information first, I would never be able to help myself or a single other soul on Earth; it was that important.

<u>Breaking Bonds</u>

For the first time, I looked at myself and asked what I needed, it was the first true charity I had ever given myself, to just look at my needs, identify them, and then either provide them or allow God to provide them for me. I was always the most difficult for others to care for because when people asked me what I needed, I would always say "Nothing" or "I don't know." I had never taken the time to get to know myself or what gave me pleasure or happiness, but in my studies, I learned about self-love, self-worth, codependency, boundaries, standards, radical forgiveness, and how to exit survival mode, and I felt humiliated for learning all of this so late in life. Having focused all my attention on getting money to solve my problems, it never occurred to me that I was the problem and no amount of money could fix that. It made me think of all the pain I could've avoided, time I could've saved, and people I must have hurt through my own ignorance, and so it was time to take my rose-colored glasses off and see the reality I had built for what it truly was.

I had to acknowledge that before, it was wrong of me to want my husband to take the responsibility of filling my tank, and it was equally wrong of me to overextend myself and fill his. I remember during a fight once, after six months of coming home to him playing *PlayStation* each day and not working, I asked him how he could disrespect me after I had given him so much, and he responded:

"I never asked you to do all this for me. It's your fault for making me feel too comfortable."

At the time, I thought he was the most ungrateful bastard I had ever met in my life, but now I know he was absolutely right; he never did ask. I had created a burden out of my love, and when he rightfully refused to participate in the situation and tended to his own needs instead, I blamed him for being selfish. I thought suffering for each other was the way you showed love, and I didn't know at the time that he was teaching me how to stop suffering and how to prioritize myself. Instead of taking his lead, I judged him.

My first attempts to fill my tank were very small. I asked my husband to watch the kids for a few hours so that I could read books and take naps. I signed up for Kung Fu classes that I had always wanted to try, and I had lunch dates with my sisters. It was life-altering. Normally, every minute of my day was scheduled to take care of someone else from the moment I woke up to the moment I put my head down to sleep. Now I was relaxing and doing things I liked during the day, something I had not done since I was 16. It made me feel refreshed and alive; I was learning about the holiness of the sabbath for the first time.

I thought giving to yourself had to be a big production, but these tiny refills accumulated, and drop by drop, they started to build the momentum of being able to handle so much more self-love. Also, by understanding that it was my job to fill myself up, it completely changed the dynamic of our relationship. Now that I no longer needed him, I had to decide if I even wanted him. He was my first love and the father of my children, and despite everything we had been through, I still believed in him and our future, but I knew now that I was in love with a version of him that didn't exist. I had dreamt of what he would be like at his highest potential, having graduated, making money, and finally supporting me, but he wasn't that person. I had to admit that although some of the things I had asked him for were not his responsibility, many others were, and he refused to do those as well.

I had to see him for what he was. He was someone who was okay with his wife taking all the financial responsibility while he coasted and who didn't help with the kids unless specifically asked. He was independent, and I needed a team player. He also didn't enjoy growth and change. When I asked him to read and learn with me so that we could grow and become better versions of ourselves together, he said he didn't need to learn anything and that I should continue to focus on myself. He was also unwilling to admit that he had a money-spending addiction and anger issues, and instead, he blamed me for those vices. He flat-out told me he would never change; he was 11 years older than me and set in his ways.

Although I started this journey to save our marriage, at the end of it, I learned that in knowing myself, I had to honor myself and my needs. When I asked him for a divorce, it wasn't because I didn't love him; we just weren't compatible anymore once I realized that if I had to earn his love, it wasn't real. He said it was my fault for changing, that men marry women hoping they will stay the same, and women marry men to change them. It was a harsh truth, but he was right; I had changed, he changed me. I had built the dynamic in our relationship where I was the giver, and he was the receiver, but I hadn't anticipated that he would take so much without giving anything in return, and in doing so, he broke me.

"The world breaks everyone.
The very good, the very gentle, the very brave.
And those it doesn't break, it kills."

Changing Core Beliefs

When I broke the old version of myself that put others first, I released the belief that love must be earned through serving others, and moved forward to the next step of charity that purifies and upgrades our beliefs to serve us.

After spending 10 years observing my ex and seeing how relaxed he always was, I asked him why he never worried about money, and he said:

"Because it always comes when I need it."

He had said this to me before when I wasn't ready to hear it, and it would enrage me.

I would think to myself, 'Ya, it always comes when you need it because I'm the one making sure we have it,' but I knew now that way of thinking was wrong. I allowed my victimhood mentality to overinflate my responsibility when the reality was that I never gave God the opportunity to care for me the way my ex did. I observed that statement differently now and realized it was my ex's core belief that he trusted God would always be there for him, and his confidence in that allowed him to physically relax and be cared for.

I witnessed this core belief manifest for years during the time we were married. I watched him sit around and play with his camera or watch videos on his computer, and never truly worry about or contribute to the household in any meaningful way, and in the end, he got half of the house that I paid off. It was like watching someone take an eight-year vacation and get a bonus at the end for attendance. As opposed to my stressful experience of working myself to death, saving every dollar I made, feeling like doing any basic thing for myself was a splurge, carrying and giving birth to our children, and at the end of it, I had to give away half of everything I worked so hard for. It was in watching our two truths manifest side by side in the same world that I understood the power of our faith to shape our daily lives.

To me, faith meant professing that there is one God, devotion through prayer, and acts in service of others. But in the course of our marriage, I never once saw my ex-husband pray, or even mention God's name, or perform any consistent charity. Yet I could feel through his calm, relaxed nature that he believed more than me. His energy on a daily basis felt like someone who knew they had a bank account they could access any time of day, with unlimited funds.

It was through his unbothered energy that he demonstrated that belief and trust weren't lip service that needed to be professed or performed but rather a quiet conviction, deeply felt. God, for him, wasn't an external being he worshipped; it was the universal force running through him. He made fun of people (like me) who constantly declared their faith or belief, comparing us to a poor man who always brags about how much money he has versus the quiet confidence of a rich man who has nothing to prove, allowing his wealth to speak on his behalf.

In his void of any form of religious traditions, he was a complete anomaly to everything I had ever learned about devotion. For so long, I was perturbed that he never thanked me, but looking back, I never heard him thank God either. He didn't 'practice' gratitude or journal, and he strongly hated symbols and labels. The thought of going to any building that labeled itself 'The house of God' revolted him; he was disgusted with the notion that God could be limited or contained in any way.

I watched him over the years with a mixture of judgment and awe. He appeared to have no relationship with God whatsoever, and yet his blessings were too obvious to deny; I watched him so many times just express his desire for something once, and then magically, it would appear. It wasn't until I had the time to look back with the wisdom I had accumulated that I saw how truly holy his void was.

He was teaching me the faith and conviction required to bring the true wisdom of the first pillar to life. No god, but God. Everything was hidden in the void of nothing. The only way to find God was to reject everything that claimed to be God.

This required me to break even further my mental idols of what true devotion and worship meant. All my efforts, no matter how sincere and informed they were now, were still just 'whistling and hand clapping' done in vain, compared to the power in his quiet conviction. I could not find what I was seeking because I had switched from working hard to accumulate money to accumulating faith rather than just having faith.

All he needed were his silent beliefs and simple joys, and in that simplicity, he demonstrated for me the power in Jesus's* words:

"For truly I tell you, if you have faith the size of a mustard seed, you will say to this mountain, 'Move from here to there,' and it will move."[7]

I look back at him now, not as a husband, but as an exceptional teacher that didn't cripple me with a dependency on him and didn't lecture me to change. He just lived his unassuming teaching that true wealth wasn't only found in hard work but in the ability to trust God so deeply that our presence becomes indistinguishable from our faith.

As soon as I awakened to his lesson about how deeply we have to reach within ourselves to break bonds from beliefs that obstruct the charity we are meant to receive from God, and replace them with the conviction that enables us to receive, like a true mystical teacher, he disappeared.

"When the student is ready, the teacher will appear.
When the student is truly ready... The teacher will Disappear."
-Tao Te Ching

Detachment and God's Will

In order to truly ingrain into me the faith that God is my provider, at the end of our divorce my ex gave me a final parting gift… an expensive and painful lesson in detachment. Once I had gone through the mental cycle of charity by breaking my idols, identifying my false beliefs, and exchanging them for ones that served me, I now had to walk that faith into my physical experience by relinquishing my expectations of how my life should be, and allow God to provide for me, which was really scary at first.

As mentioned above, per our divorce agreement my ex got half the value of the house, which I worked so hard to quickly pay off during our marriage, and it felt like a punch to the gut … I thought God was teaching me the value of a prenup.

But in taking away my hard-earned provision, what He was really teaching me was to acknowledge and accept the temporary nature of life, that tomorrow is not guaranteed, and that there must be a balance between living for today while also saving for the future. With the law of charity, giving and receiving must be balanced, and I was so obsessed with only saving for the future that I had cut off the cycle of giving to myself today.

This probably sounds like the most basic knowledge to most people, but admittedly, I was so stuck in survival mode that I needed a huge slap in the face, like losing over $100,000, to wake me up. Before, I never stopped to smell the roses; I was learning that 10 years of slaving away could be lost in a moment, and it was better I learn that now rather than 40 years from now when I was retiring and my entire life had passed me by with nothing but hard work to show for it. God was giving me the gift of today and hit His point home by having me witness an old friend go through a similar experience at the exact same time.

Growing up, one of our closest family friends was a very large and kind Syrian family. For several years, I watched them work hard, save their money, and live a modest life here in America so that one day they could build their dream home in Syria. After a few decades, that day came, and although it was hard to lose one of my best friends, we promised to see each other again one day. A few years later, I finally got to make the trip out to see them, and I was shocked. They lived in the most beautiful home I had ever seen; it was a mansion compared to the home I was used to seeing them in. Everything was custom-made and painted gold like I imagined the inside of the Trump Tower might look.

As a young adult, this experience was a core memory for me because it further confirmed my programmed belief that – if I work hard and save all my money for many years, one day I will have my dream home and that the pursuit of happiness did have a happy ending after all. However, several years later, a war broke out in Syria, and in order to survive, they had to leave everything they had worked so hard for behind and come back to start all over. They moved in with their eldest son, who had stayed in America when they moved abroad, and for a few years, while they resettled, there were four adults and five kids living in a small two-bedroom apartment.

I can't fully describe how jolted I was by this, but it was like I got to see a glimpse of my future and see that hard work didn't come with any guarantees. No matter how responsible I was, no one had any control over life.

The combination of these experiences urged me to restructure what the rest of my work/life expectations would be for the foreseeable future, because why focus on working solely for money when it is so unfulfilling and can so easily be taken away? Going forward, my passions would take energetic priority over my job, meaning while I found a way to make money pursuing my passions, I would not work overtime or accept a promotion/more responsibility at work. This was completely contrary to who I normally was, and it would be difficult for me to hold back my enthusiasm to achieve at work, but I didn't have to hold back for long.

At the end of 2020, I found myself in a situation where I was unemployed, living on my savings, and following God's will for me to write a book. I was living life on the edge of faith, and even with the steps I was taking to prove my conviction, I was still scared. I didn't have my ex-husband's cool confidence, but I figured if I kept walking, eventually, it would come. But what I also realized was being unemployed and pursuing my passions would've been unthinkable just a few years ago, and the fact that I was now okay with this level of financial uncertainty showed me how far in my faith I had actually come and just hadn't given myself credit for.

Two years later, I was faced with a huge dilemma: my savings had run out, and my CPA license needed to be renewed, which meant that I needed a job and had an easy way to get one. In my mind, this was a critical fork in the road because I had to decide whether I should stay on the course of fulfilling God's plan but be broke or go back to the world of financial stability and trust in the almighty dollar. Even though I probably could've been very reasonable about it and worked part-time and wrote on nights and weekends, by this point in the book, you have all probably realized just how intense I am. So, I took it as a grand test of faith of how committed I was to serving God and allowed my CPA license to lapse. It was scary because of all the years, degrees, money, and back-breaking labor I put into acquiring it, but I heavily relied on its prestige and ability to quickly open doors to make money.

Spiritually, it represented a backup plan that planted a seed in my mind that failing at writing was an option, because if I didn't succeed, I could always go back to being an accountant and rely on my license instead of God. After everything I learned, the one thing I knew was that, like Lot's wife, I could not look back. I had to move forward with God's plan, even if it meant poverty, and trust that He was the only one that could ever really provide for me.

"If you want to take the island, burn the boats!"
-Julius Caesar

While meditating, I asked God what he wanted me to do for money to support myself on this journey, and my intuition guided me to sell stocks held in my 401(k). A few years ago, I would've considered this committing financial suicide – yes, CPAs are that dramatic about our savings. But now that charity taught me to detach from future expectations, it felt natural and right to use the money today when I needed it, even when accounting for the penalties. I only took as much as I needed to carry me forward another year, and through releasing the deathgrip money had on me for so long, I was finally able to balance taking reasonable precautions for the future, while giving myself the gift of today, so that I could comfortably keep going on my journey.

You Give Charity to Yourself First

After all the changes I had made in my beliefs and actions, I was a completely different person inside and out. So, although it may have seemed drastic for me to file for divorce, sell the house, and quit my job in one month, at the time, I was completely ready for it. It was my next cataclysmic step in charity that required me to release everything that no longer served me, and because nothing in my immediate surroundings supported who I was as a person anymore, it was too painful to live in that lie anymore.

It was also in how quickly and easily I could destroy everything it had taken me over a decade to build that I realized how much of an illusion it all truly was, and even though I was starting over from scratch, instead of feeling loss, I felt weightless. In unloading all of that pressure, responsibility, and pain, I not only created so much new space in my life but also felt light enough to ascend to the next station of life.

I moved in with my mom and stepdad to live as cheaply as possible in order to give myself as much time to find myself and my purpose as I could, and so with no time to lose, I threw myself into learning to give charity to myself first through serious self-love.

Self-love is not Selfish

I had always believed that being selfish was a bad thing, and I equated that with self-love. I was also very extreme, so wanting to be the opposite of selfish, I became completely selfless. For two decades, I lived on the bare minimum to make sure everyone around me was okay; I only had two pairs of identical dress pumps – one brown, one black. I owned one black utilitarian purse, and when it fell apart, I replaced it with a similar one. I thought flowers were a waste of money, and my idea of fun was staying home, watching TV, and making sure everyone around me felt safe. Because I didn't know the tangible value of having fun, I had the biggest chip on my shoulder, and I expected everyone else to have the same priorities as me. So, when I saw adults who lived for fun, I equated them with being frivolous grasshoppers, only good for freeloading off the ant's hard-earned harvest.

My ex's words rang in my mind, 'I never asked for your help.' I saw others in distress, kindly offered help, and they accepted. So, my first step in self-love was giving myself permission to allow others to fail and let them learn how to solve their own problems. Before, I was like an anxious mother, hovering over her children to catch them before they fall. By doing that, I was simultaneously making myself into a doormat and robbing them of crucial life lessons to give them confidence and independence. After crippling their self-esteem, I blamed them for being too dependent. In owning my part in that equation and correcting my mentality to understand that you also help people by not helping them, I no longer felt the urgency to save everyone, freeing me to prioritize taking care of myself.

It was wild at first; just thinking about what I wanted to do for fun made me feel uncomfortable, not because I was averse to it, but because I was embarrassed to be genuinely baffled that I had no clue what I liked. I hadn't done something just for fun since before I started working at 15, and even then, it was probably in the confines of my bedroom. Funnily enough, life had brought me back to that exact same location as if I had picked the wrong 'build your own adventure' option in a game, and it forced me to restart my life from my last checkpoint.

To begin, I had to embark on a year of discovery. Trying new things to see what I liked and what I didn't like. The excitement overtook the fear of leaving my comfort zone, and I signed up for dance and spirituality classes; I bared my soul at meditation and plant medicine retreats, and I met people who felt like long-lost best friends. I also rediscovered the love I had for old friends who made the same leap and went on the journey with me. After all the theatrics were over, I finally settled into a self-love routine that was basic and fundamental. I connected with my heart often through meditation/prayer and prioritized having fun and fancy meals with friends and family at least once a month. I used exercise to learn life skills (like self-defense through Kung Fu), which made me feel both more enriched and fit rather than bored, which is the way I used to feel when I monotonously beat myself up at the gym. I also made a point to read both for research and for fun and found that I could easily classify *50 Shades of Grey* as both because of its deeply holy yet erotic take on surrender. The energy from these simple acts of indulgence made me feel like a supernova of abundance.

By taking care of myself, it resulted in a double benefit. When I was full of energy, love, compassion, passion, and inspiration, my presence alone filled those around me. My positive energy spilled out of me and motivated others to make positive changes in their lives, too, and I didn't have to nag them or lift a finger to help them. It was all self-motivated, authentic, and gave them the gift of their own confidence and self-worth. I understood now that my responsibility to others was to show them, by example, how to fish rather than give them my fish. In doing that, I gave them the greatest gift one person could ever give another. Self-Love.

After learning that giving to myself was the first and greatest act of charity that could ever be done for the world, I learned that the second kindest thing we can do for ourselves is establish boundaries.

Boundaries are not Oppression, they are Protection

Energy vampire was not a term I knew, but I was very familiar with the concept when it came up in a book I was reading about how to protect my energy. Energy vampires are people who prey on sensitive, happy people to feed off their kindness and compassion and leave them feeling drained.[2] They do it by taking in their positive energy and then killing the mood, or criticizing, or wasting people's time listening to their endless complaining without ever helping themselves. With the abundance of energy I had from filling myself up, I had attracted so many dark personalities as well. Although I wasn't trying to save them anymore, I wanted to understand what I was doing to attract them and how to protect myself from their tactics, which were more sophisticated than the vampires I had dealt with in the past. Apparently, the brighter I became, the more darkness I naturally attracted, and the way to protect myself was with firm boundaries, something I never had before.

These boundaries established limits to the kind of behavior I would and wouldn't accept from others, and if they transgressed, I had to be solid in my consequences. Establishing boundaries felt harsh and unnatural at first. My inclination was to forgive, be patient, and endure, but with my newfound ability to sense more deeply, I could no longer deny how draining it was to hang out with old friends who did nothing but gossip and complain. It hurt even more when I would try to counsel them with their problems after hours of listening to their pain with a compassionate ear and then seeing them do nothing to solve their issues despite asking me for my advice. I realized how much of my precious time I was wasting on entertaining things that drained my energy when I should've been focusing on things that filled me instead. In knowing that energy is life, what I was effectively doing was allowing them to drain my life force, and NO ONE should be given that kind of power.

It didn't take long for me to learn how to put a stop to people's negative thought patterns mid-conversation. I'd steer them in a healthier direction, and if they didn't get the gist and I felt generous, I would quickly make an excuse and leave. I also exited entire friend groups that led their chats with negativity, and for them, I made no excuses. I flat-out told people that there was a way to solve problems without being angry and hateful and that although I could lend a helpful ear for a short time if I didn't see quick realizations, they needed to direct their frustrations elsewhere because I couldn't help them. For as many friends that I lost while putting up my boundaries, I made just as many, and now that my mind was different, I attracted like-minded people. I thought that by having boundaries, I would limit the amount of love that I let through, but the cycle of renewal was teaching me that boundaries made it easier to break bonds with the old to create space for the new.

This doesn't mean that I was 'love & light' all the time. There were many times when I would meet with family and friends to deal with heavy experiences, both my own and supporting theirs, but I didn't dwell on those feelings. We unburdened ourselves freely with each other and then offered different points of view based on our experiences, allowing us to benefit from each other's wisdom. I left conversations feeling educated or resourceful rather than drained and frustrated. We also met far more often for joyful experiences, and that was the main energetic signature of our relationship. We loved being around each other, always knowing that no matter what, we were going to have a good time.

My entire idea of what charity truly was had transformed. Looking at charity as an energetic exchange, rather than monetary, the same way money is protected in a bank, energy must also be protected. Even when I considered myself completely selfless, I still didn't run around throwing money at every person I saw in need. However, I realized that I was constantly doing that with my energy.

When I unburdened myself from my false beliefs about what giving charity and being selfless means, I released the heavy emotional responsibility of carrying others and readily cut away their negative/draining company. By making the conscious choice to establish boundaries that only let in what filled me with love, I was not just protecting but multiplying my energy bank, and in doing so, I consequently established my self-worth and learned that by not giving to others that didn't value me, I was giving charity to myself.

False Boundaries

It was in learning about boundaries that I also learned about karmic relationships. These are people who will come into our lives to teach us something (often painfully), and once the lesson is learned, they either leave or their presence no longer triggers us.

A trigger - is the pain we feel inside when someone pushes against our deepest false boundaries.

A false boundary (or wall) - is a false belief created by a trauma that is so deeply buried that it becomes unconscious, and causes us to unwittingly block out the good, because we want protection from what feels bad.

My karmic relationship with my father was my first experience with true, deep masculine love. I didn't just love him; as a child, I worshipped him. I believed that no one in the world would ever love me as much as he did because I came from him, and how could someone not love their own blood? He was the only man I let into my heart completely and unconditionally. In my mind, he could do no wrong, but as I grew up, I learned how painful it was to love someone so blindly like that. Even though in that pain, he taught me how to access the true love within myself, since I didn't understand the value of it at the time, my focus was consumed with all the pain of unrequited love I was constantly feeling. Out of necessity for survival, in order to protect myself from the overwhelming amount of pain, I built a wall around my heart made of the semi-false belief that expecting to receive love was too painful when it never came, and in doing so, I created a boundary against receiving and became a giver.

As if by divine timing, two months after my father passed, my husband and I were married. God was trading one karmic relationship for another. I hadn't completed my lesson, so my husband was sent to finish the job my dad started, Teaching me that unconditional love couldn't live behind an impenetrable wall but that it could thrive with flexible boundaries.

Instead of living a black-and-white life, where I was either completely open or closed, I had to learn how to dance with life. The only way to hear the rhythm of the dance was to access my heart so that I could tune into its wisdom and know when my boundaries should be firm and when they should be relaxed. But after years of having a wall around it, I couldn't access it even though it was within me, so God sent a demolition man.

When my husband came into my life, I thought he was my knight in shining armor. Coming to save, love, protect, provide, and care for me in a way no one else ever had. When I saw his red flags, I disregarded them; they were white compared to my father's. Love was relative, and my bar was so low it was non-existent. So, I thought my low expectations were reasonable and that it would be easy for him to fill me with all the love I never had before, not knowing that it was possible to fall even lower. He was my first romantic relationship, and I had no clue what I was stepping into, nor that his real job was to cut me even deeper. I asked God for true love and thought he had sent a life vest to save me, but instead, in his mercy, he sent a knife to forever cut through the false reality I had unconsciously lived in for so long.

I loved my husband. I loved the way he smelled and his English accent. I loved his intelligence, quick wit, and creativity. I loved his eyes and how elevated I felt when they looked at me, that somehow him picking me meant that I was special because I believed he was so special. It was as if he was scientifically made in a lab to be physically, chemically, and mentally the exact type of person I would let my guard down for. Being with him made me feel whole and worthy in a way I never felt before, so I took a chance against my better judgment and gave him all of me. I asked him what his dreams were, and when he said he wanted to be a Ph.D. I supported him to go after it. After getting accepted to university, I encouraged him to save up as much money as he could until his first semester started so that he could still comfortably pay bills out of his savings while a student, and I agreed to work and live frugally in order to take as much pressure as I could off of him to provide so that he could focus on and finish school as quickly as possible.

In the beginning, before the kids arrived, it was ok. He was helping pay a few bills with his savings, and although I wasn't thrilled with his work ethic, where I had expected years of being in the corporate world to engrain within him a productive eight-hour-per-day work schedule, he was still getting his work done even though he had reverted back to his old college days night owl schedule. But then, over time, I also started noticing behaviors that I never expected to see. Very often, when I got home, he was 'taking a break' in front of the TV, then at night, he also stayed up really late watching more TV and rarely came to bed with me, which brought to life our second biggest fight. The first being that he had somehow run through his savings so quickly that he was no longer able to help me with bills; I didn't know he had a money-spending addiction at the time, and the second was that our arrangement absolutely killed our intimacy.

About four years into the program, after both of the kids had arrived, I could cut the tension in the house with a knife. We hadn't slept together in two years after my last son was conceived, and beyond the physical exhaustion and pain of becoming a working mother, the expenses were astronomical. It cost $6,000/each with insurance just to give birth to them, and after that, their daycare combined was $24,000 a year, which I paid so that he could study while at home all day. My routine every weekday was to take care of the kids after work, which I loved even though I was exhausted because I had so much guilt from being away from them all day. Then, on the weekends, to give him extra time to write his thesis, I would take them to my mom's house so that he could focus while at home alone.

I probably could've survived in that state for years if I knew when it would end and saw that he was pushing himself as hard as I was to get things done, but as time went on, I saw how remarkably different our daily lives were, I became uncontrollably angry and resentful. His normal daily routine included several breaks, naps, a two-hour gym session in the middle of the day, and way too much time watching videos on *YouTube* and other more unsavory platforms. Over time, my anger turned into a fire that was burning me in every dimension I existed in, emotionally, spiritually, and physically. I put my foot down and asked him to get a job and start working to help pay bills. That's when he became irate and told me it would "impair his quality of life," and when I retorted by asking him about my quality of life, he said to just hold on a little longer because when he graduated, I could stop working and he would support me. That was always our agreement from the very beginning, and he would throw it back at me when I demanded help from him, but I never expected our lives to be so unequal and for him to be okay with that.

Eventually, my anger got to a point where that excuse didn't work anymore, and after threatening to divorce him, he found a way to make money doing something he loved - freelance photography. But when he made money, it just went back into buying more expensive gear rather than helping with household bills. So, instead, I tried to alleviate the pressure by asking him to help me with the kids more, but he complained that it would further delay him getting his degree, and with each request for help, the finish line seemed to extend out to forever.

I didn't understand how he could allow his work ethic to stay so relaxed despite seeing me suffer in everything I was carrying for him. I thought it would be a man's nature to help support the woman he loved, especially when he saw how much I was drowning for him. By not offering help and complaining when I asked for it, I felt he didn't understand or appreciate what I had given him – Something no one had ever given to me: The time, support, and freedom to focus on going after my dreams. I know he didn't ask me to help him, and in doing so, I made a burden out of my love, but I truly believed that's what partners do for each other.

My definition of a partnership was ultimate love in the give-and-take form of endless charity. To love someone so deeply you give everything you can to them, with the complete trust that they would do the same for you, so you end up in a never-ending cycle of support you can always depend on… That is what home feels like. Bon Jovi's song *Livin' On A Prayer* encapsulates this 'stability amongst chaos, through love' feeling exactly, look up the lyrics and see for yourself… "Take my hand and we'll make it, I swear."

I didn't realize many things in this experience, and it would take a horrific bone-crushing fall for me to finally understand what God had been trying to teach me all along. That I was right in my understanding of love and charity, but that I had it backwards in that I was giving to and expecting to receive all my love externally from men rather than internally and energetically from God.

Because I shut off the ability to receive love long ago, the only way for God to open my receptors was to make me experience a bigger pain than unrequited love - emptiness. He knew that would create a life-or-death desperation for love so great it would trigger my false boundaries regarding fear of receiving love to the surface, allowing me to tear them down once and for all, and finally fill myself.

Charity requires an even balance of give and take within each individual, and when we are unbalanced we karmically attract a partner that is our exact opposite to teach us that lesson. If I was completely selfless, then I energetically communicated to the world that I needed a bottomless pit to complete me. Because of my lack of self-awareness and not yet knowing the pure physics of charity, I took his lack of initiating any form of assistance or appreciation as his own shortcoming rather than my own fault in blocking myself from receiving, and became bitter and vengeful instead.

Receiving Forgiveness

Many things happen over the course of a marriage, and when it is as toxic as mine, where one partner thrives at the expense of the other's suffering, it showed me who I could become when I let the outside world take precedence over my inner world. After 10 years of thinking I had found my prince that would save me, I had to pop that hopeful bubble and painfully admit that instead, I got the opposite: Even more responsibility, financial infidelity, deleted text messages, gifts coming home from girls he met on campus, and so many other lies that eventually came to light. By the end of the marriage, I felt as if he had ungratefully taken everything I had given him and spit in my face as a thank you. I say all of this not as an excuse but to give you an idea of the state of mind I was in when I stepped out of my marriage to have my needs met.

It was a last-ditch effort right before I filed for divorce when I delusionally thought I could have it all. I wanted to keep my family and everything I had built but also find a way to relieve the pressure and feel desired and appreciated. The essence of my mother's words from long ago echoed in my lost mind, 'If he does what he wants and only asks for forgiveness instead of permission, then for once in my life, I should do the same.' It was a very short experience, which was fueled by my need for revenge and to reclaim my power, but in lowering myself to his level and tactics and allowing my vices to move me in a way I never gave them the power to before, I didn't recognize myself anymore. I had broken everything I believed in, and instead of feeling empowered, I felt completely defeated by life.

The words of my Christian marriage counselor came to life in my downfall, "We don't break God's laws, we break ourselves on them." In order to feed my emptiness, I broke my internal laws that defined the core of who I was as a person, and he was right; in breaking them, I did break myself. But to my surprise, the break wasn't a demolition; it was a liberation. After years of judging others and believing I was sinless and superior and didn't need to ask God for anything, my arrogant inner angel had fallen, and for the first time, I had to ask God for something real - Forgiveness.

I had never lied or cheated anyone before, and so I never felt the eternal resting place of my soul as being in danger. It was in that deep realization that this was no longer a worldly game I was playing, that what I had done had eternal implications, that I initiated the deepest request from God I ever had before. The immediacy of his forgiveness amplified its sweetness, allowing me to finally taste the true nectar of life and fill myself with it completely due to the depth of my humility.

By falling so steeply from grace, the walls that separated me from receiving were shattered, and in the process, I found that I could only know the forgiver when I needed to be forgiven.

I thought I had fallen out of God's favor, only to find that this elaborate strategy to break me was done for the purpose of showing me how much more love and compassion there was to discover and receive. I thought I would only deserve love if I earned it by being perfect and that it would be waiting for me when I got to Heaven. It never occurred to me that I could sin, and despite that, with sincere atonement, I could still experience God's love while on Earth. It was in that moment of need and the millisecond it took for me to receive God's forgiveness that the true meaning of unconditional love and compassion was engraved within me.

Compassion's Latin root: 'passio' – 'to suffer' and 'com' – 'together',

means 'to suffer together.'

My understanding of love long ago, as a child, knew this. Knew that suffering for each other was an element of love, but I slightly misunderstood it. It wasn't that we suffer for each other; it's that our suffering is what brings us together not only with humanity but with God. It's through suffering and truly understanding the pain of others that we unify, collapsing the many, to understand the one.

In breaking my deepest core beliefs about right and wrong, which defined me, I learned that it is not wrong to steal bread if you are starving. God was teaching me that in fearing unrequited love, I was also blocking unconditional love, and that God would prefer a temporary break from his laws to teach a lesson about how far true love will go to rescue us, rather than for us to live a life ignorant of the extent of his loving essence.

"By Him in whose hand is my soul, if you did not sin,
Allah would replace you with people who would sin,
and they would seek forgiveness from Allah,
and He would forgive them."[3]
-Muhammad*

Moses* learned this lesson when one day he met an angel by the sea in the form of a man and asked to follow and learn from him. The angel agreed but warned him to be patient and not to question what he saw, as the angel had no free will and could only do what God commanded.

Moses* agreed, and their journey began with a walk on the shore, where they found several boats, and the angel started to drill a hole in one of them. Moses asked how he could do it, concerned that the passengers would drown, but the angel reminded him of his oath to be patient.

Later, they met a young boy, and the angel killed him. Moses* protested, 'How could you kill an innocent person?' and the angel reminded him again to be patient. Moses* apologized and told the angel to banish him if he asked another question.

When they got to town, they asked for food but were refused. Then they saw a wall, and the angel started to repair it. Moses* asked why he didn't take payment for the repair, and the angel said this is where we part ways, but first:

"I will tell you the meaning of the things you could not bear with patiently:

The boat belonged to some needy people who made their living from the sea, and I damaged it because I knew that coming after them was a king who was seizing every [serviceable] boat by force.

The young boy had parents who were people of faith, and so, fearing he would trouble them through wickedness and disbelief, we wished that their Lord should give them another child– purer and more compassionate– in his place.

The wall belonged to two young orphans in the town, and there was buried treasure beneath it belonging to them. Their father had been a righteous man, so your Lord intended them to reach maturity and then dig up their treasure as a mercy from your Lord.

I did not do [these things] of my own accord; these are the explanations for those things you could not bear with patience."[4]

Like Moses* in that story, I never understood God's plan for my life. It seemed so harsh to only know a masculine love from my father and ex-husband that was so dry that it left me dehydrated in a desert, willing to give anything for a drop of water. I thought I was being demeaned and starved, but in not allowing me to be nourished by the outside world, God was actually elevating me by never allowing me to become dependent on drinking from someone else's cup.

After years of believing I had to climb to reach His favor, it was in becoming too weak to climb that I fell and broke my false beliefs open, and found my salvation - in that the greatest thing anyone can receive is His Forgiveness, because it is proof that love is truly unconditional. It also showed me where to go within myself to access His love and endless charity, and in showing me the way He gifted me with the realization that my cup was Self-Sufficient.

Forgiveness is one of the more difficult emotions to access for so many reasons: Guilt, shame, unworthiness, or the difficulty in letting go of the pain we have been subjected to, to name a few. Yet even with the barriers we put in the way of accessing it, incredibly, it is the most quickly distributed, in that when earnestly asked for, it is received instantly. It is the fastest way to access God's charity and only requires us to be open to receive it.

Many times, when I feel my heart hardening for someone, I remember my own fall and how quickly and urgently God forgave me. There is so much power in remembering, which is why remembrance is such a holy practice; it instantly ignites the fire of forgiveness within. For so long, I heard the saying 'forgive and forget,' but that never worked for me. I couldn't forget the lessons I had learned in my life, no matter how hard I tried. They were etched on my soul. So, instead, I 'forgive and remember.'

But most importantly, I also had to learn the nuance that forgiveness doesn't mean reconciliation. Life was no longer either having a wall and not letting anyone in or having no walls and letting everyone in. I learned how to love with healthy rather than false boundaries, which meant no longer subjecting myself to relationships that constantly require forgiveness. I could instead love someone deeply, but from far away.

As soon as I accepted his karmic lessons, my ex and our relationship of 10 years abruptly ended. I entered a new dimension of life that he didn't have access to. He rejected the tenants to move into the new world of: Forgiveness, compassion, and unconditional love. So, even though he indirectly taught me all those things, he couldn't come with me, and now that I had seen the Kingdom, I couldn't go back either. My elevation in consciousness created such a vast space between us that even though we had joint custody of the kids and communicated often, our thought signatures were so different that talking to each other felt like cell phones trying to make a call to someone living on a different planet. The old Earth vs the new Earth.

<u>The Art of Receiving</u>

In charity's cycle of giving and receiving, I was a natural giver, which satisfied my inner minimalist. I loved throwing away anything that disturbed my peace because I understood that everything had an energetic effect on me. If it wasn't worth the energy to maintain, or it didn't serve me, it had to go. This is why I could forgive those who wronged me; they weren't worth the energy to maintain the resentment, and also why I was able to throw my old life away so efficiently after realizing its burden. I was not only good at releasing, but I was also incredibly generous and loved giving to others. Because all of these were acts of pushing energy out, it was learning to receive that was uncomfortable for me; I had to change my energy to go in the opposite direction.

Receiving required an inward acceptance, and it felt intimate to be energetically touched like that. Before, I believed there was only strength and power in giving out because I could touch others without being touched. This might explain why I don't like physical touch, either. I was a massage therapist for a while, so I loved providing a healing touch to others, but I recoiled at the thought of receiving it. It was a programmed response to my past, when I had let love in, and it hurt. But I knew I couldn't survive like that anymore. In order to progress in my ability to hear God and receive His favor, I needed to have the courage to open up again because receiving required a completely different type of power.

<u>Vulnerability</u>

<u>Definition</u>: The quality or state of being exposed to the possibility of being attacked or harmed, either physically or emotionally.

Although vulnerability is not gender specific, it is through the power of vulnerability that feminine energy opens to receive. I had no idea how to do this before my awakening. I had been so masculinized at such a young age through physical and emotional abuse that my receptors to receive were literally closed, evidenced by my inability to feel my own feelings and my ability to suppress physical pain. My entire mental state was consumed with disregarding my needs and giving to others.

When my dad left, I didn't complain; I just naturally took on the role of man of the house. When I entered the corporate world, everyone at the top was a man, and if there was a woman, she had to be more severe than the men to make it there. Growing up in the West at the time, there was a movement where women were fighting against sexism, unfair compensation, and prejudices of either being weak and fragile or a bitch. Being swept up in this movement, I felt I had something to prove. I was just as mentally strong or ambitious as any man, and as such, I didn't lose my femininity; I discarded it.

Although I never changed my identity, and I always considered myself a woman, nothing about me was female other than the way I dressed and the fact that I had the parts. My energy was male, and even though deep down inside I still had the desire to be cared for, I crushed it down to not appear weak. I don't want to go so far as to say that I felt cursed being born a girl, but I suspect this inclination towards masculinity was rooted in wanting to be the boy my father always wanted. My external world mirrored my internal confusion, and so I couldn't see what being feminine had to offer.

No one had taught me to value the power of being a woman. The power of the womb, which, if you remember from before, is the root of God's greatest names - The Compassionate and The Merciful, and is the only way that life can become manifest on Earth. It is through the gentle strength of Compassion and Mercy that we find the ultimate power to open people's hearts, no matter how hardened, and illuminate where God dwells within us. The masculine may take the lead, but that can only be rightly done when they allow themselves to be guided with the wisdom of an open, vulnerable heart, as evidenced by the existence of Muhammad*, who is described as a Mercy for mankind. Proving that the most powerful gift God could bestow on men was not strength or dominion but the ability to open their hearts and access God's Mercy.

For so long, I was at war with my feminine essence, not realizing that my masculine was nothing without her, and she was nothing without him. She needed him to protect and provide for her so that she could carry the awesome responsibility of keeping herself open and vulnerable to receive guidance and create a life for them to share purpose in.

Once I valued and respected my feminine powers and abilities, it was natural to shift my focus to strengthening them. Although I received a considerable boost when my receptors were blown open from the awakening I experienced during my last fight with my ex, I was like a toddler, learning how to use its legs for the first time, and my fear of falling again caused me to regress to crawling. In order to keep my senses open and heightened, I had to practice receiving often.

As a gentle start, before introducing receiving from others to the equation, I would lay out in the sun by myself. While out there, I would really focus on how it felt to accept the sun's soft light on my skin and its warmth deep into my body. Noticing how it simultaneously relaxed and nourished me while its kisses gently energized me. I could accept this love without fear that I was taking someone else's sunshine because it provided infinitely more than anyone ever needed. I also felt free of debt or expectations because even if I wanted to, the sun could accept nothing from me in exchange. It was truly a one-way relationship where I could only receive, and the only thing I could give was gratitude, which only benefitted me even more.

I believe someone should consider changing the definition of vulnerability. Currently, it is stated from a very pessimistic point of view. Vulnerability accessed from a heightened state is no longer a state of exposure to the possibility of attack; it becomes a state of openness, allowing endless benefits to be received deeply.

Accepting God's Charity

While my masculine and feminine energy kissed and made up, I felt emboldened by their united power to revisit some of my deeply embedded religious beliefs and judgments about receiving money and support, in order to heal them and enable myself to receive more.

As a kid, anytime I asked my dad for something he would give me the same trite response, "Money doesn't grow on trees."

When he would give it to me, he would remind me often that I had to 'behave,' but his definition of behave was slave. By accepting anything from him, it created an energetic debt that I could sense oozing out of him with every interaction. Most of the time, it was him making petty demands, but I could also read it in the unspoken lift of his eyebrows and focus of his eyes. Entire threats could be conveyed in the subtle tilt of his head: 'Don't forget, I'm the one who feeds you.'

He was right; he did feed me, and I was grateful for that and for him. So, despite his control issues, I respected him, man to man, even though he didn't recognize me as such. It was because of my respect and love for him that when he relayed his random cherry-picked religious wisdom to me, I accepted it. He would often say:

"The upper hand is better than the lower hand," quoting from Muhammad's* tradition:

"The upper hand is better than the lower hand (i.e., he who gives in charity is better than him who takes it). One should start giving first to his dependents. And the best object of charity is that which is given by a wealthy person (from the money which is left after his expenses). And whoever abstains from asking others for some financial help, Allah will give him and save him from asking others, Allah will make him self-sufficient."[5]

I accepted his interpretation of this saying and his superiority complex as truth and counted down the days of my youth until I was the upper hand; I never wanted to suffer the humiliation of being the lower hand again. As I grew up, I carried on my father's same belief that when I gave, I expected to receive constant appreciation for it, which we needed because by having a demeaning view of the lower hand, we cut ourselves off from receiving. In order to replenish ourselves energetically, we had to feed off the control and power we could exert on those we gave to.

It was after I awakened, when I revisited the Prophet's* traditions with the eyes of my heart, that I was able to properly extract its wisdom. As all giving is energetic and no one owns energy, it is a force that passes through us; then, by definition, God is always the upper hand, and creation is always the lower hand. There was nothing anyone gave of themselves; the source of all giving was the same. He uses people to distribute His support to us, but ultimately, it is prompted when He sends His intention to the hand to give. The drain we feel when we give is not the result of the giving itself; it is the result of not knowing how to properly receive replenishment.

The realization that God was always the giver, and we were always the receivers, regardless of whose hand it came from, dissolved any lingering feelings of guilt or humiliation I had previously associated with accepting help. Because now, I was empowered with my knowledge and belief in the law of Charity, knowing that the rain and the clouds may appear to be separate, but they are one cycle.

In that understanding, I saw so clearly how my experiences with my father and ex-husband perfectly complimented each other. In experiencing being both the lower hand with my father and then the upper hand with my ex-husband, I learned that when done egotistically, it results in humiliation and exhaustion, respectively. By playing both roles, God was teaching me what being in those positions felt like, shaping me for the future to give gracefully with my right hand and receive gratefully with my left, in compassionate balance.

"One of the seven groups of people that will be granted shade on the Day of Judgment includes the one who gives charity but hides it so that even his left-hand does not know what his right hand has spent."[6]

– Muhammad*

God had also been priming me to stay in a constant state of gratitude (receptivity) by giving me a father who always expected appreciation. Gratitude is the energetic signature that communicates to God that we like something and, therefore, we want more of it. By emitting this signal often, it acts as a magnet, attracting to us what we appreciate. Incredibly, it's also the only thing we have to give because regardless of how much we receive, there is nothing of value that we possess that communicates love back to our creator apart from our gratitude. As an adult, I only had to make a slight tweak to the consistent practice of gratitude my dad had instilled in me by changing its direction from him to God, and in doing that I solidified my state of knowing that when I need something, God would provide it.

During a meditation once, while swimming in gratitude, this lovely prayer came to me:

God give my heart the strength, to hold my gratitude,
for your greatness.

Money and Men

It was only after taking an honest and vulnerable look at myself that I understood all the issues I had with men and money before were just an external projection of the internal dominance my masculine energy was exerting over my feminine energy. When I finally started valuing my own femininity, I realized that their worth was entangled. The masculine's suppression of the feminine only weakened them both, but when they were respectfully balanced, their worth amplified. The masculine could finally give freely, without fear of scarcity, knowing the feminine was open and receiving their replenishment. They could only work properly when they were a unified team.

After making so many internal changes and aligning my inner energies, my value soared. My external reality automatically adjusted to reflect my internal state of peace and abundance, whereas before, my desperation attracted other needy people. Now, in discovering my true power and validating myself, I attracted men who were equally confident in their own self-worth and abundance.

It was refreshingly awkward at first; after expecting a man to complete me for so long, I didn't know what external love relationships were supposed to feel like anymore now that I felt complete within. So, like everything else I had done during my time of discovery, my initial encounters with others were exploratory.

First, I practiced receiving from others without feeling humiliated or in debt. It started small with allowing people to gift me things and not gift anything back. Not because I was ungrateful but because I was teaching myself that people will continue to love me even if I accept their love and just say thank you. Perhaps because I was venturing out of my comfort zone not for the purpose of obtaining things but with the sincerity of honoring my intention to learn how to receive God's charity, once I opened that channel up, God sent many people to spoil me extravagantly. It was overwhelming at first, but the more I allowed myself to receive, the more it reinforced that my mechanisms for opening and receiving were working and getting stronger.

Eventually, I became comfortable receiving larger gifts, like jewelry, a car, and international trips from people, while still not giving anything back in return other than my presence. Although I knew this was the effect of my own energy, I also became curious to understand what the mentality of these people was like, that God was accessing to give so abundantly and freely. There was one person in particular who was exceptionally generous, so I made a real effort to pick his brain. I asked him about his mindset about money, and he said:

"If money is your problem in life, then you don't have a real problem."

I wanted to say this is something only a rich person would say, but I couldn't help but admit how wise and true these words were, based on the problems I had encountered in my life that no amount of money in the world could ever fix.

I asked him what his father taught him about money, and he told me a story about how his father would never go backwards. When he joined him on a business trip once, they accidentally left a carefully packed bag behind, but his father refused to go back for it, instead opting to stop somewhere along the way to rebuy the supplies. When he asked his father why, he said because money always comes back, but time can't be replaced, and breaking forward momentum to go backwards, wasted twice as much time.

His father also demonstrated to him at a young age how to trust with certainty the law of return. He watched him spend huge amounts of money on things that brought him joy and give generously to friends and family without fear or expectation. His father had probably never picked up a book about energy or spirituality in his life, and yet he was a master of the practical application of give and receive, understanding that money was just energy and it follows the same law of momentum and return as all other energy in life.

I observed his work ethic, and as expected, he worked exceptionally hard, but I noticed it was always with a genuinely happy demeanor and sense of urgency. He also celebrated small inconsequential wins that, if I were a business owner, I never would've even paid attention to, like when he made a sale on the first day of the month, no matter what the amount, he would react with the same level of happiness and gratitude I would expect from someone who just won the lottery. I asked him why, and he expressed his belief that it was a sign that he could expect even more success for the rest of the month, because energy attracts more of the same kind of energy.

He dealt with the same everyday problems as other business owners. He was always busy and very involved with the day-to-day operations of his business, and when he wasn't working, he spent a lot of time thinking about more ways to make money. But I never once saw him stress or complain about it or count it with the worry that he didn't have enough. Instead, he loved reminiscing about times when he spent huge amounts, leaving him with nothing left in the bank, and then within a day, he would get unexpected checks from customers that completely refilled his account. When he told me these stories, they were never laced with the idea that he was taking a risk by spending the money. Instead, his words emanated an unspoken faith that came alive in his reality.

I watched him diligently, waiting for the day he would break character and have a human moment, but he never did. Not once did I feel or hear him attach a drop of negativity or expectation to money at all; it was just the natural side effect of his own energy and momentum. The more he moved forward with joy and gratitude, the more money that would come, and it was that simple to him. I watched that simple ethos translate to a life of swimming in abundance. His blessings came in from every direction due to his positive, attractive mindset, his generosity with others, and all the value he provided to his satisfied customers.

After years of having almost no standards and basing what I would accept on what a man had to offer, God had sent an angel to kindly teach me that I set my standards and that likeminded people would immediately recognize my value and never require me to earn their respect. It was strange learning a merciful and gentle lesson from a man when I was only used to tough love, but by becoming gentle internally, the world became more gentle with me as well.

By not allowing men to give to me before, assuming they would use it to control me, I limited their innate mechanism to give and provide and suppressed my natural desire to receive. In breaking this order in the law of energy, I simultaneously emaciated myself and emasculated and weakened the men around me. I had to accept that I wasn't an island and that even though I was self-fulfilling, I still needed to participate in the world as I was designed to in order to live gracefully with my surroundings.

It was in the physics of charity, and accepting that by allowing men the privilege of providing for me without expectations, that it not only benefitted me, but also created space for them to increase their prosperity even more, that I could finally relinquish my fear that I owed them anything and could rejoice in the knowledge that by being cared for I was energetically assisting them in their prosperity. There was never any deceit in my acceptance of gifts offered, and if I ever felt like there was an expectation attached to it, then I outright refused it. But as I became more experienced at reading people's energy and intentions, I chose to only interact with those with healthy, abundant mindsets because I wanted to be around other people who reconfirmed my trust in how the world actually works.

As a disclaimer, please do not use these examples as guidance to give any of your belongings away; when it comes to giving, only follow your intuition. My primary use of charity was as a tool to uncover the spiritual blockages within myself that prevented me from receiving God's love and guidance, and to make our connection stronger. Many times, this did result in physical experiences of gifts and financial support, but those were just extras and were not the purpose of my journey.

Surrender to Serve Humanity

Ultimately, I couldn't fool myself. After going on the journey of discovering myself and the true meaning of Charity, at the end of the day, I couldn't deny how much I truly loved serving others.

There is a story about Muhammad* where each day, when he would leave his home, he would have to walk past his neighbor's house, who was an elderly woman. During the early days of him spreading his message of surrender, he was ridiculed like all prophets are initially, and so she would wait on the roof of her house for him to pass, then pour trash on his head. He never looked up at her, knowing that if he gave her a reaction, it would either encourage her to do more or it would energize an awkward tension between them. Neither of those options would add to their positive energy; it would only subtract. Since he knew how precious and holy energy was, he chose a neutral option and never looked back, opting to pretend nothing happened while moving forward.

Then, one day, after passing her house and not getting his usual welcome, he became concerned and checked in on her. He found that she was sick with no one to care for her, and as it was his normal practice to care for the sick and elderly, he asked permission to tend to her, which, of course, she granted. It's no surprise that shortly after spending time with him and experiencing his mercy in gently caring for her with no regard for how she treated him before, she became a believer.

<u>The story demonstrated:</u>

- His knowledge about energy and forward movement.

- When it was important to stay silent and do nothing, and

- That his message could only come alive and change hearts when it informed his acts. Evidencing that his thoughts, words, and actions were aligned.

I relay this story and illustrate how I use the knowledge I've gained to analyze any past prophet's behavior to show my process of extracting their wisdom so that I can replicate it. Being as close to God as the prophets were is the crux of my aspirations as a spiritual person, and although I had reached great heights in my spirituality and connection, I was never satisfied. I read stories of the boundaryless giving by those bestowed with God's favor, and no matter how hard I tried, I could never reach their level. My mother's words rang caustically in my ears:

"You are not a prophet."… Sigh. I know.

My sister randomly asked me once:

"Who in the world do you admire the most? " and without thinking twice, I responded, "Jesus*."

I didn't expect her face to light up with genuine amused shock. We both looked at each other silently, stunned for a moment, until she recovered and asked with lighthearted confusion:

"Why do you want to be like Jesus*?"

But I was equally baffled by her reaction, and so I offered a question as my response.

"Doesn't everyone want to be like Jesus*?"

I had never taken the time to think about why I wanted to be like the prophets. Perhaps I believed that God loved them more. Or maybe to egotistically prove my own belief that they were sent as an example for humanity, and by successfully emulating them, I could evidence our ability to do what they did. But probably even more honestly, I was jealous of them; as a second-born child, I had never left the mentality behind of competing for Dad's love. When I reached the peak of my intuitive abilities and compared my best day to their normal day, I saw how short I fell and that I couldn't compete. I had to accept my limitations, but I just couldn't understand: "Why hath thou forsaken me?"

My answering thoughts followed in quick succession:

'I am weak. I hate being weak.'

Then, a moment of clarity opened the door for the voice to speak:

'Wait, I'm weak, but why do I hate that? Why am I judging my weakness?'

'The limitations are there for a good reason, they are trying to tell you to stop striving. Stop trying. Just be. Every time you strive, you will be pulled back because that is not what you are supposed to do. You're supposed to receive.'

I thought I had finally gotten a hold of my judgment, and yet there it was, casting stones at my limitations. However, through the skills I gained in being able to quickly realign with my heart and clearly hear its wisdom, I was able to look at my limitations from a higher perspective and recognize how they benefited me. My limitations were a natural barrier to stop me from wasting my time and effort when I had done enough, and my next step was to stop striving and to receive.

Although I had done so much work to balance the giving and receiving energies within me, I noticed that the prophets had a much larger capacity than me to give charity and receive Source energy, and it was in that observation that I realized why my comparison was unfair. For so long, I had put the cart before the horse and tried to measure myself according to their example **after** they firmly established their connection to God, without first patiently establishing the practices they took years to master before gaining the ability to serve humanity. I learned that the order and timing were crucial because although there are stories about their goodness before, it wasn't at the same level as it was after their time of solitude and enlightenment.

<u>Surrendering Self to Serve</u>

As I mentioned many times before, every prophet to ever exist, spent years cultivating their practices of intentional silence, meditation, prayer, fasting, and charity before they reached enlightenment. I thought by 'doing' the same actions, eventually, I would reach enlightenment as well, but I missed a step by not paying attention to what they were 'not doing,' which was equally important. My limits were diligently trying to teach me that I was correct to first lead with my masculine effort and establish the practices, but then eventually, I had to stop exerting and allow my feminine to be carried over the threshold.

I thought I had balanced my masculine and feminine energy when I started receiving, but there was more to it. I not only had to accept help, but I also had to relinquish any form of effort whatsoever in order to allow the flow to carry me. My feminine could only stand on what my masculine had built, but she could not build with him; she could only reap what he sowed. Otherwise, there would be no open hand for the fruits to fall into, and they would both suffer. She wasn't even allowed to pick the fruit; her only job was to stay open and patient. YIKES.

The secret was so obvious that I missed it because I judged, mocked, hated, and divorced it. But here he was, back to say his final 'I told you so.' The secret was the void.

Initially, I had loosely translated the concept of the void to mean not working hard, so I did things with ease and relaxed more. But now I had to wrap my head around its true meaning of doing nothing at all. The thought made my brain collapse in on itself. I couldn't even 'do' nothing because that was still implying an action. I had to be nothing.

In the introduction chapter, I told a story about Muhammad's wives conspiring to tell him his breath was offensive so that he wouldn't spend more time with one of his wives who had a special honey he liked, but it gets more interesting. After figuring out what they were up to, he made an oath in front of one of them that he would never eat that honey again in order to appease and keep the peace between them (and so his breath wouldn't stink). He asked her to keep it a secret, as a prophet's oath is not a light matter, but shortly after, he received a revelation that he wasn't allowed to forbid himself from something God had not forbidden him from, and so she told his secret. It was the straw that broke the camel's back because, on top of the collusion, lying, and indiscretion, for some time, they had been complaining to him about wanting to live more luxurious lives. He had access to the wealth of his nation and could easily justify spending more money on himself and his family, but he valued a simple life and wanted them to follow his example. He had finally hit his limit, and in anger, he vowed to live in meditative seclusion for a month, giving everyone a chance to think about their priorities. When he returned, he was cheerful, and in his refilled state, he was given another revelation with a generous offer for his wives. They could either choose to stay with him and live a simple life, or they could leave with a generous payout. They all chose to stay.

I like this story for the most unobvious reason - because he gets mad. It always impressed me way more to read stories of prophets dealing with real-life issues and responding in the most human way rather than with their elevated emotions of love, compassion, and mercy. It showed that they had their limits, too, and to resolve it, they had to go back to their most basic practice: silent meditative seclusion, essentially becoming nothing. The difference between us, I found, was that I judged my limits and didn't give myself enough time as nothing, and I could work on that, or more accurately, not work on it.

Once the prophets had established their daily practices to be so embedded into their lives that their actions became an automatic program. They could then surrender to the momentum their actions created, allowing God's Will to move them easily due to their total lack of resistance. They never stopped their practices; they still needed to refill, but they balanced doing with not doing.

I'm Not A Prophet, I'm A Pen

When we acquire any skill, initially, we expend so much energy to study, understand, practice, and perfect it. But eventually, a day comes when everything clicks, and we can do it with our eyes closed and our hands tied behind our backs. It's not that it doesn't take any movement to, let's say, play the piano, but it doesn't take any conscious mental or emotional exertion.

Whereas before, I might have to think about what I want to play, or which keys make which sounds, or battle with my inner insecurities about whether I am getting better or if I should just quit because I'll never be the best. All of those little internal pangs are hurdles we run into that cause us to expend energy to jump over them. So, for a long time, when we are learning a new skill, it feels like a zero-sum game. We receive as much energy from the joy of doing it as we give away to acquire it.

But one day, when the hurdles lessen and don't slow our momentum, we not only get to keep the energy we used to expend on them, but we also get to add the energy of the joy we've cultivated. This doubles the energy of that momentum and fills our cup so much that it has no choice but to spill over. It's like the difference in effort between building a boat and riding it. We can't build forever. Eventually, we have to let go of perfecting the boat so that we can enjoy the ride but know that all good boats require maintenance.

Like when I acquired the skill of writing, for so long, I practiced and was terrible at it, but then one day, everything clicked, and while writing, I just disappeared for a while. When I came back, hours had gone by, and there were words on pages that I knew I typed, but when I read them, it was as if I was just the first one to discover them rather than the one who wrote them. I didn't even feel tired, just content. By allowing the momentum of my writing practice to take over and being an empty, willing vessel for words to pass through, I could access unlimited words and give them without feeling drained or needing boundaries.

In trying to emulate every aspect of the prophet's existence, I sold myself short in believing that I was lesser because I could never be them. When I stopped comparing myself to them and what they could do, it opened my mind to find my connection to Source and purpose in life and made me realize how ridiculous being jealous of them was because we all have our own unique ways of serving God and humanity, and mine was to surrender to God's charity of words that came through me.

"If all the trees on the earth were pens,
and the ocean with seven more oceans were ink.
Yet these would not suffice to record all the Words of God.
God is Majestic and All-Wise."
- Quran 31:27

For so long, I had the deep longing desire to serve people, but I didn't know how to do that in a way that left me feeling energized and not drained; I began to think I might be too sensitive to ever be around anyone else's energy. But then, a few days ago, I experienced my own revelation from my younger sister, but it felt so divine it may as well have been from God.

She had volunteered to proofread my pages, so immediately, when I completed a chapter, I would send it to her to provide notes. She would probably never read a book like this of her own choice, as religion and God held no interest for her. She is the same sister who, shortly after her child was stillborn, declared that 'God is Evil,' but she loves me and would do anything for me, so she read.

After a while, I noticed a peaceful change in her and asked what she was doing differently. She tucked her head slightly down, an unconscious maneuver indicating she was bracing herself, knowing that her words would even surprise her, and said:

"I started praying."

There is neither enough silence nor enough words in the world to convey what hearing that has done for me. If God has sent this entire book and all the experiences I had to endure to write it just for her. Then, I can say, with the most certain conviction, that it was all worth it.

What Success Looked Like

My mom and I were sitting outside together on a beautiful sunny day when she casually looked at me and made an observation and then a suggestion:

"You pray a lot. You should start looking for a place to live and get a job."

"Ouch, are you just kicking me out like that." (covering my hurt with a soft laugh)

"There is no honor in praying all day; even the Prophet* and his companions worked."

Trust

It had been a year since my divorce, and although it stung an old memory to feel my mom pull her support from me, by this point in my studies and self-discovery practices, I knew what was happening. God saw that I was becoming dependent on her charity, and he wanted to remind me that it only ever comes from him.

Without delay, I looked for a job and a house, and only one week later, by divine timing and will, I signed both contracts. By the end of the month, I was gone.

Because I didn't have a job when I first bought the house, I couldn't get a mortgage, so I found one I could afford to buy with the cash I had in my savings. I spent every penny I had, so the house was completely empty for a long time until I could afford furniture. We slept on the carpeted floors for a few nights until a floor mattress arrived; a couple of weeks later, my sister gave me her patio table so we didn't have to eat sitting at the fireplace. As a housewarming gift, my mom bought me a couch. Slowly, it was becoming a home rather than a shelter. Then, one day, a friend I hadn't spoken to in 17 years randomly reached out to me.

As we were catching up, I mentioned that I had just bought a house, and he kindly interrupted me to ask if I needed any work done on it. He just so happened to be in the home remodeling business, and I thought he was selling his services, so I honestly told him that I couldn't afford any remodeling at the moment but that I would keep him in mind when I was ready. He laughed and then corrected my understanding. He started by reminding me of a big favor I did for him long ago; he said that he never forgot about my kindness and wanted to repay me now by remodeling my house for free. I was shocked; I hadn't thought about what I did for him at all; what registered for him as big was just normal for me.

I thanked him for his generous offer and accepted it. The house was built in the 70s, so there was a lot of dark wood paneling on the walls, a bar in the middle of my living room I would never use, and the kitchen was very dark and closed off. It drove me crazy, so I asked if he could make it brighter and more open. The next day, he arrived, took measurements, and two weeks later, I had a brand-new kitchen, soft white walls, a beautiful simple lighting fixture where the bar used to be, tile in all the bathrooms, and curtains on the windows, and he wouldn't accept a penny for it.

It was a watershed moment. After years of being closed off from receiving, when I initially opened up, there were years of suppressed emotions (and lessons) that came to the surface in quick succession, needing to be healed. I spent that entire year living with my mom in my room, just processing what had happened to me up until that point in my life and mentally unraveling the pain so that I could see the truth of what those experiences came to teach me about charity.

In discarding my childish beliefs about giving being about exerting power over others, and receiving being humiliating, and accepting that give and receive energy must be balanced within and outside of us, I theoretically knew and understood the concept of charity, but now God wasted no time in my intellectual stagnancy. He immediately uprooted me and put me to the test, saying: 'You say you trust that I will provide for you, but are you willing to step into the unknown, with the certainty that I will catch you'?

I could see his hand guiding every step in my progression; it was by his divine timing that he inspired my mother to give me a gentle push out; it was by his will that I found a house and a job waiting for me and it was by his charity that he sent people to support me abundantly.

He showed me that what I had learned about charity was useless unless I walked in my conviction of its truth, which, as with every lesson - required deeper and deeper levels of trust to be successful. Charity was one of the scariest of all the pillars for me to adapt to because although it is nice to receive, I had a fear of receiving, which made giving easier for me. For others, it is frightening to let go of our belongings and beliefs because we earned them painfully, so being asked to release that hard-earned wealth or knowledge at the risk of being exposed to pain or loss again can feel vulnerable and unsettling.

But it is when we toe the fine line between detachment from the physical world and refocuse our faith in God, that the laws of give and receive come alive within us. In feeling that shift and balance within myself, it transformed the way I value myself, strengthened my connection to God, and changed my relationship with the world around me from feeling like I was in a harsh foreign environment to a gentle, loving (albeit temporary) home. The impact of understanding and grounding the lessons I learned about charity was tangible, deep, and personal. This is why everyone's journey through charity will be different and according to their soul's needs, and as such, success will look different for someone else than it does for me. But for me, success is trusting that when I need help, someone comes.

God took me on this journey of charity to show me that charity is not turning the other cheek and allowing others to use me as a doormat. That misunderstanding of what it meant to be a kind and charitable person made me resentful, angry, and empty. God was showing me that charity didn't just mean the rich among us giving to the poor. We are all poor compared to God, and in order to love others unconditionally, I had to receive His charity first through becoming vulnerable enough to allow love in again. By being brave and diligent enough to fill myself first, I gave to others by just showing those around me the power of self love, flexible boundaries, and forgiveness, and demonstrated how to use that energy to receive the unlimited gifts and charity within ourselves.

"Every act of kindness is charity."[8]

-Muhammad*

Charity Flow

The whole time, I thought with my honest heart I was giving.
I was actually expecting.
My sin.
Not allowing dreams to die.

Dreams of limitation and scarcity.
Caused me to believe that when I gave,
I should be appreciated, I should be obeyed.
"Money doesn't grow on trees."

Mistaking giving for Charity.

Not all giving is charity, but all charity is giving.
An understandable mistake,
For a child to make.

I was 33 years old the first time I experienced true Charity.
I had experienced kindness and giving before then,
But the true essence of the word Charity. I finally felt.

Charity is standing in the presence of God.

We give to taste,
to remember,
that everything will be ok.

When you come back,
You realize it's everywhere.
Every breath,
Every drop of water, a charity.

An endless supply that keeps recycling itself.
The intelligence crippling.

We don't notice it, because its normal.
The normal state of our existence is to be drowned in Charity.
Asking why nothing good ever comes to me.
While breathing.
While witnessing.
While understanding.
Only possible through Charity.

Believing it is ours to own.
Not knowing it's borrowed on borrowed time.
One day the Charity will end, and we will know just how much
we had.
That we had no hand in creating.
Created on our behalf. For our pleasure.

How much would you sell your awareness for?
Priceless. Yet it was given freely.
Charity.
If you had to make a new one, would it be superior or inferior?
Charity.

Charity is not just giving a few dollars away, or feeding the poor.
It is also not just about love, or care, or kindness.
Charity is detaching from what is false, so we can remember
what is real.

Curious about what it would be like to not have everything all
the time.
We play the game of rich and poor.

Needing this point of relativity,
To appreciate our eternal truth.

In this game we mistakenly believe we own the things on loan,
Either giving them away sparingly,
fearing we won't have enough for tomorrow,
Or giving generously,
Only to learn that Vampires are real.

The truth
We don't give Charity, Charity gives through us.
Nothing is ours to give.

In the process,
Of allowing charity to give through you,
You also open the portal to receive.
It is one in the same.

The more you give, the more you get.
The less you need, the more you gain.
The rich get richer. The poor get poorer.
A universal law, witnessed by all.

A medieval castle with a long tower appeared on the screen of my mind. I entered it. The cold, dark emptiness welcomed me in.

Every footstep echoed on the bare walls, and I found myself drawn toward the tower's winding staircase. It started off wide with little windows on the outer facing wall, but as I walked up and got higher, the steps became narrower, and the windows became smaller, eventually disappearing.

Compelled by an impulse to keep going up, I didn't know what I was looking for or why I was there, but instinctively I knew to keep walking higher.

Gradually, without noticing, I found myself walking in pitch-black darkness.

It was so dark; the only way I knew I existed was because I could sense my foot on a step.

Overcome with fear, I yelled out:

"Jesus*, Muhammad*, please come help me!"

To my surprise, they came immediately.

I recognized them by their presence without being able to see them.

Jesus* instinctively knew what was wrong, and before I could speak, he sympathized:

"You're afraid because it's dark, you don't know where you're going, or if there is something out there that will hurt you. Don't worry. Keep going."

The reassurance of his presence took me forward another few steps.

Alone again, I looked out and saw nothing. It was so disorienting I couldn't differentiate between outside and inside myself anymore.

I was about to tremble when Jesus* came back, having sensed my fear again. His presence strengthened me once more. I felt myself uncurling and standing up straight, I looked out with him into the vast nothingness when he gave me his final departing words:

"I know you are looking out and seeing darkness,

but the darkness is looking at you,

and it sees the light.

Keep going."

Chapter 5: Pilgrimage

"Even if they place the sun in my right hand, and the moon in my
left, on the condition that I abandon this path,
I would not abandon it, even if I perish in the course of it."[1]
-Muhammad*

I never felt any different when I turned 18 and legally became an adult. But two years prior, when my father left us, and I stepped into his role as man of the house, I felt a huge shift. It was the day I officially stopped being a child and became a man.

I also never felt any different after my wedding day. I thought in marriage, I would feel like a woman, but it wasn't until my son was born that he made me know what being a woman truly meant.

They were my rites of passage, and although they are different for everyone, they all have the same three phases: Separation, Transition (testing, growth, and learning), and Return.

My first rite of Separation was my birth and childhood. My mother delivered me from eternal love to a cold, harsh world, and it was during those difficult childhood years that I shut down my senses to block the pain, and by doing so, I also unintentionally blocked the love.

My second rite of Transition occurred when my father left and my son arrived. The two most important men in my life shaped and opened me, preparing me for the final phase of my journey - Knowing Thyself.

Because it is only by remembering who we are, that we Return.

What is Pilgrimage?

Pilgrimage is a commitment.

Traditionally, it is thought of as a path or road, but whether we are aware of it or not, we are all on the path. The difference between a path and a pilgrimage is our commitment to keep moving forward, regardless of hurdles or whether someone offers to put the sun in our right hand and the moon in our left. It is also not a one-time commitment; we recommit with each step in our journey, one right after the other.

Every day is Day 1. Every step is the first step. The commitment is what binds us to our destiny.

For some time, while on the path of life, I was just walking aimlessly. I thought I was chasing my dreams, but what I was actually doing was swaying with the external currents of other people's expectations. It seemed like a fun sport at first, where I competed with them and their definition of success to prove my worth, but eventually, I lost interest in the game when I realized it was a never-ending dead end.

I have no doubt that getting lost was necessary for my self-discovery because I needed to experience what doesn't fill me to find what does. The pain of emptiness was the catalyst that snapped me out of my external delusion and forced me to change the direction of my consciousness to look where I never thought to look before: inside. At first, looking inside felt dark and foreign, so initially, my commitment was just to take the steps necessary to find my internal guidance. But as that guidance grew stronger and louder, my commitment changed from finding it to following it, regardless of where it took me.

After making the commitment to being led from within, I had to enter a state of ihram, which is a sacred spiritual purification beautifully captured by its ritual cleansing ceremony.

This is necessary because when I first made the change to prioritize my inner world, I realized just how neglected it was. I had thoughts and memories from way back in my childhood that I had never dealt with, and because they were ignored, they kept coming up and poking at the surface of my mind to get my attention. This caused so much noise inside that I knew before I could properly discern and follow my internal guidance, I had a lot of cleanup work to do.

So naturally, we start the purification ritual with a physical shower, which symbolizes our inner spiritual cleansing away from judgment and attachment. That way, when my memories resurfaced, they were no longer distorted by false beliefs and could be observed impartially.

The next step was to cloak myself in a garment so humble it does not even contain a single stitch – Humility. Regardless of whether a person is royalty or a slave, we all wear the same cloth, which is the same one we are wrapped in when we are buried. As a mental state, humility opens the door for our consciousness to transition from the limited perspective of our ego to an expanded state of our higher consciousness. Humility worn as a cloak allows us to safely revisit our childhood memories so that we can understand the lessons that were missed due to our limited understanding of life, while also protecting us from the fire and pain that comes with those memories.

We must do this because, as children, the lens we captured our lives with was so small, and as adults, we have bigger lenses now, so we can look back at old memories with a wider frame and see the bigger picture of our experiences. When we don't go back to look with our higher perspective of life, then it is as if our lens has gotten bigger, but the aperture we capture life with is still small, and although we are capable of seeing more, we limit ourselves. Wow, who knew all those times my ex-husband spoke his camera jargon at me I would actually retain it, and that it would come in handy one day. Even his addictions and constant need for the newest and best camera on the market held spiritual lessons for me.

When I looked back with humility, all I had to do was watch as the light of truth burned down all the veils of ignorance and false beliefs that maliciously enveloped my inner child for so long, which allowed me to clearly see with an elevated perspective the memories that used to plague me, transform into invaluable lessons and wisdom.

"The child who is not embraced by the village,
will burn it down to feel its warmth."
-African Proverb

Once my inner world had been purified, I instinctually desired the next step, which was to cut my hair. Since hair retains the energy of the thoughts stored in our head, because my thoughts had been negative for so long, I craved cutting it all off. However, women are only required to cut an inch off, while men are required to shave their heads.

After completing this sacred ritual, I was finally ready to step over the holy threshold with clarity and respond to the all-consuming call coming from deep within my heart. It was an intention guiding me on my life's true path with clear instructions. It was asking me now to consent through my free will, to commit to and obey my inner guidance for the rest of my life. My heart was ready, so it responded immediately, with each beat forever chanting internally the holy commitment of all pilgrims:

"Here I am, O Allah, here I am,
I submit and submit again."[2]

Mysticism of Pilgrimage

Hagar*

Abraham's* certainty was impenetrable. God tested him time and again, and each time, he reaffirmed that the only life he wanted was the one God chose for him. Without expectations or attachments, he lived off his trust, and in doing so, he was elevated as the father of three nations, Judaism, Christianity, and Islam, which account for over 50% of the world's population today.

But this story is about his second wife, Hagar*, whose name means flight or forsaken. In it, she personifies the rites of passage while establishing the most physically intense aspects of our modern-day pilgrimage.

The Separation:

Her story begins with a terrifying command: God instructs Abraham* to take Hagar* and his infant son Ishmael* to a remote part of the desert and abandon them with no visible resources for food or water.

By obeying the command, he triggers the first rite of passage. The masculine becomes separated from the feminine, and as a refugee in a foreign place, she wanders aimlessly, eventually settling in a valley between two mountains.

When the water she was left with runs out, and she can no longer nourish herself to breastfeed her baby, she painfully leaves him behind to search for help. To get a better vantage point, she runs to one of the mountains and climbs to the top. When she sees that the desert is desolate, she climbs back down and runs across the valley to the other mountain, but again, she sees no one who can help her.

The Transition:

Even though she was dehydrated and exhausted, the sound of Ishmael's* desperate cries in the distance pushed her forward. Fearing his imminent death, her survival instincts kicked in and filled her with an energy that she did not have. It gave her the power to run back and forth between the two mountains - 7 times, and although it was fueled by her desperation, it was her hope that would get her to the top of the mountain. Once at the top, her hope would be crushed by her disappointment when, each time, she found no one who could help her.

Not only is her transition memorialized in the physical act of Hajj each year by millions of Muslims, but she also perfectly captured humanity's daily plight. The two mountains she runs between spiritually represent the extreme ends of our emotional pendulum, positive/negative, high/low, feast/famine, and hope/despair, which whip us back and forth in life. The cycle begins when we believe the external illusion, causing us to reach so high in our pursuit of happiness, and then crash back down into despair when we find out that all our hard work has been for an illusion. The cycle continues with each new hope and ends when we realize it always results in a dead end.

There is also deep meaning in her 7 trips back and forth. The number 7 is a universally holy number that means completeness and perfection. It is not only holy within a religious context, like the 7 days of creation or the 7 heavens, but also within the fabric of our universe. Just to name a few, there are 7 colors in a rainbow, 7 musical notes, 7 oceans, 7 days in a week, 7 chakras (energy centers) in the body, 7 visible planets in the sky, and every 7 years, there is a total spiritual change within our body, which is mirrored by the fact that every cell in our body replaces itself within 7 years.

When Muhammad* was asked how to raise children, he said:

> "Play with them for the first 7 years.
> Then teach them for the next 7 years.
> Then advise them for the next 7 years."[3]

We live our lives in these 7-year cycles, and our body is programmed to naturally release the energy necessary to push us forward through our stages of transition and evolution. Similar to how Hagar* was pushed forward by a force within herself to keep running between and climbing the mountains in search of help, even when she thought she had nothing left in her. In the present day, we experience this energy in the form of crisis years that cause us to have massive transformations to get us to the next stage in our rite of passage. I experienced this when I was 33 and had an explosive midlife crisis, which caused me to question the meaning of life and throw everything I had built away in search of the truth, despite being completely drained.

The Ptolemaic system calls these "The Seven Ages of Man"[4], and notes that each stage coincides with a planet and a chakra (energy center) within the body. For example:

The first stage lasts from 0 – 7 years old, and is associated with the <u>moon</u> and the <u>root</u> chakra.

This stage represents our state of innocence, and because we are born into a world that we have no knowledge of, our first goal is to root and ground ourselves to it. In our childhood, our mind is like a dark, clear sky, due to our limited knowledge and experience, and it's also when we form our first perception of life. So when the moonlight is the first light we see, we mistake it for the true light, not knowing that the moon has no light of its own, and only reflects the light of the sun. By accepting that false belief, we form and become rooted in our first innocent illusion.

Abraham* was 14, the age when a boy traditionally becomes a man, and at the end of his second 7-year stage, when he found enlightenment using a strikingly similar logic:

"So also did We show Abraham the power and the laws of the heavens and the earth, that he might (with understanding) have certitude.

When the night covered him over, he saw a star, he said: "This is my Lord." But when it set, he said: "I love not those that set."

When he saw the moon rising in splendor, he said: "This is my Lord." But when the moon set, he said: "Unless my Lord guide me, I shall surely be among those who go astray."

When he saw the sun rising in splendor, he said: "This is my Lord; this is the greatest (of all)." But when the sun set, he said: "O my people! I am indeed free from your (guilt) of giving partners to God. For me, I have set my face, firmly and truly, towards Him who created the heavens and the earth, and never shall I give partners to God." [5]

We see him move through the same stages of innocence, mistaking false light for God's light, and then when the largest one sets, he realizes that they were all temporary illusions. He then makes an oath that he is free of illusion and, going forward, will only face one God.

Although we don't call our external attachments and beliefs our Lord, when we innocently accept them deeply, we

312

unknowingly allow them to control our behavior. When anything controls us, whether consciously or not, it becomes our master, and in so, we have adopted 'partners' with God.

Many think that polytheism is the simple belief in more than one God, but for me, it was much more sinister than that, because it wasn't something I was conscious of. I truly considered myself a monotheistic believer until I tried to change my habits and focus on my inner guidance, only to discover that my intentions, thoughts, and actions couldn't align because of all the false beliefs and addictions I held inside. Abraham* described the telltale sign of polytheism as there being 'chaos and no peace' in the world if there is more than one God, which exactly described my inner world, and it was then that I woke up to my own hypocrisy.

Abraham* was obviously wise and gifted at a young age, but within that short story of his enlightenment, he perfectly captures the essence of what the Ptolemaic 7 stage system explains. Which is that as we age and move up through the 7 energy centers from the bottom root to the top crown, we continually upgrade our beliefs until we reach the final stage of complete self-knowledge.

The Return:

It was after Hagar's* 7th trip up the mountain, while fully exhausted and defeated, that she finally accepted there was nothing out there that could save her. As she absorbed the weight of what her failure meant, she looked down at Ishmael*, and to her great surprise, there was a stranger standing over him. Running down to them, she arrived and found it was Angel Gabriel*, who then struck the ground with his heel, causing a spring of water to gush forth.

In Mecca, that same Zamzam well still provides abundant water to this day, and it truly is physically located between the two mountains, spiritually symbolizing life's secret. That the source of life is hidden between the two extreme ends of the energetic pendulum. In order to find the middle way, we have to balance our energy and harness the power of peaceful momentum.

The fact that it is hidden reveals two lessons:

<u>First, it serves as a reminder to humanity that we were never forsaken:</u>

Although the well wasn't immediately visible until Gabriel* brought it to the surface, we must note that Hagar* was actually standing on top of it the entire time.

It is in this epic game of hide and seek where we allow our knowledge of source to be hidden, to catapult us into the first stage of separation. Here, we play by going far and high into the illusion, searching for the help and happiness that we know is our birthright, but after long enough riding the painful rollercoaster of hope and disappointment, we realize that we must do something different in order to have a different outcome. It is when Hagar* accepts that there is no water out there that the spark of inspiration within her is lit, and she learns to transition the direction of her consciousness from outside to inside. This return to her inner reality (through intuition) allows her to find that she already has everything she needed right underneath the surface and reassures her that it was all just a game.

Another random but interesting similarity worth noting is that both Muhammad* and Hagar* received Gabriel's* help when they were in near-death experiences. Muhammad*, when he tried to throw himself off a mountain due to his despair, and Hagar*, who was also on a mountain experiencing despair and dehydration. As we know, the brain releases its highest levels of DMT, the molecule that pierces the veil between the physical and spiritual world, right before death. So this could also explain why her senses were so heightened that she could pierce the veil of the spiritual world and physically see an Angel. In a way, it's comforting to know that if we never learn to turn our attention inwards, right before death, we release the chemicals necessary to do it on our behalf, and perhaps that has saved many people.

<u>Secondly, it illustrates the holy nature of duality:</u>

Duality creates relativity, without which knowledge of self is meaningless. Einstein knocks on the door of my mind as I say this, but I only nod to him, knowing the depths he can go into when he speaks about relativity, so instead, I settle for a simple example: magnets.

Duality is comparable to a magnet that experiences the illusion of separation (time and space) through a split in consciousness. Each of its north and south poles is given half the total awareness, and because their perspective is so opposite, they cannot fathom that they are connected to one another, and experience the world completely differently. It isn't until the consciousness that was split, finds the hidden center of the two poles that the time/space illusion of two collapses, and returns to one whole consciousness.

The reason this duality is necessary is because our eternal state is oneness. In order to gain a complete understanding of ourselves, we must know what we aren't to value what we are.

"Travel (safar) is named by this name,
because it reveals (yusfir) the true character of men."[6]
- Al-Qushayri

Finally and poetically, the well is named Zamzam, because once Gabriel* struck the ground and the water appeared, Hagar* fearing they would lose it, cried out, "Zom! Zom!" (Stop! Stop!), then created an enclosure with sand to stop it from spreading too far. Years later, Muhammad* would observe:

"May Allah have mercy upon the mother of Ishmael. If she had not hastened to take water, the Zamzam well would have become a flowing spring."[7]

I had been on that rollercoaster my entire life, allowing the momentum of my hope and despair to fling me back and forth. Then, just like Hagar*, when I would get a little taste of love, I would cling to it like my life depended on it, suffocating how vast it could get. At the beginning of my journey, I thought that traveling along a path only meant effort and hard work, but I learned the hard way, when my limits hit me, that although I wanted to climb so much higher, I was forced to stop. In that, I mistook God's favor for me to relax as a punishment since he did not give me the power to work harder. It was in that still and silent state that I learned how to energetically open up to receive from Him the water I needed and not the help I wanted. By immortalizing the name of the well, Hagar* forever reminds us that after all our hard work, the only way to find the water is to "Stop! Stop!"

Muhammad's* Night Journey

The Heart and Middle Way

Muhammad's* tradition is centered around moderation, which was tested by Gabriel* the night he experienced the journey up and beyond the 7 heavenly realms to commune with God. Before he could start the journey, he was given a choice of beverages: Either a glass of water, milk, or wine. His natural instincts told him not to pick the very rich nor poor options, and so he reached for the milk.

Gabriel* affirmed that he made the correct selection, and together they accessed the heavens. At each of the 7 levels, he found a different prophet waiting to meet him, and they all shared the same loving greeting with each other:

"Welcome, O pious prophet and brother."[8]

Heaven	Prophet	Name Meaning	Chakra
1 – Lowest	Adam*	Ground, Earth	Root
2	Jesus* John*	Savior, and God is gracious	Sacral
3	Joseph*	God will give	Solar Plexus
4	Enoch*	Dedicated	Heart
5	Aaron*	Teacher, Exalted, Mountain of strength	Throat
6	Moses*	Drawn out of water	3rd Eye
7 – Highest	Abraham*	Father of many	Crown

	Muhammad*	His praiseworthy characteristics are abundant	

When he reached the highest heaven, he found Abraham* leaning against a structure called the 'Much-Visited House,' which is replicated here on Earth as the Kaaba (House of God) in Mecca. Its spiritual counterpart is said to be energetically located directly above the Kaaba, and angels are constantly circling it, just like the pilgrims do during Hajj. It should be no surprise that we go around it - 7 times.

Since all physical structure only exists as an image of its spiritual origin – "As above, so below"[9], it is very significant that Muhammad* found the spiritual Kaaba after traveling all the way up to the highest 7th heaven. Because we are made of a mind, body, and spirit within ourselves, all of those elements are tied together in such a way that through our body, we can access our spirit. Since the house of God on Earth is just a physical and external representation of His spiritual home, which we know is in our hearts, when we access our physical heart through prayer to connect with God, we are also directly connecting with His home in the highest spiritual heaven, no night journey required.

"The kingdom of God is within you."[10]
-Jesus*

The heart holds many mystical meanings, one of which is hidden in the names of Abraham* and Ishmael*, who built the Kaaba, and their names mean the "Father of many" and "God listens." God alludes through metaphor and the combined essence of their names that 'The Father of Many Listens' is symbolically the energy that built our hearts (the house of God), meaning that when we speak to our hearts in prayer, it was built by God to listen. It is only recently that science has finally discovered that water has memory; just wait until they discover what the heart is truly capable of.

During our pilgrimage to Mecca, we are required to physically revolve around the Kaaba, which reminds us of the two commitments that we and God have made with each other:

1. Our commitment to put God in the center of our life.

When we walk around the Kaaba, it symbolizes our free choice to make God the center of our lives. With each step, we reaffirm that we willingly want to obey the guidance from our hearts, and

2. God's greater commitment to live within us.

We may choose whether or not to walk around the Kaaba, but since it spiritually represents our heart and that is where God always resides, He shows us that we have the free will to choose to make Him the center of our lives, but He never leaves our center. Reassuring us that if our hearts are beating, He is with us; regardless of whether we commit to Him, He is always committed to us.

<u>**The Spirit and Consciousness**</u>

Muhammad* continued his journey to the top of the 7th heaven until he reached its uppermost boundary. There, he discovered the *Furthest Lote Tree*, which no One can pass, as it is the final limit before arriving at the throne of God. This tree is mentioned often by Buddha*, and his description is similar to Muhammad's*:

It was so huge "A rider could travel in the shade of one of its branches for 100 years," and it was so beautiful: "It was surrounded with golden butterflies and had colors which I did not know, and none amongst the creation has the power to praise its beauty."[11]

The Arabic word for this tree directly translates as – "terminates" because it terminates everything that comes up from below it and everything that comes down from above it.

Because angels do not have the 'knowledge' to go beyond its boundary, Gabriel* had to stop there, and Muhammad* had to travel the rest of his journey alone.

This pattern of "Stop! Stop!" presents itself once again.

Before being able to access the source, all awareness must stop, which is why angels cannot cross this boundary, they are not consciously aware beings. But before we lose our minds talking about annihilation and nothingness, I want to talk a little about the concept of consciousness, and its boundaries. I've said it before, but as a reminder, the mind is not our brain; it is our awareness.

When we focus our consciousness on anything, we naturally tune to its wisdom, such as when we pray/meditate with a gentle focus on the energy in our hearts. By matching into its soft and subtle frequency, we find that our thoughts are influenced to be more inspired and loving.

<u>The mind has three major sections of consciousness:</u>

God/Allah/Yahweh/Absolute Light/I AM

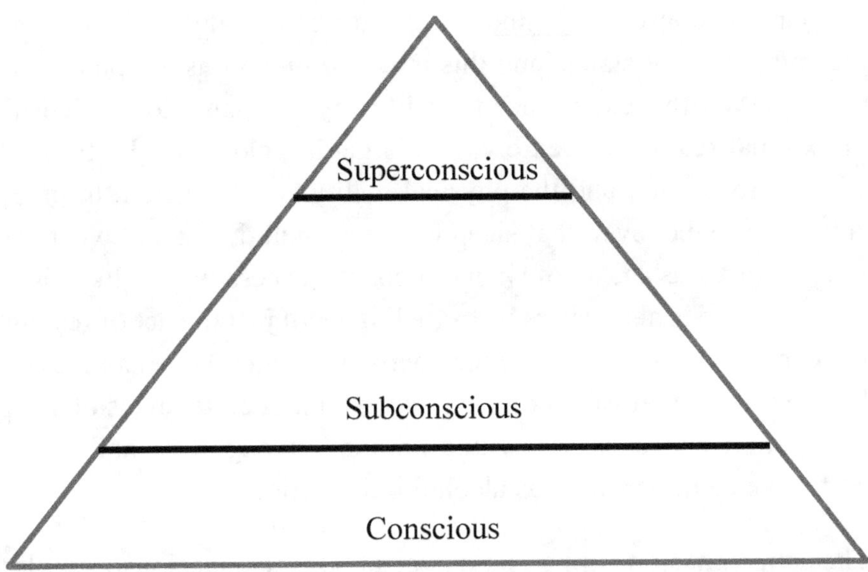

As we go up, the density of the information lessens, and there are boundaries between them. The conscious mind cannot travel to the subconscious and so forth. The major sections are further divided, for a total of – 7 states of consciousness[12], or "heavens."

Christ/Cosmic/Buddha Consciousness	Superconscious
Causal	
Mental	Subconscious
Higher Astral	
Lower Astral	
Emotional	
Physical	Conscious

<u>In our conscious mind,</u> we experience the densest reality through our five senses: touch, taste, smell, sight, and sound.

<u>In our subconscious mind,</u> we experience our imagination, dream/meditative states, and this is where intentions are planted in us. However, this experience feels illusory compared to the density of external reality. Incredibly, this is getting closer to the truth of who we really are, and the physical reality is the illusion. In many cultures, it is believed that sleep is like a small death, and when we sleep, it gives us a taste of what our consciousness will be like when we die. Sleep is also where we refuel; it is not just the act of resting, but connecting with the spiritual energy of home that revitalizes us. It is so critical that we reconnect, that even moderate levels of sleep deprivation can cause the same amount of cognitive and motor performance impairment as alcohol intoxication.

<u>The superconscious mind</u> is a universal cosmic consciousness, also known as nirvana or 7th heaven, which is appropriate because that is exactly where it is located, at the very highest level of our mind. Once our conscious and subconscious minds are aligned, i.e., our intentions match our thoughts, words, and actions. We can then attune to our superconscious mind anytime we are fully absorbed in doing anything that we truly love. A good indicator that we are there is that we feel lit up inside or we enter the flow state where we forget about time, rewards, and the world.

At this point, we reach the final boundary of the mind, and in order to discover the secret hidden beyond it, we have to annihilate what we perceive as self and leave separation behind so that we can return to Union. We've heard it called so many things: ego death, the void, terminating, becoming nothing – which is why Islam (surrender) was the last religion to be revealed to humanity. It is the final step that must be taken to experience our last rite of passage and return us to oneness - the complete surrender of self.

After Muhammad* surrendered his five senses, his intentions, dreams, thoughts, and awareness, he terminated everything that made him separate. Allowing him to successfully cross the boundary of duality and relativity, and merge into oneness. Little was said about this union, apart from one sentence in the Quran:

"Then Allah revealed to his servant what He revealed."[13]

The secret must stay a secret because no one likes a spoiler.

After he returned from this epic night journey, he didn't furiously lecture about the experience or double down on religious mandates to push others to experience oneness quickly. It was the exact opposite. He returned with only one piece of knowledge to share with humanity – Pray.

Serving as the single greatest tool to directly communicate with God, no matter what level of consciousness or surrender we are in, and confirming for us after seeing it for himself - That when we speak to our heart, God listens.

<u>How I Failed</u>

It was the nightmares about my son. Those were the worst.

Beyond the sleepless nights, the sickness, and the urgent care visits, and that one time, my nine-month-old fell off the bed at 3 am and hit his head on the tile, and we had to keep him up for an hour to make sure he wasn't concussed.

It was the nightmares that no one prepared me for.

I didn't know I could love someone that much, and because I didn't know how to love without attachment, the idea of losing them crippled me with anxiety. No one ever told me that was a normal part of your life after having a baby. I thought kids were physically and mentally demanding and exhausting, but I had no clue the toll they would take on my spirit. The amount of energy I spent keeping them from dying each day was constant, but I never calculated that I would spend my nights dreaming about losing them as well. I couldn't escape the fear.

The dream starts with me arriving at the scene of a car accident. I don't know how I got there, but I know it's him. He is 17 and just got his driver's license, and I just knew something like this would happen. He is not diagnosed as autistic, but he's always been different. He loves lining everything up, especially in order based on the colors of the rainbow. He doesn't like to socialize, always preferring his own company, and he is refreshingly honest in a painful way. We were playing together once when he told me:

"I wish there were two of me."

"Why?"

"I don't like playing with anyone else."

What he meant by that was, 'no one else knows how to play games the way I want to play them,' but his short, simple statement was the true essence of his point.

He made up games and worlds in his head all the time that were too elaborate for his limited language skills to convey. Often, I would see him sitting too still with his eyes softly unfocused, living in imaginary worlds that I couldn't join him in, no matter how badly I wanted to. I don't know if you have ever been around a kid like that, but their light is so pure. No matter how old they get, they never lose their innocence. His presence reminded me of a light within myself that was snuffed out so long ago, the stars in the sky seem nearer, and the air around him tastes like the juice of a cool Honeycrisp apple, so light and refreshing you can drink it in without ever getting full. He didn't like being touched or hugged, so I was never able to get my fill of him, the taste of his air was all I ever had.

Normally, just arriving at the scene of the accident was enough to jolt me awake. I would sit up to bring down my nausea and calm myself by repeating, 'It's just a dream,' but tonight was different. I was deep enough in my studies at this point that I knew this would haunt me forever if I didn't face it, so I allowed the nightmare to continue on.

I run to him. He's lying on the ground, face up and to the side. His body is too relaxed, sharply contrasting the severity of the scene, making me more alert, like when a mom realizes it's too quiet. I get closer and see that his eyes are closed, and he is completely still. I already know. I lower myself to kneel beside him, then gently hold his head between my hands, hoping he will react to the touch. Despite so much blood all around, I can't stop looking at his face, and I know.

The light is gone. His light is gone. My light is gone.

Although there is so much commotion around, no one dares to come near us. Without looking away from him, I sense them slow to witness a pain so holy and universal not a single word can convey it.

The feeling is so primitive, it takes me back to a time before words, only expressible by a howl, that comes from a place so deep and singular, it might be the sound that created the world.

The howl of separation.

He was gone.

My son had set.

It wasn't enough time, we needed more time, but it was my time now.

I had to sacrifice the largest sun in my dark sky.

I had to face the cold, dark, emptiness.

<u>What I Learned</u>

Big things start with a dream.

Abraham* also had a dream about his son dying, although his was different from mine. He believed he was being commanded to sacrifice him, a masculine take on the same idea. The man is asked to kill, while the woman is asked to let go. Illustrating again that masculine energy is active, while feminine energy is passive, but the pain we endure unites us.

His dream was so strong that he conveyed it to his son, who immediately accepted it and told his father to do as he is commanded. Abraham* knew his son's reaction was so unusual it had to be inspired by God, so he accepted it as a confirmation, and together, they went up the dreaded mountain of hope and despair for the final time.

For many our children are our first experience of true unconditional love, and spiritually, they represent our hope for a brighter future. Which is why we give everything we have to give them a better life than we had, and our primary instinct of survival diminishes when they are around because we would even willingly give our life for them to live on.

But I knew by this point in my journey that God uses dreams as metaphors to guide us, and that happiness cannot be found in the future. So, like Abraham*, I was also sent a dream forewarning of the death of my future as an initiation into the final stage of my pilgrimage.

Because in order to get past the last boundary that terminates everything and reunite with eternal oneness, I had to surrender everything, even my hope.

To Love and Be Loved

I had been on the journey to enlightenment my entire life, but it wasn't until I had my kids that I consciously committed to my pilgrimage. They were my first taste of holy unconditional love, and the intensity of that awareness altered me from being cold and detached from life, to finally having something I was afraid of losing. The nature of being a mother is within itself a pilgrimage because, essentially, it is a lifelong commitment to serving love, and so by becoming a mom, I activated the second phase of my pilgrimage, that transitioned me from ignorance to knowing.

I remember after I gave birth to my first son, when the nurse put him in my arms, I looked at him, and something in me ended. The wall I had spent years building to protect myself from love shattered in an instant, like magic, one look at this unbelievably small and perfect being that carried the whole of my love in him, and I was gone. I became as vulnerable as he felt in my arms, and although I experienced a love I never thought possible, with it came an equivalent amount of fear that completely consumed me. I was attached to him at a level I didn't even consciously understand, as if our DNA hadn't split and we were still somehow energetically entangled with each other. Even though he had a separate body, he felt like a raw piece of me, that was outside of me.

The love was sharply anchored in the depths of an ethereal place only mothers know. The womb has an intelligence of her own, and no one in existence has ever taught her more, or touched her more intimately than her children that come through her. They teach her the power she is capable of, that she doesn't just hold; she manifests the unmanifest. It is only through her merciful self-sacrificing essence that life is brought to the world, which is beautifully captured in a quote by Khaled Hosseini:

"A man's heart is a wretched, wretched thing.
It isn't like a mother's womb.
It won't bleed. It won't stretch to make room for you."

Which is why the first question anyone asks when a child is concerned is, 'Where was the mother?.' It is also why when we hear stories of mothers harming their children, it shakes us to our core. It goes against the fabric of the one truth we know about the world, that a mother's love is the highest, purest form of selfless love we experience on Earth. The connection between a mother and child is so strong, that the spiritual act of letting go of that connection is so painful, it would almost be more merciful to kill her.

This may explain why, in Islam, heaven is guaranteed for No One, apart from the woman who loses her child. There would be no point in sending her to hell, no matter what her misdeeds, because there is no fire that could burn her more deeply than the pain of losing her child. Muhammad* deeply understood this pain, he buried six of his seven children with his own hands.

I muse to myself and wonder, if that is why we seldom hear stories of women who have achieved ultimate unity, because of the almost insurmountable bond between a mother and child that must be broken to reach it. The Buddha* called his son, his 'ball and chain,' but was still able to leave him for years in search of unity. I never heard a similar story about a woman.

In Islam, the mother is elevated so high that Muhammad* used to say:

"Your heaven lies **under the feet** of your mother."[13]

He was also once asked by a man:

"O Messenger of God! Who among the people is the most worthy of my good companionship?"

Muhammad* responded: "Your mother."

The man said, "Then who"?

He responded again, "Then your mother."

The man further asked, "Then who"?

Again, he responded, "Then your mother."

The man asked one more time, "Then who"?

Finally, he said, "Then your father."[15]

In Islamic households, we hear the shortened version of this discourse echoed over and over: 'The mother, the mother, the mother, the father.'

This is not to take away from the father, who, as masculine energy, is so revered and elevated that even when we refer to God, who is genderless, we say 'Him.' My intention is not to pit energies against each other or determine who has it harder than the other. Both experiences to oneness, whether coming from the masculine or the feminine side of the magnetic poles, are equally harrowing; they are just different.

The reason I stress the feminine experience is because, in my research to gain enlightenment, it was so rare to see the plight and perspective of how feminine energy achieves oneness. So, since this is my story, and I am a woman, I wanted to illustrate what it feels like when a woman has to let go of everything and stress how difficult that is when it comes to our kids. At this state of consciousness, it feels cruel to force us to love something so much, only then to be forced to surrender it.

But as my journey of motherhood unfolded, I got to see the duality of loss from a heightened perspective, and from there, I could unlock the symbolism of my dream. For so long, as an individual, I had only ever experienced life as 'the one who is lost.' But when I became a mom terrorized with nightmares of losing her son, I got to experience what it was like to be 'the one who has lost something.' There is a merciful ignorance in being lost because, in that innocence, I didn't know what I was missing. But when I experienced losing someone I love, I knew what I was missing, and by far, it was a much more wretched experience.

It was with this fresh perspective that I could witness a higher truth, and where before I thought God was cruelly asking me to let go of my son, now I saw that He was just using the image of my son to convey a feeling to me in a way I would understand. By reversing our roles in my dream, God was inviting me by way of compassion – the shared suffering that unites, to experience the pain God felt when He lost me. It was an alchemical experience I had only experienced once before when, during the height of my physical suffering as a child, me and my father's pain would somehow merge us.

With that compassion, the *Genesis* story of creation comes to life because after biting the apple that reveals the knowledge of good and evil (duality), and being cast out of heaven (separation), to experience life (suffering). The only way to return home (to unity), is to realize that the knowledge given by the apple is a lie. It blinds us to only see half-truths until we figure out that compassion is the only tool that can combine and return us to seeing the whole truth.

I was so concerned with my own plight that I never considered that perhaps God felt pain too, but it made complete sense now; how could He not? He was everything. In using compassion through my dream and motherhood, He reunited us by teaching me that separation from oneness is painful for both parties involved. I had only understood separation as a theoretical and mechanical process before, as it had never occurred to me that I could commiserate with the Big Bang. Many religious beliefs and scientific theories agree that the world was created with a sound, but I never assigned a sensory experience with this sound because who would've been there to experience it? Like when a tree falls in the forest, and no one is around to hear it, if there is no witness, then does sound exist if it isn't heard?

But God wanted to be heard now, and so when, in my dream, something primal screamed through me, His ancient pain became Our pain. The sound carried a familiarity with it, as if it was so old it predated the mind and could only be understood by the soul, and as it pierced to the depths of me, I recognized it for what it was. The sound that started the world was like a universally understood siren because no matter what language we speak, we all know the sound of losing a child, and it is with that same sound that God calls us to come back home.

In becoming a mom, I got to experience both roles of life, the lost child and the parent that loses a child, and learned the bittersweet meaning of 'to love and be loved.' This made whole my knowledge of the dark and light side of love and loss, and by completing my transition phase I was ready to take the final step of my rite of passage - the return to unity.

However, in order to do that, I had to surrender the last illusion that separated the lover and the loved and understand that my son and I are one, but even with my new perspective, it was difficult because the fear of losing even the idea of my son was so great it still consumed me. And although it was reassuring to know that God loved and missed me, the intensity of symbolically experiencing God's loss in my dream only amplified my terror. It was in this place of limbo, where I understood oneness but had not truly accepted it, that I believe God sensed my hesitation.

Because I believe he was as desperate as I was for our reunion, I felt the intensity of my nightmares increase, leaving me with no choice. He made my inner world so unbearable that I was forced to face my fears to survive the misery, and in that way, he chose me by not giving me the option to give up.

The only way to transcend the pain of duality was to take the next step and to make love a state of being rather than treating it like a subject. Because of my experience with my children, I wholeheartedly knew now that everything was made of little broken-off pieces of the same one greater love, the way I felt my sons were made from pieces of me. So, with that knowledge, I was being asked now to return my life to its most singular state and make the terrifying leap from 'To love and Be loved', to just 'Be.'

"Kun Faya Kun"[16]

- Be, and so, it Is -

Acceptance

So, at this point in my pilgrimage, I understood that all material forms are illusions of the same oneness, that God loves me and wants me to come back to him, and that in order to return to him, I had to collapse love and pain into one, which is all good from a theoretical perspective, but from a technical perspective how does a mom stop loving her kids? I had no clue how to detach from their love, nor how to embrace the fear of losing them, and because it was their love that opened and transitioned me through my second phase, my gratitude for that made it that much harder to acknowledge that they were now the barrier between me and my final return to oneness.

Along the path, I surrendered attachments to not only my most basic needs of food, financial stability, and relationships but also deeply buried false beliefs and past versions of myself that I truly loved. With every release, I got a small manageable taste of death, but now I was being called to surrender my greatest attachment of all, to my sons, and through its difficulty, I realized that I loved them more than food, money, and safety.

The crux of my problem was that before the kids, I closed myself off from feeling love completely, in order to not pay the price of losing it. But I couldn't close myself off from loving the kids, and even if I could, life in that state was a cold, shallow existence that also cut off my ability to commune with God, and I was committed to getting that back, but I needed God to show me how.

In order to fully live, I had to find the balance between being open to love, while simultaneously accepting that not a single day or hour was guaranteed. In the 7 stages of grief, the final step is acceptance, and of all the steps towards death I had taken on my journey, this was the hardest. I knew death was inevitable, but I had to stop hoping that it would not come for my kids, and accept that one day it would. I asked God to help surrender this last hope within me, and because I was so far along on my journey of heightening my senses, I was clairvoyant enough to palpably feel when His hand reached through my dream, and grabbed me to focus my attention and stabilize me, while he upgraded me.

That night in my dreams, I was strengthened to fully look at the terrifying scene unfolding in front of me, and in just looking at my worst fear, I accepted the loss of my son's sweet, innocent light and opened myself to the message from God carried in the pain of the cold dark emptiness my boy left behind. In my final act of surrender, I let my heart ache, my stomach curl, my legs get weak, and my head bow in defeat as if every cell in my body emitted, 'you win world, I couldn't keep you, no matter how hard I tried.'

In his death, just like in his birth, I physically did very little. I never consciously grew him in my womb, or broke my water, or started contracting, or even pushed him out, my body knew how to do all of that on its own. The nurses told me on the day of my labor that my only job was to breathe through the pain, and now, in surrendering him, it was the same. I could only breathe while I allowed the pain of facing my fears to burn me alive, while simultaneously shivering in the cold he left behind. God had to use every kind of flame to cleanse me of my attachment, and in accepting this experience, rather than walking, I learned that the only way to cross the final step, was to allow myself to be carried across.

Enduring that ultimate pain forged into me the lesson life had been teaching me over and over again:

'Everything external is temporary. Keep going - inside.'

The severity of how deeply I downloaded this acceptance created a palpable change in the energy in and around me. I was at peace with my pain, and just to be clear, the pain was very much still there in every cell of my body, but by accepting it, it didn't burn anymore; it lit me up from the inside.

My decision to 'Zom, Zom' fighting created the crack God needed to bring His living water to the surface, so that He could nourish me and put out the fire within. Because He could not do it without my consent, He honored my free will and waited until I energetically told Him I was ready, which I did by surrendering and just looking at the dream He sent me.

After years on the spiritual path, and knowing that in surrender, we never truly lose anything; we only trade up, I couldn't imagine anything that could replace the love and pain of the heartbreakingly beautiful hope and future I surrendered… Until the value of something truly remarkable that I have possessed my entire life, was revealed to me.

Certainty

'I had to kill your hope, so that you could become certain.'

It was a truth that had been carved into me since my earliest memories of life because, just like Abraham, I had also witnessed the Ptolemaic rising and setting of many lights in my life, my first being the light of my father. The love I had for him filled my dark inner sky with a soft, pure light, but because his love was very rough and painful to accept, it burned me as well. It was a confusing time in my life because although I loved him so deeply, I also felt the need to be saved from him, and while I was trying to unravel that, I was also trying to make sense of the harsh world I was born into.

In the midst of that chaos, I tried to reach out to the larger-than-life savior God I was taught about, but because I expected something outside of me, when no one came, I felt completely abandoned. So it is no surprise that during this murky and disorienting time in my life, when God sent His word through me, I didn't recognize it as His presence watching over me, nor did I translate it correctly. The subtle essence that came to me was one of silent solitude pulling me to go inside, but because I urgently needed a physical provider and protector, I didn't value the invitation in, and instead, I translated the silence as *'No one ever comes,'* killing all my hope. When what it was actually trying to tell me was that *'no one needs to come, I'm already here inside of you.'*

Remarkably, even though I felt alone and was mistranslating the words coming through me as a child, it was so natural for me to absorb the deeper essence of its wisdom (through my gift of claircognizance) that even though I didn't understand the message, I knew exactly how to apply its wisdom. By not sending physical help, God was intentionally killing my hope of finding an external source of love, and in that harsh mercy, I was guided to know with certainty that my dad would never become kinder, that he was the only dad I would ever have, and because he was always sick, his life would be short. These truths forced me to step into the only logical option I had if I wanted to survive, and ever experience love for my dad – I had to change myself.

I had to let go of all my expectations of what I thought a dad should be, and bend my childish perspective from seeing life as something that lasts forever to seeing it as a radically temporary reality. In doing that, I stopped believing that dads should be kind, and started believing that it's because of their harshness that they make kids strong. My new bias was confirmed every time I saw a spoiled child unable to cope with even the smallest amount of adversity and when underdogs used all their hardships to bewilder the world with unbelievable achievements. He made me strong and confident, and I was proud of myself for that. I didn't want to be any other way, and I knew how to give credit where it was due.

Also, with constant visits in and out of frigid hospitals, the crisp smell of hand sanitizer, latex gloves, and bland, uneaten vegetables filled his rooms with the taste of death around the corner. Making me always on guard for the reality that I may have to bury him soon, which made anger and resentment completely pointless in a very temporary world. Why waste time being angry today when I viscerally knew for certain that tomorrow was not guaranteed?

So I not only forgave and loved him, I cherished every lesson he had given me. Because by being born to an iron-fisted father who was difficult to love, just like Hagar*, I was forced to dig deep to find the living water in the harsh desert of my environment, and through that, God gifted me with the ability to find the buried love in any situation.

"It is better to teach a man to fish, than to give a man a fish."
- Lao-Tzu

When my dad died, I had sorrow in my heart, but I was not devastated. Although he was young, it happened with the natural order of life, we expect the parents to die before the kids. But also, I buried him knowing I had given him everything I could; I didn't hold back, and in that, I felt contentment, and he left this world in peace, knowing he was loved. But that was just it, he knew he was loved, but I didn't know if I was, and because of that, I assumed the mechanism of love within me only lit up when it was giving love out to others. So when he died, so did the biggest light inside of me, because I assumed he was the source of the light he inspired within me.

In making that innocent mistake of believing that love was only accessible when inspired by others, when no other light as big as his appeared, I joined the example set by my society to seek happiness externally. I lit up on my first date with my ex-husband, on my graduation day, when I accepted my first job offer, and over time, I forgot about all the lessons I learned as a child, and traded love for comfort and stability. But after years of working a job I hated and being overburdened with responsibilities, I found that I was ravenous for love, and was living off the light of single-use matchsticks. It was in that state of deep need that my sons were born, reminding me of what real love was supposed to feel like, and in my desperation, I believed I had found the biggest lights of them all.

The sun dictates everything in our physical world, as such, it would be remiss of me not to mention that in the ancient days, there were cultures that used to worship the actual sun, and I understand why. Without it, the world as we know it would cease to exist, it would descend into a freezing darkness, that couldn't support any meaningful form of life.

Spiritually, the sun, like my son, is also a promise of tomorrow. Its sheer existence anchors me with the truth that no matter how dark it gets, the sun always promises a new day, and, with it, the only opportunity we have to live.

Religiously, the sun's location in the sky dictates our five prayer times each day, telling us when it is time to connect with our Inner Light, to remind us of our true purpose in being gifted this life. In witnessing the holiness of the sun's daily rise and fall, we hear it beckoning to us while inclining:

'Today is a new opportunity to wake up, live, and know yourself,'

and while declining, we hear its urgent reminder:

'The day is almost over, hurry and live, time is almost up.'

The 3rd prayer of the day, when the sun is in its declining stage, is called *Al -Asr*, which literally translates as 'the declining day,' but it can also mean 'time that is limited' or 'something that is pressed and squeezed.' It is also the title of a chapter in the *Quran* that is only three verses long, but through its brevity, it presses us to realize that the pilgrimage of life is short, and it guides us on what we should do while we are here:

"(I swear) by the passage of limited time.
That mankind will experience a grave loss.
Except those who live the truth, and do good intentional
acts. Whose honesty and patience is so genuine, it wills
others to want to do the same."[17]

Incredibly, even with all the knowledge accumulated over the thousand-five hundred years since these words of guidance were given to us, I was no different from the ancient cultures that worshipped the sun. In making my sons the source of light in my life, I unintentionally fell back into a state of ignorance, where I was depending on something external to nourish me, and because of that, I unknowingly worshipped my sons as if they were my idols.

In my own defense, at this point of my journey, I was uninitiated into the mystical aspects of religion. I still only knew a silent God that was unreachable, and I was desperate for love. So it never occurred to me that by making them the center of my world, I was revolving around them, and making them partners with God. But intuitively, I knew something was wrong and that I needed help, because even in that state of ignorance where I was dazzled by the brilliance of the light they inspired within me, I couldn't enjoy it due to the constant crippling certainty I had that one day they would set.

It was in that state of fear and desperation that my first conscious steps on my journey to finding God were ignited. I was ravenous for knowledge, and in a very short time, I absorbed wisdom from every corner of the Earth. But I quickly learned that acquiring knowledge meant nothing if it was not applied, because I knew a lot, but was still suffering.

I was encouraged on my path when I experienced moments of clarity, and I knew that if I stuck to it, I would see true, undeniable benefits, not just intangible ones. Such as, a night I mentioned before, when I was at a meditation retreat, and I had experienced such a heightened state of consciousness, that even though I was disappointed in not seeing a dolphin I had requested to see from God, I felt content because He had given me the breathtakingly beautiful light of two moons.

Contrasted with my state now that I had the abundance of two sons, and rather than enjoy the magnitude of light they shined on me, I mourned the light of the sun when it rose each day. Rather than seeing daylight as a promise of a new day, my mind was warped by my fear, and instead saw it as a signal that I was another day closer to losing them, so instead of seizing the day, I grieved it. I felt helpless; I couldn't stop the sun from rising, and the pain seemed endless, because even if I could control it, it didn't matter, even forever with them wasn't long enough.

Living with this amount of love and crushing grief on a daily basis was impossible, something had to break, and once again, I knew that the natural laws of the world would not change for me, and the only way to survive was to break myself. By bombarding me with images of loss night after night, God relentlessly chased after my attention until I stopped running away from the pain, and looked at it. In facing the death of my son, I burnt alive his false light inside of me, and from under those ashes, the truths I buried with my father long ago were resurrected.

'Life is short, the only time to love is Now.'

I had no choice but to accept that life was short; it was so apparently true that it would've been insane for me to continue fighting that, and although that acceptance gave me peace, I was still filled with pain. However, with years of added experience to pull from since the last time I heard these words, my claircognizance guided me through my problem by presenting to me a comparison.

As a child, I was forced to break my expectations because I didn't have enough light and needed more, and the only way I could do that was to relinquish my idea of what it meant to be a good father. In doing that, I could love him unconditionally, with a light heart not weighed down by resentment. Whereas now I had too much light, but feared losing it. Making me realize that it wasn't the amount of light that nourished me; it was the confidence in knowing I could access it as needed. Just like when I was yo-yo dieting before, when I would eliminate foods, I created a mental scarcity that I couldn't have something, and it made me want it more and binge eat. Whereas when I told myself I could have anything I wanted whenever I wanted, the abundance that belief created allowed me to surrender control to the wisdom within me, which self-regulated my eating, brought me out of survival mode, and into the best health of my life.

I was being guided now to do the same, to stop believing that my ability to love was dependent on others, and that there was a power inside of me that I could access whenever I needed, no matter who was around. It was then that I realized I had a tiny, misinterpreted belief, that limited my ability to access the love in my own heart. Before I had mistranslated *the only time to love is now* as *love him now because he will be gone soon,* and in doing so I relinquished my power to inspire my own light, to my father and son's. But I saw now that the true essence of the wisdom had nothing to do with them at all, it only said love now without needing a reason.

By breaking my misunderstanding, and knowing with certainty that I could access my own love whenever I needed it, my desperation fell away and left behind a great gift - transmuted pain.

In accepting that the world was temporary, and that the things I loved would leave, but that I could always access the love within me, the pain of loss transformed from a crippling fear, to a current of urgency that forced inspired action from within. Like when Hagar* was in a deep state of exhaustion, but could still run from mountain to mountain, because she was propelled by an unknown force within her. I, too, experienced a similar mystical force that refused to allow me to quit when I was so close to the finish line - Certainty.

In the dream of accepting my son's death, I thought God was trying to teach me not to make partners with Him, and not to love things that set. But it was the opposite, He was trying to show me how to 'fear not'[18] so that I could more fully love my sons while I had time to do so, and that it wasn't only the permanent and eternal that deserved love, but that everything deserved it. It was with certainty's final push that I unlocked and embodied my fearless essence of unconditional love, and finally completed my journey and reunited with One Love.

I thought about what that moment of reunion would feel like for so long, and romanticized it into thinking it would be an epic night journey into the heavens, where my body disappears and my soul merges in with a higher power. But in taking all of these steps in order to completely transform myself, it was just with the subtle act of aligning with unconditional love, that I realized God's presence is everywhere. I didn't have to go anywhere to feel it, the first step and the final step of the journey were the same; it was just a process of slowly unfolding our truth, and returning to our natural state of unconditional love, to remember how to 'be in the world, but not of it'[18].

The Technical Steps to Transmute Fear to Love

If you are anything like me, the esoteric can seem very fluffy and hard to apply, so I have created this section to give direct instructions on exactly how to make this emotional climb, of 'breaking' ourselves. I will admit that the ability to do this was only possible for me after I established the five pillars in my life as a daily practice, because they are the vehicle I used to heighten my senses and ground myself, giving me the strong and clear intuition I needed to sense the subtle changes happening inside of me, and the discernment to know the difference between a true thought versus an old program. Some people are naturally born with a strong intuition and can apply the formula I present below immediately, but for me, I noticed that when I tried to apply it before my foundation was built, it felt like a hardship where I was constantly jihad-ing against my lower nature. But after the pillars were firmly in place, my resistance to change fell away naturally, and rather than apply the formula through will and hardship, I lived it with ease.

In the ancient days, alchemists were obsessed with the idea of finding a magical *Universal Elixir*, also known as the **Philosopher's Stone**, which was believed to have the awesome power to turn base metals into gold, cure all diseases, and was the fountain of eternal youth. The name Elixir comes from the Arabic word *Al-Iksir*, which means 'potion,' but the root of it - *ksr*, means 'to break.' Implying that in order to change something into its perfected form, the inferior form would have to be broken. To this day, I believe we are still trying to find this heavenly state because something in us knows that is our true reality, and that the whole point of going on this journey is to find our way back home.

For so long, I had been looking for an external heaven, so the first step on my pilgrimage was to reverse my attention to focus on my inner world and make my internal peace and felt connection to God my priority in life. This proved difficult in the beginning because each time I tried to look inside myself, a tremendous barrier of pain was there that I had spent most of my life numbing and avoiding. Just paying attention to it would fill my body with a fear so intense that I could feel it coursing through my veins, and my fight or flight instincts were instantly ignited.

Although I believed those instincts were valid, I also believed that fear was the lesser form that needed to be fought and broken in order to achieve enlightenment. So, when I became brave enough to fight it, I learned the same lesson Jacob* did when he got his limp, that God and the natural laws of existence always prevail in the end, and I had no control over anything. I couldn't write the perfect book on my own, and I couldn't stop the people I love from dying, and initially, I resented that fact.

Before awakening to the reality of life, it was my arrogance that caused me to be resentful. In my judgment that the world was not fair enough and needed to be changed, I was emitting a constant unconscious signal to God, saying: "You did a terrible job by creating so much pain in this world," implying that I could do a better job than Him. But after I awakened to the temporary nature of the world I was in, and realized that it was intentionally created that way to force me to refocus my attention on my eternal inner world, my logic couldn't hold on to that resentment anymore. It didn't make sense to hate the way the world was by design.

So after my first step of looking in, my second step was to accept the nature of existence, which includes beauty, fun, and love, but also loss and suffering as well. By fully surrendering to that truth, the resentment had no choice but to fall away on its own, and left in its wake was curiosity and humility. I had to admit that I didn't know more than God about how to create a perfect world, and that if he was willing to show me, I was now willing to learn.

It was with the open willingness that comes from humility that the chemistry in my mind changed. I felt my mind relax and drop its defenses, my heart became lighter, and my eyes relaxed from an intense cynical focus to being softer and naturally opening wider so they could take more in. It was in that state of being that I looked at the pain inside of me once again, and gave my attention to all the things I hated about the world, but this time not with judgment, but with a willingness to understand. What I found was that at the root of everything I hated, was fear. I feared not having control – and I hated that; I feared that I would lose my children - and I really hated that. No matter what pain was inside of me, it all boiled down to fear, it was the biggest barrier between me and my inner Light. So with humble curiosity, I tried to break down the idea of it, and asked myself: "What is fear?."

Before, I naturally had prejudices against fear because it feels so awful in the body. It spikes our heart rate, makes our thoughts run uncontrollably wild, and shows us images that make us nauseous and want to avoid sleep so that we don't have to close our eyes, which makes us feel even more emotionally volatile and unstable. Fear, when given unchecked control, can make us its absolute slave, urging us to develop addictions to anything that numbs our inner reality even for a moment, and that was the only relationship I ever had with fear. Either as an enemy to be conquered, or a state of deep devotion – in that we should only fear God.

But going in now, without judgement or reaction to the way fear made me feel inside, I faced it to see what my fears wanted to tell me. All I did was just physically sit there while its intensity wreaked havoc on me. I looked at all the gut-wrenching images it sent, I allowed my body to thrash, shake, and scream while it surged through me, without trying to numb or run away from it. In just allowing the feelings to exist and to witness them within me, I found on the other side that fear was like any other emotion, a communication from God. It also followed the same method in that when I blocked His messages, their intensity would grow bigger and stronger until I couldn't ignore them anymore, and so I learned the hard way, like Hemmingway observed, that my only options were to either break my resistance to His messages, or die. I chose to break the resistance and allow the feelings to flow through me, and through that openness, I found that fear was actually a holy servant with a sharp and beautiful reminder:

'Life is short. All you have is now.
Don't delay your happiness to the future, it doesn't exist.
Love now, Live now.'

With this new perspective and the confidence that comes with facing my fiercest opponent only to find it is my greatest ally, I felt set free. In surrendering my resistance, I paradoxically became unconquerable, and the obstruction between me and my highest power had been lifted. I didn't just feel alive, I AM life.

Life is defined as: the condition that distinguishes animals and plants from inorganic matter, including the capacity for growth, reproduction, functional activity, and continual change preceding death. I had finally seized the opportunity that daylight promises us and changed from a small, terrified walking corpse, to living life with the enthusiasm of someone who had been given a second chance, which came from my certainty that the part of me and everything else in this world that mattered, was eternal.

To be clear, I was still experiencing the exact same pain as before when I thought about losing someone I loved too soon, but because I now understood the true message the feelings carried, I no longer translated the fear as 'Don't love, you'll only lose them in the end,' now I understood it was truly telling me 'Loss is certain. Love Urgently!.' With that refinement, the energy of the pain transmuted from one that used to cripple me, to one that served as a constant inspiration - to love unconditionally immediately. The intensity I translated as pain before now served as energetic fuel that propelled me to be present and live life fully, while I had time.

So the last step on my pilgrimage was to surrender, or 'break' my resistance to fear, and to realize it was never my enemy.

"In Hinduism, there are nine steps to the realization of Oneness with God. And the ninth and final step is Surrender. Hence, in Hinduism, "Islam" - this state of total surrender to God - is the final and last stage of worship. This is the reason why Islam is regarded as the final and last message of Allah to humanity because it represents that highest and final form of worship on man's journey to God."[19]

When I looked at fear in my surrendered state, and saw the complete spectrum of what it could do in my life when I harnessed its power, instead of defeating me, it transformed me, which gave me a first-hand taste of the alchemical wisdom of "Love your enemy." In that softer, more unconditionally loving approach towards fear, it also adjusted my view that it's not that we should fear God, but that even our fear should serve God.

As you can see, I actually did very little in the latter part of my transmutation process; all I had to do was allow myself to feel my pain, and absorb the wisdom that came with it. Most of my work was at the beginning of my journey when I was establishing the five pillars in my daily life, without which I wouldn't have been able to heighten my senses or intuition enough to understand the messages coming through me. I note this because I don't want anyone to think that breaking ourselves is this huge herculean effort that only spiritually adept people can do - anyone can feel their feelings.

But it was only by going through this process that I figured out how to technically apply the same Universal Elixir that Jesus* and so many others found long ago, in their ability to instantly collapse pain and pleasure into one experience. If you remember Buddha's* four noble truths: Life is suffering. Suffering is caused by craving. The end of craving is the end of suffering. There is a path that will lead one away from craving and suffering.

It was when I stopped craving control of my external world, and started walking the path of moderation through to my inner world, that I found the Elixir that breaks us free of our attachments. Boiled down, my entire process is contained in one simple ointment that I constantly apply:

Make any thought, feeling, or emotion,
either amuse or educate you.

That is it. That is how we break the density of our heavy emotions, so that we can rise and evolve to our highest potential in life. The entrance to the Kingdom of God, where we experience only love, is one thought away when we humbly ask ourselves - "What is this trying to teach me?."

It was a formula I heard repeated by so many spiritual teachers over the years, but because it was so simple and understated, it felt wishy-washy and not useful for true transformation. But it's because it's so simple that it's so powerful, and all of its magic was hidden in its small and consistent application. As soon as we apply the formula to our thoughts even once, the ease of our mental burdens is physically felt, and we get an instant taste of our peaceful mental nature, and the more we apply it, the more this state becomes our default again.

Although I had experienced this so many times on my surrendering journey, I had never felt it at this scale. It wasn't until the very end that I had put the two ideas together, that the universal elixir of life was surrendering my attachment to the validity of my own thoughts. Which I had been doing from the very beginning of my journey, but the momentum of that surrender continued to grow the further I walked, and by the end, I could see how powerful it was when I was able to challenge my biggest and scariest thoughts.

With every break and skeptic examination of my own false beliefs, expectations, judgments, and even dreams, I kept witnessing how either illogical or misinterpreted they were, and I gained the ability to see more truth, until I finally found the only truth – Love Unconditionally Now.

When I was unaware of what was happening to me during my periods of forced surrender, where I felt I wasn't given a choice, it was terrifying to feel weakened by the emotional pain that beat me up inside. But I know now that our spirit is just like our muscles, where in order to grow in strength, a muscle must first be torn, so instead of fearing the inner burn, I appreciated it, further collapsing my experience of pain and pleasure.

After coming back stronger, I could see a distinct difference between my energetic state before and after my break. Before, my attention was scattered, thinking about past and future pain, causing my energy to be spread so thin over time that only existed in my imagination, leaving me with very little to invest in my present day. But by the end of my journey, after breaking my attachment to my wasteful habit of projecting my thoughts out and bringing my attention back inwards to my life now, the momentum of my spiritual strength had grown and felt like a thick inward, focused laser, intent on living my highest expression of love now.

This reclaiming of my energy automatically aligned me with my intuition, which not only caused my senses to heighten and enhance my experience of daily life and connection to God, but it also changed every aspect of my outer world too. By embodying this intensely focused energy, a singular focus was created – like tunnel vision, and I could look directly at the light at the end of the tunnel without distractions or noise, and without looking away I received its words and instructions on how to bring my dreams to life today, and never again waited until tomorrow. I moved from trying to being, instead of hoping I would eat healthy tomorrow, I ate healthy today. The energy felt like willpower, discipline, trust, mercy, and love all rolled into one.

Einstein knocks once again, but this time, I let him in. He comes to present to me the immensity of what I have discovered, by offering the spiritual meaning of E=mc^2.[20]

E = energy (immaterial)
M = mass (material)
C = speed of light

In this scientific equation, energy and mass are interchangeable, revealing the spiritual truth that everything is energy.

C, the speed of light, is a universal constant, and the fastest speed known to man. However, in 2022, the Nobel Prize in Physics went to a group of scientists who proved the incredible phenomenon of quantum entanglement, which states that two particles can instantly affect each other, even if they are light-years apart. With this, we understand that there is something that travels even faster than the speed of light:

Speed of Sound	750 miles/hour
Speed of Light	186,000 miles/second
Speed of Thought	Instant

I don't understand the physics of the connection, or how messages can travel from one impossibly distant location to another so quickly, but I do know that when I ask God a question, I receive His response instantly.

When I received my final gift of Certainty, the best description of the way I experienced it was 'Love Urgently,' which came with the energetic signature of calm but urgently focused attention, that was so strong, it felt much faster than the speed of my normal thoughts.

When I apply all of this spiritual knowledge to $E=mc^2$, I note that:

E – Energy (which is interchangeable with Mass), is our attention, and

C - Certainty is a quality that focuses and speeds up our energy.

So when I take the Energy of my inward-focused attention, and multiply its speed by the exponentially faster quality of urgent love - Certainty, I solve for the secret E-lixir that Einstein hid in his equation, which unlocks the doorway home… Fiercely turn your loving attention inward.

<u>Surrender All 'things' To Know Thyself</u>

I had completely underestimated Abraham's* sacrifice before and only seen it for its most shallow meaning of being a test of trust, or obedience to God's command, which is huge, but Abraham* had nothing to prove. He had already reached enlightenment when he was 14, and had worshipped only one God ever since. He had left the traditions of his forefathers, broken idols, been thrown into a fire that didn't burn him, and left his wife and infant child alone in the desert. He had proven his trust and devotion to God many times over the years, but this final act of sacrificing his son was revealing something truly monumental that I had missed before because I had no frame of reference for understanding it, until I had a son of my own, and a dream of losing him.

When Abraham* took his son up the mountain, it was with no doubt fueled by the greatest sorrow a parent could ever contain, which he transmuted into an energy of Conviction that was so dense, it even made the air around him thicken, collapsing under the weight of his surrender. When he laid his son and final false hope down in front of him, and raised his knife of truth up, his actions were done with such focused, solemn intention, that it made words unnecessary to convey his obvious swear:

'I will never look anywhere, but within'

… He was showing us the way back home.

Al-Haqq (The Truth) is one of Allah's 99 names, and is known as the sharpest knife. It has the ability to slice through anything false, no matter how dense, to reveal the truth hidden within, and romantically, it's described as a knife because everyone knows that the truth hurts, but it also sets us free.

When Abraham accepted the painful truth of life, his physical sacrifice of his son became a metaphor. By slashing through his emotional attachment to the false idea of tomorrow, he set his energy free from the illusions that imprison us to this world, and, instead, laser-focused his energy on his eternal and direct connection to God Now.

So the point of his dream was not the physical sacrifice of his son, as evidenced by the fact that his son was replaced with a ram at the final moment; it was to demonstrate how to sacrifice the less dense 'idea' of his son. When we break the word idea down, its root meaning is:

Id – which is the part of the mind that manifests the innate.

Ey – is the root sound of me or my.

Ah – is the sound of the outward breath, which indicates you, other, or an outside projection.

So an idea - manifests our innate qualities, by creating an image of our inner desires and projecting them out.

Generally, Ideas are nice and wonderful because they allow us to peek at what we contain within ourselves. Everything starts with an idea or a dream, even this book. My point is not to demonize ideas as this false devil enemy that we must slay. It is only to illuminate that on the journey to enlightenment, when we are no longer looking out, and we've reached far into our inner spiritual depths, there is a final step our spirit must take in order to cross the final boundary that terminates everything.

In our outer world, it is such a paradox to know that everything feels so dense and real, yet in every spiritual, religious, and scientific school, it is universally acknowledged that it is all just an illusion of energy. In our inner world, ideas also carry with them the density of illusion, for two reasons:

1) The nature of an idea is our attempt to take the immense unmanifest potential within us, and reduce it to something small enough that our mind can hold, and

2) Then, it is further distorted by the limited perspective we see it with.

As such, our ideas become the final false veil that we must slice through, in order to clear anything that obstructs our direct connection to the source. In that state, we are able to clearly know the truth of the One Light, and since there is nothing left between us, we merge into one.

This non-concept is most beautifully described by Abu Bakr*, who said:

"Praise be to Him,
Who has granted His creatures access to the knowledge of
Himself, only through their inability to know Him!"[21]

During Hajj each year, we sacrifice a lamb to remember and reenact Abraham's* sacrifice and God's Mercy. By accepting the death of his hope for tomorrow, he became the 'Father of Many' today, and demonstrated to all his children for the rest of time, how to adopt through conviction the density of nothingness, in order to cross the ultimate final boundary and complete our last rite of passage - The Return to Oneness.

May God have the most delicate mercy on Abraham* and all parents.

<u>What Success Looked Like</u>

In order to test whether this discovery was only significant to me, I immediately called and asked my sister to apply the logic. I asked her to take any emotion, feeling or thought she had right now that she perceived as negative and find a way to make it amuse or educate her. She said she didn't really understand how to apply it, so I offered to walk through an example with her, she agreed, and the following climb occurred:

"OK, how do I stop myself from hating being inside all the time during the winter?"

I asked why she hated it, and she said: "Because I miss nature."

"So then your hate of the indoors is actually just your love of nature in disguise. Instead of focusing on the hate part of the pendulum, take one step closer in between them and say the more true statement: 'I miss nature'."

"But that doesn't change that it's still a negative, I'm still not in nature where I want to be."

"If you were in nature all the time, wouldn't you wish you were home?"

Her instinct to fight new thoughts before letting them in immediately softened when she saw how apparently true that statement was for her.

"The time we spend away from the things we love builds a delicious anticipation within us. The longer we delay the gratification, the more pleasurable the experience becomes. You're interpreting that anticipation as pain, but really it is excitement."

"But the energetic difference between 'I hate being stuck inside,' and 'I miss nature,' doesn't feel that different; it isn't big enough, is it? It still seems negative, and if I'm trading thoughts, shouldn't they be for positive ones?"

"It's a ladder you climb. You can't energetically go from 'I hate being stuck inside' to 'I'm grateful for everything,' it will feel fake, and life is not about being fake, it's about being more real. Saying you miss nature is more honest than saying you hate the indoors. You are judging the subtlety and magic of taking the first step, when that's literally all life is - taking one step at a time until you climb the ladder up to a 'heavenly' perspective."

Uh oh. I felt the well-intentioned preacher within rising.

"When I started writing this book, it was an outline, and I could've hated it and said, 'You aren't good enough, you aren't big enough.' But instead, I understood that the outline is the spine of the book. It was all I needed for the roots and branches and leaves and fruit to grow. We have to find the spine of our words and true feelings, because a single seed of truth is all we need to grow an entire tree."

We both erupted in laughter.

"Did you scratch your itch sis? If you got everything you needed to prove your point, I'm gonna get back to work now. Call me if you need anything else; I love you."

Although I was still laughing for a long time after the call, I also felt a bit disappointed because I didn't feel like I succeeded in convincing her about how special and useful this process was, nor did I feel like I helped her at all. It made me realize just how desperate I was for someone to understand, which quickly evolved from feeling like I was sitting on a jackpot of wealth, to wanting everyone I know to hit the jackpot too, but not knowing if I was conveying it correctly.

Eventually, I surrendered that feeling of responsibility, too, knowing and believing that because the words were written in a language for people like me, that they must understand. Then I surrendered even further with the realization that I hadn't written this book for people like me at all; I just wrote it exactly for me. I wrote the book I wanted to read.

I took diligent care with including words that were strong and logical enough to penetrate my heart, which had hardened over time, and needed a verbal sledgehammer to break its walls. I also danced with words sweet and soft enough to lure me in when I was so lost and blind, that I wouldn't have been able to recognize light by sight, but only by its taste and caress.

There were parts where I shook myself awake, the way I wish someone had shaken me, and alerted myself to the fact that this was a call to action and not a fun idea to toss around in my head. I also wrote about subtle realizations with so much emphasis to show myself that this was humbly it; the secret to life was plainly there all along. I had such a hard time figuring it out before because I was expecting a big and sudden eureka moment of enlightenment or an alien to show up with money to change my life, but the true reality was that the magic of life was hidden in the mundane acts of my everyday thoughts and actions.

It wasn't until I committed to the slow and painful process of aligning my thoughts and actions to fulfill my intention to write this book that I finally understood the power the mundane could wield over time. My older sister summed up the essence of this when she was just a child at our cousin's birthday party, and at the end of the night, our uncle asked her how she liked it. In her innocence, she made a brilliant observation and told him:

"This boring party turned out to be a lot of fun."

I included the words of so many (but not all) that guided me along the way, and although they were not all prophets, it didn't make their words any less prophetic. Their messages were all different, and yet they pointed me in the exact same direction.

The pilgrimage, the commitment to taking the step, is the self-contained secret. The steps go higher than anyone can know; it's infinite, and there is no end, but the point of this game is not only to keep climbing and discovering new facets of love. It is also to realize that no matter what step I am on, the same magic elixir that gets me to my next and all steps is right underneath my feet; all I have to do is stop running from it. Zom! Zom!

My hands shake as I write the last few words of this book and think about what I'm supposed to do next now that I have completed the biggest achievement of my life. Then I remember every day is Day 1, so I reaffirm my commitment to walk one step after another in obedience to the guidance from my heart.

"Here I am, O Allah, Here I am.
I submit, and I submit again."

A Summary of My Surrender Pilgrimage

Once, while I was meditating, I asked Jesus* to appear to me, but instead, a single white rose appeared. I looked at it perplexed, not understanding why I associated Jesus* with a flower, but as I silently absorbed its beauty, the lesson that came with it gently and silently seeped into my mind:

'God is the one plant, we are His roses.'

Buddha's* flower sermon was alive and well, still preaching 2500 years later, and after two years of radical transformation, growth, and learning, my own rose had bloomed, and I finally had my book.

Initially, I thought there was no way it could ever be physically as good as it felt energetically within, but when it was inside, I only got to see small glimpses of it at a time. It felt so large and random that when I tried to envision it all, I would become overwhelmed and feel crushed by its great weight. I couldn't understand how stories of my life, modern and ancient spiritual teachings, religion, science, and *The Cat Kid Comic Club* would all fit together, and yet here it is. Now that I get to see it for the first time as a fully formed being, it's even better than I was capable of imagining. Perhaps that's because all mothers think their baby is the most beautiful in the world… even the mother of Goliath.

The most resounding gift the journey has given me is the ability to hear and trust my inner knowing. No matter how much I studied and learned, when it came time to write, if I tried to pull from my own thoughts, I knew nothing, and the words were flat and boring. But as soon as I tapped into my intuition, it shocked me with the way it was so independently intelligent and organized. It tied up thoughts even if they were chapters away from each other, and when I thought it was getting lost telling stories, it would actually end them in a way I didn't expect and convey teachings that hit the nail on the head. I also can't even begin to count the number of times it urged me to look up the lyrics to random songs or the root meaning of words, which it was so passionate about. Words cannot describe the thrill of discovering this precious gift within me, and being able to access it unlimitedly fills me with an abundance I have never felt before.

My self-love habits primed me for this gift, and for a while, that's all my life was: just establishing habits. I didn't know the fruits and flowers they would produce when consistently applied. I thought they were an end in themselves, only to find that once the pillars were firmly in place, they were both the tools that I would use to build the house and the foundation the house would stand on. My tools were inward attention (intention), love (prayer), silence (fasting), openness (charity), and commitment (pilgrimage). My Fruit is the words that come through me and being able to hear and convey them.

My biggest surprise on this journey was how failure was my best friend on this path. I despised it at first until I learned its holy purpose, which was to first teach me what I am not so that I could know what I AM. The pain of negation carves the hole first to make space, to be filled with the pleasure of knowing. No God, but God.

Finally, I learned that happiness doesn't feel anything like I expected it to; it wasn't a spa day or a nice dinner. It felt like sacrifice and hard work, waking up at 3 am to write before the kids got up, exercising every day to make sure my body is settled and my mind is silent, eating less junk, and drinking more green juice so that my energy stays as high as possible, but also doing that with balance and ease. Happiness feels like vulnerability, being compassionate during the struggle and growth, forgiving myself when I fell off, getting back on, realizing I have limits and can only go so far, trusting God to work out the details, and so much dark chocolate.

The side effect of all that happiness was confidence, health, fitness, a constant glow from within, contentment, and the ability to be in constant communion with God.

This epic journey of slowly trading up temporary pleasures for eternal happiness taught me how to play with my pain. Eventually, not being able to differentiate between pain and pleasure - Two became one.

Pilgrimage flow

My kids are the love of my life,
Detaching from them was hard.
But if I didn't detach,
Life would be harder,
Like being stuck between two mountains.

They taught me a pure love.
The type of love that weakens you,
before it makes you stronger.

I was here to learn to unconditionally love the temporary,
without trying to own them.
The elegance of borrowing and sharing,
allowed me to become unstuck, and evolve.

There is so much to feel.
But when I found my favorite flavor,
I wanted to try it more than once,
and in that innocence, I became attached.

Only knowing how to see outward, blinded me,
to what I have within.
So after enough pain of them leaving,
I started the internal journey.

It got much worse, before it got better.
Every ghost and monster appeared, two, three times.
Making sure I had learned my lessons well.
Testing me before allowing me through the gates.
My fears were just my training ground,

preparing me for take-off.

I learned the lesson of – Let go of everything.
I didn't know I was holding on to so much.
But once I made that first breakthrough,
I knew there was no going back.

My highest,
became my new bare minimum,
and it's easy to fly,
weighing nothing, with new wings.

 I was equipped. I was ready.
I knew how to navigate the way.
I knew how to avoid the pitfalls.
How they were healthy for you either way.

I knew how to organize, and heal,
With compassion, and perseverance,
I found the fountain.
The one I was forever seeking.

I found it in myself.
In my happiness.
Not the pursuit of it.
I am it.

The lesson at the end,
Is hidden in the beginning.
The point?
To go on an epic journey, to Know Thyself.

"Perseverance is half of faith; Certainty is all of it."

-Abd Allah ibn Masud

One night before bed, my son asked me what heaven was like. I told him in heaven, anything you ask for instantly appears. His eyes grew in wild excitement, and he asked:

"So if I want a dog, a dog will appear."

"Yep."

My older son caught the excitement and joined our conversation:

"Wait, can I have infinite Robux?"

"Easily. At the snap of your fingers."

They both went on to list things they would ask for until it was time to go to bed, and I watched them fall asleep to dreams that left soft smiles on their faces. The next morning, on the drive to school, my youngest son asked wistfully:

"Mom, wouldn't it be cool if there was a portal to heaven?"

"Well, I'm kinda a portal. You and your brother were in heaven until you came through me to get to Earth."

"But I wish we could have a portal back to heaven."

"Aww baby, we're just visitors here. Eventually, we all go back home."

"But I wish I could go now."

There was a true sadness in his voice that resonated with an old sadness within me but for the opposite reason. So, my response was just as much for myself as it was for him.

"Don't worry baby, life is short."

<u>Index: 99 Names of Allah</u>[1]

It is believed that our souls are made of a unique combination of the energy in these names. Read them and feel which ones resonate with you to discover your essence:

#	Name	Meaning
1	Ar-Rahman	The All-Compassionate
2	Ar-Rahim	The All-Merciful
3	Al-Malik	The Absolute Ruler
4	Al-Quddus	The Pure One
5	As-Salam	The Source of Peace
6	Al-Mu'min	The Inspirer of Faith
7	Al-Muhaymin	The Guardian
8	Al-Aziz	The Victorious
9	Al-Jabbar	The Compeller
10	Al-Mutakabbir	The Greatest
11	Al-Khaliq	The Creator
12	Al-Bari'	The Maker of Order
13	Al-Musawwir	The Shaper of Beauty
14	Al-Ghaffar	The Forgiving
15	Al-Qahhar	The Subduer
16	Al-Wahhab	The Giver of All
17	Ar-Razzaq	The Sustainer
18	Al-Fattah	The Opener
19	Al-`Alim	The Knower of All
20	Al-Qabid	The Constrictor
21	Al-Basit	The Reliever
22	Al-Khafid	The Abaser
23	Ar-Rafi	The Exalter
24	Al-Mu'izz	The Bestower of Honors
25	Al-Mudhill	The Humiliator
26	As-Sami	The Hearer of All
27	Al-Basir	The Seer of All
28	Al-Hakam	The Judge
29	Al-`Adl	The Just

30	Al-Latif	The Subtle One
31	Al-Khabir	The All-Aware
32	Al-Halim	The Forbearing
33	Al-Azim	The Magnificent
34	Al-Ghafur	The Forgiver and Hider of Faults
35	Ash-Shakur	The Rewarder of Thankfulness
36	Al-Ali	The Highest
37	Al-Kabir	The Greatest
38	Al-Hafiz	The Preserver
39	Al-Muqit	The Nourisher
40	Al-Hasib	The Accounter
41	Al-Jalil	The Mighty
42	Al-Karim	The Generous
43	Ar-Raqib	The Watchful One
44	Al-Mujib	The Responder to Prayer
45	Al-Wasi	The All-Comprehending
46	Al-Hakim	The Perfectly Wise
47	Al-Wadud	The Loving One
48	Al-Majeed	The Majestic One
49	Al-Ba'ith	The Resurrector
50	Ash-Shahid	The Witness
51	Al-Haqq	The Truth
52	Al-Wakil	The Trustee
53	Al-Qawiyy	The Possessor of All Strength
54	Al-Matin	The Forceful One
55	Al-Waliyy	The Governor
56	Al-Hamid	The Praised One
57	Al-Muhsi	The Appraiser
58	Al-Mubdi'	The Originator
59	Al-Mu'id	The Restorer
60	Al-Muhyi	The Giver of Life
61	Al-Mumit	The Taker of Life
62	Al-Hayy	The Ever-Living One
63	Al-Qayyum	The Self-Existing One
64	Al-Wajid	The Finder

65	Al-Majid	The Glorious
66	Al-Wahid	The Unique, The Single
67	Al-Ahad	One, The Indivisible
68	As-Samad	The Satisfier of All Needs
69	Al-Qadir	The All-Powerful
70	Al-Muqtadir	The Creator of All Power
71	Al-Muqaddim	The Expediter
72	Al-Mu'akhkhir	The Delayer
73	Al-Awwal	The First
74	Al-Akhir	The Last
75	Az-Zahir	The Manifest One
76	Al-Batin	The Hidden One
77	Al-Wali	The Protecting Friend
78	Al-Muta'ali	The Supreme One
79	Al-Barr	The Doer of Good
80	At-Tawwab	The Guide to Repentance
81	Al-Muntaqim	The Avenger
82	Al-'Afuww	The Forgiver
83	Ar-Ra'uf	The Clement
84	Malik-al-Mulk	The Owner of All
85	Dhu-al-Jalal wa-al-Ikram	The Lord of Majesty and Bounty
86	Al-Muqsit	The Equitable One
87	Al-Jami'	The Gatherer
88	Al-Ghani	The Rich One
89	Al-Mughni	The Enricher
90	Al-Mani'	The Preventer of Harm
91	Ad-Darr	The Creator of The Harmful
92	An-Nafi'	The Creator of Good
93	An-Nur	The Light
94	Al-Hadi	The Guide
95	Al-Badi	The Originator
96	Al-Baqi	The Everlasting One
97	Al-Warith	The Inheritor of All
98	Ar-Rashid	The Righteous Teacher
99	As-Sabur	The Patient One

References

<u>Semantics – An Opening Message:</u>

1. *Matthew* 5:43–44.
    "But I say unto you, ***Love your enemies***, bless them that curse you, do good to them that hate you, and pray for them which despitefully use you, and persecute you."

2. *Zaad Al-Ma'ad* 3/60.
    https://rasoulallah.net/en/articles/article/2054/

A letter from Muhammad* to King Negus:

"In the name of Allah, the most beneficent, the most merciful.
From: Muhammad the messenger of Allah.
To: Negus, King of Abyssinia (Ethiopia).

Peace be upon him who follows true guidance.

Salutations,
I entertain Allah's praise, there is no god but He, the sovereign, the holy, the source of peace, the giver of peace, the guardian of faith, the preserver of safety.

I bear witness that Jesus, the son of Mary, ***is the spirit of Allah and His word which He cast into Mary,*** the virgin, the good, the pure, so that she conceived Jesus.

Allah created him from His spirit and His breathing as He created Adam by His hand. I call you to Allah alone with no associate and to His obedience and to follow me and to believe in that which came to me, for I am the messenger of Allah. I invite you and your men to Allah, the glorious, the all-mighty. I hereby bear witness that I have communicated my message and advice. I invite you to listen and accept my advice.

Peace be upon him who follows true guidance."

3. Mark, J. J. (2021, July 22). Four Noble Truths. *World History Encyclopedia.*
    https://www.worldhistory.org/Four_Noble_Truths/
4. *Bukhari* 3461

Chapter 0 – Introduction:
1. *Quran* 8:35
2. *Declaration of Independence.*
    https://www.archives.gov/founding-docs/declaration-transcript
3. Ramadan, Tariq. *In the footsteps of Muhammad*, Page 30. (Source: *Bukhari* 4953)
4. *Matthew* 4:4
5. http://www.buddhanet.net/e-learning/buddhism/pbs2_unit03.htm
6. Hazrat Inayat Khan.
7. *Bukhari* 7405
8. *Quran* 37:103
9. Ibn Ishaq's biography, *Sirat Rasul Allah* (*Biography of the Prophet of Allah*):

    https://jamesbishopblog.com/2019/01/29/why-did-the-prophet-muhammad-try-to-kill-himself/

'[Muhammad said,] "So I read it, and he departed from me. And I awoke from my sleep, and it was as though these words were written on my heart. Now none of God's creatures was more hateful to me than an (ecstatic) poet or a man possessed: I could not even look at them. I thought, Woe am I a poet or possessed—Never shall Quraysh say this of me! I will go to the top of the mountain and throw myself down that I may kill myself and gain rest. So I went forth to do so and then when I was midway on the mountain, I heard a voice from heaven saying, "O Muhammad! thou art the apostle of God and I am Gabriel"'

10. John Newton. https://hymnary.org/text/amazing_grace
11. *Quran* 1, Author's translation

Chapter 1 - Intention:
1. *Quran* 12:8-14
2. *Quran* 12:43-49
3. *Quran* 27:18
4. *Quran* 59:21, https://sunnah.com/bukhari:2
5. *Quran* 21:107
6. *Matthew* 6:33
7. *Quran* 96

Chapter 2 - Prayer:
1. Hadith Qudsi, https://rumisgarden.co.uk/blogs/traditional-meditations/hadith-qudsi-neither-my-heavens-nor-my-earth-encompasses-me
2. Onwuchekwa, John. *We Go On*. Zondervan, 11 Jan. 2022. (Source: *Ecclesiastes* 1 NIV)
3. *Matthew* 7:7
4. Wally Amos, Adapted from Winston Churchill.
5. *Romans* 8:31
6. Clendenin, Dan. "The Limp and the Blessing." www.journeywithjesus.net/essays/2703-the-limp-and-the-blessing.
7. *John* 8:7
8. Modern English Version
9. *Matthew* 6:10
10. *Luke* 23:34

Chapter 3 – Fasting:
1. Abu 'L-Qasim Al-Qushayri, *Al-Qushayri's Epistle on Sufism*, Garnet, 2007, page 176.
2. *Bukhari* 6465
3. Abu 'L-Qasim Al-Qushayri, *Al-Qushayri's Epistle on Sufism*, Garnet, 2007, page 170.
4. Puckett, Susan. "Intermittent Fasting and Your Health: What You Need to Know." www.bouldermedicalcenter.com/intermittent-fasting-and-health/,
Link, Rachael. "8 Health Benefits of Fasting, Backed by Science." www.healthline.com/nutrition/fasting-benefits.

5. *Bukhari* 3419
6. Yogananda, *Autobiography of a yogi*. Self-Realization Fellowship, 2014. Page 163.

Chapter 4 – Charity:
1. Onwuchekwa, John. *We Go On*. Zondervan, 11 Jan. 2022. (Source: *Ecclesiastes* 1 NIV)
2. "Energy Vampire: Definition, Signs, & Traits." The Berkeley Well-Being Institute, www.berkeleywellbeing.com/energy-vampire.html.
3. *Muslim* 2749
4. *Quran* 18:66-82
5. *Bukhari* 1427, 1428
6. *Bukhari* 660
7. *Matthew* 17:20-21
8. *Bukhari 6021*

Chapter 5 – Pilgrimage:
1. Safi Al-Rahman Mubarakfuri, *When the Moon Split: (a Biography of Prophet Muhammad)*. Riyadh, Darussalam, 2002. (Source: Ibn Ishaaq in *al-Maghaazi 1/154*)
2. *Talbiyah: What Does Labbaik Allahumma Labbaik Mean?* - Muslim Ink. 23 Mar. 2022, www.muslimink.com/islam/hajj/talbiyah-labbaik-allahumma-labbaik/.
3. Lail Hossain. "Principles of Islamic Parenting." With a Spin, 22 Dec. 2019, withaspin.com/2019/12/22/principles-of-islamic-parenting/.
4. "These Are the Seven Cycles of Life... And Then Some." Gaia, www.gaia.com/article/seven-cycles-of-life.
5. *Quran* 6:75-79
6. Abu 'L-Qasim Al-Qushayri, *Al-Qushayri's Epistle on Sufism*, Garnet, 2007, page 300.
7. *Bukhari* 3183
8. *"Al-Isra' Wal-Mi'raj: The Story of the Ascension to the Skies,"* Muslim Hands UK. www.muslimhands.org.uk/latest/2021/03/al-isra-wal-miraj-the-story-of-the-ascension-to-the-skies.
9. *Matthew* 6:10, "On earth as in heaven."

10. *Luke* 17:21
11. *Jami at-Tirmidhi* 2541
12. Gregg, David. "*7 Planes of Existence.*" The Michael Teachings, www.michaelteachings.com/7planes.html.
13. *Quran* 53:10
14. *Sunan al-Nasa'i* 3104
15. *Bukhari* 5971
16. *Quran* 2:117
17. *Quran* 103, Author's translation, with help from my mom:)
18. Adapted from *John* 15:18–19:

"If the world hates you, know that it has hated me before it hated you. If you were of the world, the world would love you as its own; but because you are not of the world, but I chose you out of the world, therefore the world hates you."

19. The Enigma of Islam... Enlightened by Sai https://archive.sssmediacentre.org/journals/Vol_06/01MAR 08/03-coverstory.htm
20. "*E=Mc2: Everything Is Energy - Why Do We Continue to Ignore the Energetic Truth*?" Universal Medicine, www.universalmedicine.com.au/articles/emc2-everything-energy-why-do-we-continue-ignore-energetic-truth#.
21. Abu 'L-Qasim Al-Qushayri, *Al-Qushayri's Epistle on Sufism*, Garnet, 2007, page 309.

Index:
1. https://nooracademy.com/99-names-of-allah/

"Are they desiring some religion that is not Allah's?

All in Earth and Heaven have surrendered to God either
by compulsion or on their own."

- Quran 3:83

About the Author

Nahida Nabulsi is a writer with a Masters Degree in Metaphysical Sciences, and a passion for world religions. Her first book seeks to serve people of all faiths to access their inner gifts, so that their light can shine so bright, it shows others the way back home.